T0339781

Darkest Europe
and
Africa's Nightmare

DARKEST EUROPE
AND
AFRICA'S NIGHTMARE

A CRITICAL OBSERVATION OF NEIGHBORING CONTINENTS

Akinyi Princess of K'Orinda-Yimbo

Algora Publishing
New York

© 2008 by Algora Publishing.
All Rights Reserved
www.algora.com

No portion of this book (beyond what is permitted by
Sections 107 or 108 of the United States Copyright Act of 1976)
may be reproduced by any process, stored in a retrieval system,
or transmitted in any form, or by any means, without the
express written permission of the publisher.

ISBN-13: 978-0-87586-518-8 (trade paper)
ISBN-13: 978-0-87586-519-5 (hard cover)
ISBN-13: 978-0-87586-520-1 (ebook)

Library of Congress Cataloging-in-Publication Data —

K'Orinda-Yimbo, Akinyi von.
   Darkest Europe and Africa's nightmare: a critical observation of the neighboring
continents / by Akinyi Princess of K'Orinda-Yimbo.
      p. cm.
   Includes bibliographical references and index.
   ISBN 978-0-87586-518-8 (trade paper: alk. paper) — ISBN 978-0-87586-519-5 (hard
cover: alk. paper) — ISBN 978-0-87586-520-1 (ebook) 1. Africa—Civilization. 2. Europe—
Civilization. 3. Africa—Social conditions. 4. Europe—Social conditions. 5. Africa—
Relations—Europe. 6. Europe—Relations—Africa. I. Title.

   DT14.K66 2007
   960—dc22
                                   2007021627

Front Cover: *Kenyan Kikuyu girl with blue eyes* (photo by author)

Printed in the United States

Dedicated to the memory of my mother

For my husband Erich Harald, the gift of Nature to me
as my best friend and confidant,
And for my son Christopher "Nicc" Nicholas,
the bearer of all that I am and ever have been.

TABLE OF CONTENTS

In my book I call a spade a spade. I will not equivocate. I've quite frankly had enough of the African people's moaning and whining and the pointing of fine accusing fingers at just about the rest of the world — while cringing even at the very thought of confronting their own leaders who are deliberately keeping them poor, uneducated and misinformed. At the same time I'm also weary of the West's bizarre attitude towards Africa and Africans. In the last ten or fifteen years I have watched the West's media training its citizenry to become absolutely misinformed about, and served a particular image of, Africa and Africans — a training I had hitherto only experienced in Africa, a training both insidious as well as amoral. I get asked, in the Western world, the most inane questions about Africa as well as about myself and my family. Somebody, apparently, must take the bottom rung of the ladder to support somebody else to be on the upper rungs. But does the ladder need its rungs at all? Can't we all simply pull and push each other along the sides? There is a saying: When you point a finger at someone, at least three of your own fingers are pointing at you. I'm equally indignant at the cocoa farmer who will never eat chocolate for the whole of his life but lets his children starve in order to have a bit of change in his pocket, and the chocolate manufacturers and eaters who turn around to blame Africans for adhering to the monoculture instead of growing something to feed themselves and their children.

From time immemorial, Africans always knew each other as Luo, Ibo, Yoruba, Ashanti, Zulu, Xhosa and so on. Then the West, in their feverish endeavors to classify humankind, brought in the B and the W notions and the rest of the world picked it up from there. I don't think any African person has a quarrel with being identified as an African. Then the skinless ones — that's the Luo term for pink-skinned people — turned the world into a grading scale, about three hundred and fifty years ago. Humankind were suddenly black, white, red, yellow and brown. I have a problem with our being labeled black just so that somebody else can keep the image of being spotlessness and purity personified. But why do we ourselves refer to ourselves as blacks? Who is it who insists on firmly taking up a stance at the bottom end of the ladder of coloration — if that is a relevant grading point at all — and referring to themselves as "blacks" and thus voluntarily remaining the counterpoise of "whites"? The color white in the African Union flag "represents the purity of Africa's desire to have genuine friends throughout the world." Would anybody in his right mind refer to himself as "impurity"?

The principle on which the United States of America was based is: All men are created equal. Then how did it all go wrong? The West preaches democracy but behaves very undemocratically when its "interests" are at stake. That has always been the rule of the day. The Western citizenry think their countries are wealthy because of the sweat of their brows or their brains — all connected to the color of their skin. This is the deliberate belief to support their hegemonic delusions. The truth is that they are rich because they have robbed and still rob their wealth from the rest of the world, creating the "poor countries" who should not be poor at all. Take Equatorial Guinea, for example, a small country on the Guinea Coast of Africa with a population of ca. 445,000 people, earning from its oil resources alone around $7 billion a year. It is the third poorest country in Africa, while Chevron & Co. are busy extracting the resources. And when Patrice Lumumba wanted a democratic Congo whose wealth would be controlled by and would bring prosperity to the Congolese instead of the Europeans and Americans, Belgium, France, Britain and America "got rid of" him. Both Europe and America have histories of violent opposition to African and other societies aiming to be independent and democratic. The elected nationalist Prime Minister of Iran, Mossadegh, was "got rid of" by Americans because he wanted Iran oil to be under the control of Iranians. In the words of John Perkins, author of *Confessions Of An Economic Hit Man*, in an interview by Amy Goodman for *Democracy Now!* on 5 November 2004:

> Well, I was initially recruited while I was in business school back in the late sixties by the National Security Agency, the nation's largest and least understood spy organization; but ultimately I worked for private corporations. The first real economic hit man was back in the early 1950s, Kermit Roosevelt, the grandson of Teddy, whose overthrow of [the] government of Iran, a democratically elected government, Mossadegh's government who was Time's magazine person of the year; and he was so successful at doing this without any bloodshed — well, there was a little bloodshed, but no

military intervention, just spending millions of dollars, and replaced Mossadegh with the Shah of Iran. At that point, we understood that this idea of economic hit man was an extremely good one. We didn't have to worry about the threat of war with Russia when we did it this way. The problem was that Roosevelt was a C.I.A. agent. He was a government employee. Had he been caught, we would have been in a lot of trouble. It would have been very embarrassing. So, at that point, the decision was made to use organizations like the C.I.A. and the N.S.A. to recruit potential economic hit men like me and then send us to work for private consulting companies, engineering firms, construction companies, so that if we were caught, there would be no connection with the government.

Very good Christian fishers of men and wealth — if you follow them. John Perkins said, further, when asked by Goodman to "explain this term, 'economic hit man', 'e.h.m.', as you call it":

Basically what we were trained to do and what our job is to do is to build up the American empire. To bring — to create situations where as many resources as possible flow into this country, to our corporations, and our government, and in fact we've been very successful. We've built the largest empire in the history of the world. It's been done over the last 50 years since World War II with very little military might, actually. It's only in rare instances like Iraq where the military comes in as a last resort. This empire, unlike any other in the history of the world, has been built primarily through economic manipulation, through cheating, through fraud, through seducing people into our way of life, through the economic hit men. I was very much a part of that.

Iranians then got a Western stooge thrust on them — the feudal tyrant shah who had nothing against leaving his people in abject poverty while American and European corporations whisked away the country's resources to enrich their own economies. Fidel Castro was once an idealistic democrat bent on ridding the Cubans, even risking his own life, of a bloodthirsty dictator, Fulgencio Batista. But the United States, forever undemocratic when dealing with other sovereign states, had other "interests" so they pulled all their might in support of Batista. Castro turned to the Soviets for support. Americans and Europeans do not balk even at murdering civilians, men, women and children, when a country wants to control its resources for the benefit of its citizens instead of enriching Euroancestrals. The war in DRCongo was and is the West's war by proxy.

One supposedly humanitarian and devoted League of Nations supporter, Gilbert Murray, proclaimed:

There is in the world a hierarchy of races...those nations which eat more, claim more, and get higher wages, will direct and rule the others, and the lower work of the world will tend in the long run to be done by lower breeds of men. This much we of the ruling color will no doubt accept as obvious.[1]

Perhaps in this third millennium nobody, I should hope, would dare publicly utter, let alone put into print, such words. But that's what is engraved in the pink psyche from infancy. The words remain branded in all our psyches — the one psyche nodding agreement and basking in it while the other — especially that of Afroancestrals, wherever they may be — either nodding in silent agreement and thus "accepting" their "predestined" place in the ladder of human hierarchy, or vehemently quarrelling with it and being inundated with impotent rage and hate.

In this book I'm going to present my views. I do not intend to deliberately insult or hurt the sensibilities of anybody. My convictions are predominantly anchored on "vehemently quarrelling with it" but I seek to explain it without "impotent rage and hate."

If the reader believes I'm about to pull down those at the top of this artificial humankind hierarchical ladder, then the reader is mistaken. I intend to elevate and/or pull down everybody. I intend to rationalize the action and/or reaction of the entire spectrum of us — Homo sapiens — who have conquered and subjected the planet earth so (un)successfully. It takes a poisonous snake to produce snake poison, which poison can cure or kill. Yet it can more likely only cure or kill one bitten by a poisonous snake, not one bitten by a rabid dog. My main field of interest is of course the African turf, mainly in Africa but also in the Diaspora.

There is this self-hate that is the curse of Africans and people of African blood. I make no bones about it. I will refer to us collectively as Afroancestrals™. Deep down, the majority of us are angry with and hate ourselves more than everybody else does. And generally more than we hate and are angry with everybody else who is not one of us. I'll support these arguments later with anecdotes that will be very familiar to Africans and those of African ancestry. I use the term African to describe us because it is a fact, if a generalized one. I completely avoid the term "black" because it is an untrue label.

This self-hate has led us to an unequalled ability to embrace political, social and intellectual apathy. Furthermore it has led us to an equally unbelievable self-imposed idleness and what I term the mother of fatalism and resignation — the good old *inshallah*. The paranoiac conspiracy theories. Yet we have quite *actively* strangled our ancestral as well as national patrimony and are still inanely throttling whatever vestiges of these that may still be evident around us. We have

---

1 Murray, Gilbert, *Liberality and Civilizations: Lectures Given at the Invitation of the Hibbert Trustees in the Universities of Bristol, Glasgow, and Birmingham in October and November 1937*, London: Allen & Unwin 1938

personally burnt down our precious house! Who is conspiring with whom about the all-round misery of Afroancestrals and Africa?

It is also my conviction that this self-hate has imbued us with a self-disrespect that is unparalleled among any other people on earth. And such reflection of oneself does, from a psychological point of view, lead to one's loss of basic human moral principles, loss of self-worth, loss of any remnant of personal dignity. It leads to the kind of abhorrent toadying Ghana's former President Jerry Rawlings inanely spewed in November 1999 to Queen Elizabeth II at an official banquet in Ghana, one of the few African countries still commanding some measure of self-esteem: "Your Majesty, we cherish gold very much but the Ghanaian industry is infested with criminals." Some skeletons must remain in the family cupboard.

And as already mentioned, I also have a bone to pick with the rest of the world, especially the West. This attitude of My Way is Good and the Only Way and Your Way is Bad and Must Be Chucked Out Of You Forever is thoroughly assumptive and paternalistic. The West neither created nor gave birth to Africa and Africans; it is actually the other way around. And Africa is still the pillar upon which the West is perched and scavenging like the carrion bird. Africa's social, political, economic and psychological problems sprout more directly than indirectly from outside the continent. The West seems to have cultured a conscious and an unconscious ignorance and arrogance about Africa and towards Afroancestrals™ in order to soothe their troubled subconscious and to justify inhuman atrocities. With capitalism "amoebaing" across the entire planet, Africa is increasingly voiceless but has long been staggering under the burden of the planet's multitudinous "Good" and "Evil." Yet we humans are sitting in one and the same boat, so if it capsizes we are all going to get wet. Some will have swimming vests while others will drown. I, for my part, don't intend to be the first one not to receive a vest simply because I belong to what some avaricious Euroancestrals™ have manipulated to be the "wrong" side of the color scale.

Christianity came from and thrived in my corner of the world first, and I seriously doubt that the Good Carpenter is happy with those calling themselves Christians but acting like insatiable wolves set loose on a flock of new-born lambs.

PART ONE — AFRICA'S NIGHTMARE

Asia is called the cradle of mankind. The times change. People change. But the belief in the Asiatic cradle has not changed.

> — HANS VON WOLZOGEN, 1875
>
> (in J. P. Mallory, *In Search of the Indo-Europeans*, p. 24)

Chapter 1. Rise to Bipedalism and Modern Humankind

It is somewhat more probable that our early progeni-
tors lived on the African continent than elsewhere.

CHARLES DARWIN *(Descent of Man, 1871)*

The 19th century achieved for African geography what the 20th century has achieved for the continent's history ("men whose heads do grow beneath their shoulders," misleading maps, etc.). Humankind with no history or any achievements beyond that which a beast is also capable of, or to use the words of David Hume, "I am apt to suspect the negroes, and in general all the other species of men (for there are four or five different kinds) to be naturally inferior to whites. There never was a civilized nation of any other complexion than white, nor even any individual eminent either in action or speculation. No ingenious manufactures among them, no arts, no sciences. [...] there are NEGROE slaves dispersed all over EUROPE, of which none ever discovered any symptoms of ingenuity..."[2] Or, in the words of Trollope, [the Afroancestrals possessed] "No approach to the civilization of his white fellow creatures whom he imitates as a monkey does a man"[3]. But historians and archaeologists are unearthing highly civilized African societies of thousands of years ago.

Most Africans also knew their family histories going back thousands of years. But these the Euroancestrals rejected because they were not in the written form. The fact that ancient African writing existed in Benin and

---

[2] *The Philosophical Works of David Hume*, ed. T. H. Green and T. H. Grose, Essay XXI, *Of National Characters*, 1964

[3] *OneWorld Magazine http://www.oneworldmagazine.org/focus/etiopia/lost.html.* Accessed 14.11.2006

Meroe, as well as the recently uncovered Banum script in Cameroon, was ignored by Euroancestrals or they found it convenient to audaciously attribute such writings to non-Afroancestral people. Africans also had society members whose sole duty was to remember the past and pass this on over thousands of generations in oratorical speeches, stories, fairy tales, proverbs and songs, or "written" by artisans in pottery, bronze, musical instruments, woodcarving and architecture — all long since pillaged and kept in the West as "collections" in museums or private homes.

A million years ago the earliest (hu)manlike ape or apelike (hu)man lived in Africa. Whether nearer to apes or nearer to humankind, these beings, to use the words of Professor Raymond Dart, "trembled on the brink of humanity."[4] Over the last estimated half a million years, four main pluvial periods in East Africa have been distinguished and named after the sites of the fossilized evidence or tools found; they are known as Kageran, Kamasian, Kanjeran and Gamblian. They led to the principal reasons for asserting that humankind first occurred in Africa. Stone tools have been recovered from deposits that formed during the earliest of these pluvial periods; stone tools found in Europe turn up much later. The East African tools are the oldest ever found anywhere. In the Gamblian period (12,000 to 14,000 years ago), the homo sapiens inhabiting Africa were stepping into the Old Stone Age on their way to modern humankind. They had survived their rivals and learnt effective ways to kill, trap or domesticate other threatening species.

They were firmly established by now and could in all peace and quiet cultivate their potentialities, migrate, multiply and populate the earth.

The new humankind types to emerge in Africa some time around 5000 BC included the "Negroid" type. These multiplied in the years subsequent to 5000 BC. Pre-dynastic Egypt (lower Nile Valley before 3000 BC) skulls, 800 in all, point to the fact that one-third of them were "Negroes" or ancestors of today's Africans. The study of languages confirms that the remote ancestors of modern Africans contributed dominant elements to the populations that sired the civilization of ancient Egypt. By 1200 BC the ancient Africans were not only great artists, as shown in the French explorer Henri Lhote's collection from the Sahara in 1958, but had acquired horses. The San or Khoisan and the Pygmies have a close link to the ancient Africans. The dominant stock of today whom Euroancestrals called "Negroes" are another great African breed. The Cushitic speakers of East Africa may have been influenced by immigrants from western Asia through sea trade routes but archaeolo-

---

4   *OneWorld   Magazine:*http://www.oneworldmagazine.org/focus/etiopia/lostl.html. Accessed 14.11.2006

gists baptized them "Hamites," divided into eastern and western "Hamites," who had in some dim past entered Africa, mingled with, and "civilized" the "Negroes." A mingling of "Negro" and "Hottentots" apparently produced the Bantus and a lot of other combinations. The Bantus are predominant in the southern half of Africa, and the "pure Negroes" in western Africa, according to language distinctions and anthropological convention. In this particular case, these contribute little to the precedence of ancient migration and settlement, and definitely nothing to "inferiority" and "superiority" notions. The achievements of Africans are forever held aloft in search of some unexplained mysterious "people from outside Africa" such as the "Hamitic" Egyptians and Berbers of the Nile Valley. In fact, according to Rodney Collomb in his book *The Rise and Fall of the Arab Empire and the Founding of Western Pre-eminence*, "The Berbers, of unknown origin, appear to be pre-historic migrants into northwest Africa." Whenever something remarkable turns up in Zimbabwe or Mica, an entire universe of non-African ("non-Black") people are dragged in to explain matters — Egyptians as the painters of the White Lady in southwest Africa, Hittites, Greeks and Portuguese as teachers and inspirers in terra cotta works and in bronze in mediaeval West Africa. One wonders why, then, the "superior Hamites" of Ethiopia, Eritrea or Somali are in such chaos for decades, the Somali not even counting as a nation, while "inferior Bantu" states like Botswana are so progressive.

Since the days and endeavors of Darwin, social scientists have been involved in a cumulative process to present evidence about humankind's evolutionary development and thus produce an increasing awareness of ourselves as a species, and a pretty young one at that. It is now clear that people of different continents today, the so-called modern human beings, have a common ancestry millions of years old and that this is to be found in Africa. We have a closer evolutionary kinship than a group of gorillas living in the same jungle and sharing the same grazing land — even though there is a section of scientists who on the other hand attempt to discredit the Out of Africa evidence and who would have us all evolving separately in various nooks and crannies of the earth. Anthropological (study of the human ethnic groups), archaeological (stones), paleontological (bones) as well as the more recent DNA (genes — the units in chromosomes which controls inherited characteristics) evidence, to name but the more controversial examples, support the African origin of modern man. It has been a protracted tug-of-war.

Human evolution is a subject understandably veiled in cosmic mysteries.

During the period known as the Miocene many millions of years ago, the apes, i.e., our group of primates, existed in the warmer zones of the Old World — which in this context refers to Africa, Asia and Europe. Then about 10 million years ago their number began to dwindle and they became isolated, for reasons that are as yet unclear but that anthropologists guess to be connected mainly with climate change — the earth began to get cooler and drier at the time. This has left us today with just four species of the great apes, the chimpanzees, gorillas, bonobos (pygmy chimpanzee) and orangutans. Our ape ancestors finally descended down to the ground from their trees and developed a bipedal mode (walking upright on their two hind limbs), then later developed their distinctive hominid features of large brains and tool-making skills.

The exact period in which these hairy ancestors of ours opted for the ground and the upright gait, leaving their cousins — the ancestors of the chimpanzees, gorillas and associates — up their trees, is still a mystery. However, according to researchers we can be sure of the fact that as human beings we have today a biological proximity with the African apes of about 98 percent of our genes. The oxygen-carrying protein in human blood, which is termed hemoglobin, is identical in all its known 287 amino acid sub-units with the hemoglobin of the chimpanzee. The human pool of genes — known collectively as genomes for the animal kingdom — differs from that of the chimpanzee by a mere two percent. It is therefore estimated that we, "the apes who left the trees," separated from our tree-dweller kith and kin as recently as 5 million years ago (a more recent consensus based on molecular evidence places the date at close to 7 million years ago) and began to roam the landscape that would one day be the African savannah. Geneticists thus discredited and disproved the earlier suggestions, derived from fragmentary teeth and jawbones, that the ancient *Ramapithecus*, 14 million years old and found in India (1932), Turkey and Pakistan (in the 1980s), as well as *Kenyapithecus* from East Africa, were ancestors of the hominid branch later leading to the rise of *Homo sapiens.* Indeed, *Ramapithecus* fossils were humanlike in certain ways, but the species were tree-dwellers and have been proved to be the archaic ancestors of the orangutans. Therefore the chimpanzees are our evolutionary first cousins, the gorillas our evolutionary distant cousins. The Darwinian anthropologists devotedly embraced his so-called "package" — a sort of blitz development of bipedalism, large brain and technology, making our ancient ancestors cultural creatures. The *Ramapithecus* discourse just about forced anthropologists to abandon their earlier theories of the distinctiveness of humans from the apes since 15 to even 30 million years ago, as opposed to 4,5 to 5 million years ago, and to recognize that similar anatomical features do not necessarily support common evolutionary ancestry.

Furthermore, international researchers unearthed over 40 fragments of bones including teeth, arms and jaws, at Aramis in Ethiopia in 1993. They named them *Ardipithecus ramidus*, the first word meaning "Wise Man" and the second meaning "roots" in the language of the local Ethiopians. These finds were fossils, had both human and ape-like features, and were subsequently analyzed as having lived in Africa at around 4.5 million years ago — a date uncannily close to the date the future African-savannah upright swaggerers waved *kwaheri* to their quadruped tree- and forest-dweller cousins.

CHAPTER 2. THE FRUITS OF BIPEDALISM

*In our school days most of us were brought up to regard Asia as the
mother of the European peoples. We were told that an ideal race of
men swarmed forth from the Himalayan highlands, disseminating
culture right and left as they spread through the barbarous West.*

JOHN RIPLEY, 1900 *(in J. P. Mallory,
In Search of the Indo-Europeans, p.66)*

Our nearest living relatives, therefore, are the four great apes, all of which
are confined to Africa, a fact that together with the fossil evidences then proves
that the earliest stages of human evolution took place in Africa. Following our
swaggering ancestors waving *kwaheri* to their primate cousins, human history (as
opposed to and removed from animal history) began in Africa around 5 to 9 or
10 million years ago. In the cosmic cycle where a million years could represent
the blink of an eye, this split-off population of African apes branched into several
groups, one of which evolved into gorillas and a second into the two modern
chimpanzees and the third into humans. The gorilla group possibly split off a
little before the separation between the chimpanzee and human branches. But
at this stage even the human (or hominid, an expression preferred in order to
distinguish them from the later modern man) branch was still an ape-man with
distinctly humanlike features.

It is not known how many human species lived and then became extinct, but
it is guessed that from six to a dozen human species failed to make it. Amidst the
various human species, one of them developed significantly 3 to 2 millions years
ago to finally attain the Homo stage, proceeding on to the *Homo erectus* and *Homo
sapiens* stages that led to modern humans.

The juiciest fruit of bipedalism is that we as human beings give birth to "premature babies" that need constant nurturing and care if they were to mature into adulthood.

The upright posture was followed by the development of increased body size and small ape-sized brains around 2.5 million years ago. The general names for these proto-humans are *Australopithecus africanus*, meaning Southern Apes, *Homo habilis*, and *Homo erectus*. They are believed to have evolved into each other in that order, reaching the *Homo erectus* stage around 1.7 million years ago. The Turkana boy who is more than 1.5 million years old, first noticed by the Kenyan Kamoya Kimeu on August 23, 1984, in the Lake Turkana region of northern Kenya, is a *Homo erectus* born and bred. At the time of his death it is estimated that he was a tall, narrow-hipped, long-legged boy of about 11 years, five-foot-three and thus possessing a physique pretty similar to that of today's East Africans. His brain is said to be two-thirds that of the average modern human and double that of the ape.

The *Homo erectus* are the closest to us in body size. They are judged to have been more than an ape but less than modern human beings, in zoological terms. They are also judged the first humans to use fire, to run like we do, to develop stone tool technology, and to begin hunting for their subsistence; they are the first human ancestors to make the exodus from Africa, destination Asia. It is also suggested that they had some degree of spoken language, which would further indicate the prerequisite for consciousness or self-awareness. Exactly when they first landed in Asia is not clear, but two of the oldest Javanese *erectus* skulls have been dated to about 1.6 to 1.8 million years ago.

But he or she of the African landscape was the first colonial *bwana* or *memsahib*.

The colonialist bwana and/or memsahib's safaris finally brought them to Europe as recently as around half a million years ago, or a bit earlier than that. Eurasia being a single landmass with practically no great barriers, some scientists argue that, leaving Africa, the erectus long-distance walkers probably forked off with one branch heading to Asia and the other to Europe, and thus colonized Asia and Europe simultaneously. In 1907 a jaw was found near Heidelberg in Germany. This jaw is apparently about 500,000 years old; its owner has been named *Homo heidelbergensis*. A cave at Atapuerca in Spain has yielded the largest single collection of early human bones (about 1,300 of them) in the world, which have been dated, together with finds at Dmanisi, in Georgia, at around 800,000 years. In the words of Jared Diamond:

> Whenever some scientist claims to have discovered "the earliest X" — whether X is the earliest human fossil in Europe, the earliest evidence of domesticated corn in Mexico, or the earliest anything anywhere — that announcement challenges other scientists to beat the claim by finding something still earlier.[5]

Be that as it may, the original colonialists were Africans, and their brain capacity continued to expand until this organ was about 1,300 ml, which is about the average brain size of modern humans. The skulls of Africans and Europeans of 500,000 years ago were similar enough to those of modern humans to warrant them being categorized in modern human's arena of *Homo sapiens* as opposed to *Homo erectus*. As we already saw, the *erectus* evolved into the *sapiens*, with the exception that details of the early *sapiens'* skeleton still were different to that of modern humans, their brains were still noticeably smaller, their behavior and very crude artifacts — such as choppers from pebbles, scrapes and flakes — significantly different from those of modern humans.

But as said in the previous chapter, they had attained that important acquisition: fire. Right back there in Africa.

The big question is, why did these African ancestors develop their technological skills 2.5 million years ago and with it the expanding brains — when their fellow apes did not? What made them abandon quadrupedalism and leap over to bipedalism and possibly the ability to communicate in spoken language? Scientists offer various explanations, some of which are rather speculative. Communication for example must have remained stagnant for hundreds of millennia as evidenced by the fact that the stone tools unearthed have remained the same for hundreds of thousands of years. Desmond Clark of the University of California at Berkeley states, "If these ancient people were talking to each other, they were saying the same thing over and over again."[6] Jokes aside, maybe they were — compare this to what babies do when they start to learn speech — once they've learnt to pronounce a particular word (no matter how they pronounce it), they simply love to repeat it over and over again and their parents as a rule joyfully oblige them by joining in this "repetition" ritual. If these babies didn't live in a world where they were constantly exposed to other sounds and words from parents and other sources, they would require a very long time indeed to cultivate or develop the next new sound or word. I can imagine these ancient apes simulating the roar of a lion and physically imitating its gait to mean: "I smell a lion so pick up the kids and let's hurry off to safety." These fellows had developed more complex social societies requiring

---

5 Diamond, Jared, *Guns, Germs & Steel*, p. 37
6 as quoted in Stringer & McKie, *African Exodus, Fitzhenry & Whiteside, Ontraio, 1996,* p. 42

the complementary organization and team work. They had learnt to care for each other and foster a tighter relationship within their respective groups.

Bipedalism was a very significant achievement. How was it attained? Scientists' arguments range from the fact that ancient granddad and grandma needed their upper limbs free in order to carry things, to the fact that they could better gather food, throw stones at prey or in defense, and to keep cool by minimizing the area of skin surface exposed to the African midday heat, conserving water by sweating less, and keeping their brains from overheating — when the sun's rays would fall vertically on the small area of their heads instead of on the larger surface of their backs. Furthermore, much more of their bodies would thus be raised above the heat radiating from the hot ground at their feet.

The most plausible impetus for bipedalism would seem to be the biological and geological arguments, which brings us to the Great Rift Valley of East Africa.

Around 15 million years ago, the African continent was blanketed from west to east with dense forests housing enormous varieties of primates which included apes and monkeys. It is asserted that the ape species greatly outnumbered the monkey species. Then Mother Africa began to experience her special kind of hiccups, and the crust beneath the eastern part was ripped asunder in a line beginning from the Red Sea down modern Ethiopia, Kenya, Tanzania and into Mozambique. The result was the land-rise in Kenya and Ethiopia, forming a giant highlands 9,000 feet high on either side of the Rift Valley, a result of the seeping magma that leaked out from the rip of the crust, and which changed both the climate and the topography of Africa. Mighty lakes were born and rivers began to flow down the Rift Valley from north to south, and the previous uniform airflow from west to east was disrupted. The eastern lands were thrown into rain shadow and thus finally lost their dense forests as these turned into mere patches, scrubland, woodland, with limited open grassland. By 12 million years ago, two tectonic plates had drifted apart to create fissures and upheavals which led to further environmental and evolutionary changes. The formation of the Great Rift Valley caused on the one hand a formidable east–west barrier and on the other hand fostered the development of a rich mosaic of ecological conditions. This east–west barrier then played a crucial role in the separated evolution of apes and humans — the two species became divided, with the ancient arboreal progeny of the apes finding their ecological niches in the forested humid west and center while dwellers of the now drier east became isolated in their less densely forested ecological niche. The impressive highlands generated cool forested plateaux with hazardous slopes dropping down to 3,000 feet into hot, arid lowlands. Different kinds of habitat began to proliferate. And perhaps the prehistoric ancestry of "racial competition" was also born, fuelling evolutionary innovation.

To survive, our distant ancestors had to create a completely new repertoire that would help them make it through this new life in an open environment. Getting on their feet was the most advantageous asset in overcoming the hazardous stance the environment had assumed. But anthropologists are still challenged to find out what advantages enabled this chimp species to emerge into the silicon chip species. They were still trillions of miles away from even the rudiments of a "United Forests Environmental Program." Exit *Ardipithecus ramidus*, enter the earliest known hominid, *Australopithecus afarensis* (Australopithecus = Southern Ape, "afarensis" for the Afar region in Ethiopia where the best-known fossils were unearthed).

And the time of this "early morning" is about 4 million years ago.

The celebrity among *Australopithecus afarensis* is Lady Lu. Officially known as "Lucy," that 40% complete skeleton was recovered in 1974 at the Hadar region of Ethiopia by a team of French and American scientists led by Maurice Taieb and Donald Johanson.[7] The lady was a mature adult hardly three feet tall at the time of her death, a little more than 3 million years ago. The male of the species was apparently considerably taller than her. Moreover she is found to be extremely ape-like in build, with the usual indications of the cocktail of ape and human characteristics: long arms and short legs, the ape's pyramid-shaped chest, hand bones that are fairly curved, short thumbs that could still be of assistance in supporting the body from tree branches, but shorter yet broader hipbones much like those of modern humans. The fossils of Lucy and many others in the Hagar region gave birth to the name *Australopithecus afarensis*, although the first scientific nomenclature of this hominid line had been coined, so to speak, in 1924 with the discovery of the front half of a child's skull (part of cranium, brain case, lower jaw and face) in the Taung limestone quarry in South Africa. This child's skull was named *Australopithecus africanus* (Southern ape from Africa) and is estimated to be 2 to 2.5 million years old. *Afarensis* is suspected of being *africanus*' ancestor and it possessed similar physical characteristics. In addition the Australopithecines were upright creatures who had developed large jaws and had mixed diets but were mainly vegetarian, still far removed from deliberate hunting. However, *afarensis* and *africanus* were termed graciles while their third, stur-

---

7 *Nature Magazine*: http://www.nature.com/nature/journal/v443/n7109/full/443268a. html. Accessed 12.6.2006

dier relative with big back teeth and thicker jaw was referred to as *Australo-pithecus robustus*. The dozens of finds, following the unearthing of the Taung child, in the South African sites of Makapansgat, Sterkfontein, Swartkrans and Kromdraai prompted the scientists involved to conjure up a plethora of names for their scores of finds.

Robustus, faced with the increasing arid climates in South and East Africa (presumably exacerbated by the growth of ice caps at the South and North Poles), evolved his and/or her "millstone molars" in order to cope with the kind of hard nourishment that could be obtained from such an arid climate 2.5 million years ago. Surviving this aridity till one million years ago, *robustus* finally branched off from future *Homo sapiens*. For meanwhile, around 2.3 million years ago, another branch had evolved which, rather than develop "millstone molars" in order to cope with the climate change, embarked on a more flexible strategy of gathering a variety of food, which included meat. This was the branch of the genus *Homo* that became the first human beings.

The first fossils of this genus was found in 1959 at Olduvai Gorge, East Africa, by a team led by Dr. Mary Leakey. It was an even more robust variety than the South African *robustus* and was named by Louis Leakey, Mary's husband who was a member of the team, *Zinjanthropus* (East African man) *boizei* (for their benefactor Charles Boize). The hominid *Zinjanthropus boizei* dated from around 1.75 million years ago and finally was renamed *Australopithecus boizei*. All the Australopithecines so far revealed males of more than five feet tall, who were larger than their females (less than four feet tall). This is taken to indicate that the fellows competed for females and kept harems, the females preferring the larger more able-bodied males.

In 1960 Jonathan Leakey, son of Mary and Louis and older brother of Richard Leakey, found the cranium of another variety of hominids at Olduvai Gorge which was less robust than all the other *Australopithecines* known so far. But its brain was a whopping 50 percent larger. Louis Leakey judged that this new find was the branch that eventually became the modern humankind and named it *Homo habilis*, meaning "handy man" on the assumption that this hominid was a toolmaker.

The earliest tools made by humankind that have been found so far are dated at 2.5 million years old and include stone flakes, scrapers, choppers and polyhedrons — solid geometrical figures with many (more than six) faces. In the world of science this earliest technology, in vogue until about 1.4 million years ago, is referred to as the Oldowan industry, and is argued to have been stumbled upon accidentally, so to speak, rather than having been deliberately and consciously designed by the toolmakers. The succeeding Acheulian industry, which began 1.4 million years ago in Africa, displays for the first time the deliberate intent of the toolmaker, most evidently in the tear-drop shaped hand axe. Later versions of these tools were discovered at a site in St. Acheul in northern France, hence the name Acheulian industry.

There is overwhelming evidence of humankind's origins millions of years ago heavily concentrated in Africa. The earliest human fossils known are all from East Africa. Scientists however lament the complete lack of fossils in the period from 4 to 8 million years ago, since this period is of enormous significance in the evolution of the human branch. This lack of fossils in itself has fuelled differences of opinion where it is argued that several hominid groups evolved simultaneously, including two groups of *habilis* and a third group, the *erectus*. Each group, according to available fossil evidence, possibly practiced slightly different lifestyles up until the stage when intentional design and manufacture of tools such as the hand axe gave one group a powerful advantage. Its members were able to introduce animal protein into their diet, through either hunting or scavenging or both. This advantage led them to use wider foraging grounds but also enabled an increase in population as they reproduced more successfully. But which group was it? Writes Richard Leakey:

> We know from the prehistoric record that after 1 million years ago only Homo species existed, and we also know that they made stone tools. Until there is good reason to suppose otherwise, it seems cautiously wise to conclude that only Homo made tools earlier in prehistory. The australopithecine species and Homo clearly had different specific adaptations, and it is likely that meat eating by Homo was an important part of that difference.[8]

Another characteristic of *Homo* that is of significance and points them to the road towards modern humankind was the fact that, as the earliest toolmakers, they were predominantly right-handed. In other words the *Homo* — as opposed to the Australopithecines — was becoming more and more like you and me. *Homo habilis* was equipped to manipulate their environment to suit their needs. Their brains had increased to over 600 cubic centimeters from 450 cubic centimeters. They no longer needed sturdy nails to claw the earth but had tools — stone picks — for digging. Meat helped to free them of the powerful metabolic resources of the digestive systems needed to process vegetables, which in addition are low in nutritional value. Mothers had high quality food to foster the brain development and continued neurological sustenance of their offspring from conception to early infancy and childhood. Adding bone marrow and fat to the food supply led to the development of smaller stomachs that utilized less energy for digestion, leaving whatever surplus energy to be channeled into brain development. In

8 Leakey, *The Origins of Humankind*, HarperCollins, New York, 1994, p. 39

the words of Leslie Aiello of the University College of London, "We started to eat meat, got smarter, and thought of cleverer ways to obtain more meat, although learning to obtain other rich, but easily digestible foods such as nuts was probably also involved."[9]

So much smarter they got that, 1.4 million years ago in Kenya, these proto humans tamed fire! They had no horns, but through their newly invented technology they came up with spears, which no other species possessed, and therefore no other species could encroach on the hominids' ecological niche and drive them out of it. Their brains stored records of where and whom to hunt, how to improve the success rate, and thus how to organize effective hunting and scavenging strategies.

9 Stringer and McKie (1996) "African Exodus," Fritzhenry & Whiteside, Ontario 1996, page 35

Chapter 3. The Eternal Mitochondrial DNA

> *Herodotus saw the matter very clearly when traveling through Egypt not long after 450 BC, for he had no difficulty in concluding that Egypt's cultural origins lay in continental Africa. On the subject of circumcision, for example, he remarked that "as between the Egyptians and the Ethiopians [by which he meant those since called Negroes], I should not like to say which learned from the other..."*
>
> BASIL DAVIDSON (*Africa in History*, revised and expanded edition, Touchstone 1995, p. 15)

We were a rather crowded family but with distinct differences. For example our chimp cousins are adept at using tools they find: rocks to crack nuts, sticks to poke at termites, and leaves as sponges for water. Not so with our human branch. We began not only to use but also to manufacture tools 2.5 million years ago and kept at it right up to Ford's conveyor belt and Silicon Valley's microchips. But it all started with scrapes, choppers, flakes and a variety of polyhedrons. Yet today's humankind are still snarling at each other over prehistoric fossils, bashing each other's heads with archaeological bones, rattling ancient pots and pans, raking up ancient fire places in Kenya's Lake Baringo area and injecting their various meanings into cave paintings, whether found in southern Africa or southern France. In this entire *succès fou*, archaeologist David Lewis-Williams of South Africa puts it succinctly: "Meaning is always culturally bound."[10] So

---

10 David Lewis-Williams is well-known in rock-art circles as the author of a series of articles drawing on ethnographic material and shamanism (notably connected with the San rock art of southern Africa) to gain new insights into the Palaeolithic cave art of western Europe.

---

proponents of the so-called Out Of Africa theory continue to contend with those of the equally vague multiregional-evolution model.

Let us substitute the term *race* with the modern geographical populations, and then come back to these two main proponents. The multiregionalists maintain that anatomical characteristics seen in modern "races" should be visible in fossils found in their very regions as far back as 2 million years ago when *Homo erectus* first set its voyage to destinations beyond Africa.

"Sorry, no such regional continuity can be expected over time. And if anything, then all 'races' should indeed have African characteristics," retort the Out Of Africa proponents.

The Out Of Africa model has the best standing up to now won because of the famous laboratory research of the University of California (Berkeley) and Emory University into mitochondrial DNA. Studying the specialized DNA structure within cells, they found that following the fusion of a mother's egg and a father's sperm in the newly formed embryo, only the mitochondria from the egg became part of the new cells. Ergo, this DNA can only and utterly be inherited from the maternal line. Nature has a marvelous way of putting us in our place. If this DNA can only be inherited from the maternal line, the researchers argue, it could in theory be traced back until finally it led to the "original" ancestral mother. Indeed researchers now say that modern humankind can trace their genetics to a female who lived (among thousands of other females and males) in Africa around 150,000 years ago. For this research, more than 4,000 people from all over the world — according to Kenya's Richard Leakey — have so far been tested to establish any genetic mixing between modern humans and archaic sapiens. No such ancient mitochondrial DNA has been found. "All mitochondrial DNA types from modern populations [read: "races"] that have been examined appear to be of recent origin. The implication is that modern newcomers completely replaced ancient populations — the process having began in Africa 150,000 years ago and then having spread through Eurasia over the next 100,000 years."[11] And the proponents of the Out Of Africa model are of the opinion that all present-day humans are descendants of that African population. So much for putting everybody in his place in the pecking orders.

Written facts have long revealed that stories of the life of Jesus are plagiarized from Mithras, the Persian God of Light, right from the twenty-fifth of December birthday to the shepherds arriving at Mithra's birth, all the way to

---

11 Leakey, *The Origin of Humankind*, HarperCollins, New York, p. 61

the Ascension, Holy Trinity, and the Eucharist complete with the bit about eating "the flesh" and drinking "the blood" of the Lord for everlasting life. These mimic the words that Mithras' prophet Zarathustra chanted centuries before the birth of Jesus. Later the Euro-Christians simply took over the pagan winter solstice celebrations, cleverly adding Jesus Christ to existing festivities, including the mistletoe. And not all Euroancestral™ Christians celebrate Christmas, the alleged birth of Jesus, on December 25 of the very young Gregorian calendar (introduced in 1582 by Pope Gregory XIII as a revision of the Julian calendar). Orthodox Christians have their own dates (January 7 for Christmas) based on the calendar of Julian the Apostate, or in Latin, Flavius Claudius Julianus, who was Roman emperor from 361 to 363 and who attempted to revive paganism while remaining tolerant to Christians and Jews.

In volume 8 of UNESCO's General History of Africa series,[12] Theophelus Tshibangu writes in his article: "The African is profoundly, incurably a believer, a religious person. To him, religion is not just a set of beliefs but a way of life, the basis of culture, identity and moral values. Religion is an essential part of the tradition that helps to promote both social stability and creative innovation."[13]

The ancestors of Afroancestrals™ taught the Greeks religion, and the Ethiopian alphabet assisted the Armenians in forming their own alphabet. Pharaonic Egypt, who called their land Kemet, meaning "land of the dark-skinned" — even according to Herodotus — not only gave the Euroancestrals™ the roots of civilization, geometry, astrology, astronomy, and all that, but also just about all the names of their gods. While also learning from the Europeans other sciences and medicine, they taught the Greeks, Phoenicians and Hebrews how to write in alphabet form. The world's greatest mathematician, Euclid, who wrote "The Elements," was born 2336 years ago in Africa, lived in Africa, studied in Africa, taught in Africa, and died in Africa without ever once traveling out of Africa. Afroancestrals taught the Greeks, among thousands of other things, how to conduct litanies for the gods, the art of solemn assembly, and even gave Euroancestrals the calendar and exchanged with them forms of philosophy. Just as not all of Europe was "civilized" during the periods of Greek and Roman civilizations, not all of Africa was "uncivilized."

---

12 Volume 8 of UNESCO's General History of Africa series, James Currey, London 1992, chapter 17 (ed. A. A. Mazrui)
13 Ibid. Tshibangu is a theologian from the DRCongo.

The *Systema Naturae* of Linnaeus (a.k.a. Linné) later graded Africans AF-TER *canis familiaris* — the domestic dog. The Bible started getting steamroll-ered to make room for the theory of polygenesis. In it one finds nothing about the ever-present Holy Trinity — the father, the son and the holy ghost — as a trinity. This trinity came into existence in the Mediaeval Ages when a lot of trinities were suddenly in vogue: the Three Wise Men (the Magi: Balthazar, Caspar and Melchior), and the division of the world into Africa, Asia and Eu-rope. Simon Peter went even further back than Noah, to the so-called First Murder or Fratricide, and pronounced: "Know that Europeans are the sons of Abel...Asia and Africa inhabited by descendants of Cain. See how blood-thirsty Africans are. Note the indolence of Asiatics."

The last people I would have graced with indolence are Asiatics!

The story of that biblical ancestor of us all, Noah, as we can all read in *Genesis* 9: 18-27, and his three sons, Japheth, Shem and Ham, is a familiar one. Noah seems not to have appreciated the humor of the situation, and after-wards Shem he praised, Japheth he blessed, and Ham he cursed by inform-ing Ham's son, Canaan, that he would be *the servant of servants* of his good brothers. Moreover, those who later interpreted the scriptures for English-speakers decided to equate the three sons with the three estates of society: nobles (warriors), clerks (priests), and serfs (herders/cultivators), that had been prevalent in all human societies from ancient times. "By some absurd logic," writes Dr. Quist-Adade, "Euro-Christians came to believe that Afri-cans are descended from Ham."

Which soon led to what Africa's first Pan-Africanist, Kwame Nkrumah, termed the "foulest invention by man" — racism. Euro-Christianity had snatched Jesus Christ and made him a Nordic fellow, blond and blue-eyed. Then the Vatican began misappropriating and hoarding every piece of writ-ing, scripts, parchments or relics around the Eastern and Southern world that it could get hold of. Europeans injected Euro-Christian symbolism into all sorts of tales, including Noah's punishing Ham and God's punishing Cain. And Jesus' Jewish origin had to be obscured. It was not the color imagery and symbolism of Christendom that was adopted but the color imagery and sym-bolism of Eurocentrism. The latter was then injected into lame justifications for slavery and colonialism, plunder and cultural misappropriation that had been going on since the antiquity.

The spin that interprets Bible passages as foundations for racist attitudes has since been accelerated and edited by all sorts of later writings, from trav-elogues and popular fiction to news reports, research by pseudo-scientists, and documents penned by petty rulers. Some were plain old devilish like

King Leopold II of Belgium, Carl Peters, Paul von Lettow-Vorbeck and the German Herero terminator General von Trotha, who believed that "kindness" shown to the "natives" is interpreted by them as "weakness." Some were wantonly imaginative liars like Henry Morton Stanley, Joseph Conrad or H. Rider Haggard. Tarzan was thrown into "darkest" sunny Africa, an orphan brought up by apes but able to teach himself how to read and write because ... he is snow white. And where ol' Tarzan "kills," the indigenous Africans "murder." If I had lived at the time and met that chap, I'd say Tarzan was the living image of the devil and his blonde Jane the embodiment of my darkest nightmares.

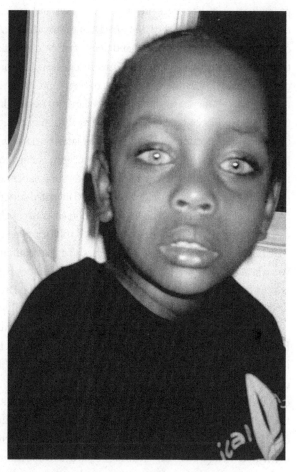

Kenyan Kikuyu girl with blue eyes

But humankind are relatively young and have therefore not had time to evolve into distinct "races," as such. My DNA sequencing as a Nilotic Kenyan of Luo descent will Confirm that comparison of human genomes — with Africa having the gene pool whose contents are more varied than elsewhere on the planet — would probably show me to be more closely "related" to a Dane (not the canis familiaris variety!) than to another Kenyan. Genetically, all humans are Africans, whether living in the continent or outside of it.

The saying that color is skin deep is dead right. And the genes "responsible" for the color of eyes or the texture-form of hair, intelligence, blood type, body shape, musical talents, genius at tennis and so on have nothing to do with those influencing the color of the skin. Most variations of humans are existing *within* the "races" (about 85% existing within any local population), and not *between* them. Small as the total human variation may be, as much as 94% can be found in one and the same continent.

In fact, Africans often have green, and occasionally blue eyes. I know a 100% Kenyan Kikuyu girl with blue eyes. The genes responsible for the color of the skin are not responsible for the color of eyes or hair.

The human invention of classification of their kind into "races" was and still is a tool for the promulgation of an idea of racial inequality, and from there the promulgation of bondage, predator capitalism and mercantilism as well, as if these were "natural" — ordained by Divine Providence. Although there is but one human "race," racism is real and does exist. We will discuss this in more detail in the section on the "Aryan" myth. Euroancestrals™ have used their "superiority" to justify robbing the Mexicans of their land, enslaving Africans, exterminating Native Americans and keeping Asians out of the global market economy. Charles Darwin's complex theory of the evolution of plants and animals as species, through selection and struggle, was later purloined and vulgarized by an English sociologist named Herbert Spencer into the neologism, "survival of the fittest."[14] Social Darwinism was hatched out of a sober theory, and twisted to mean that some societies *had* and thus had *inherited* superior genes well suited to survival, giving them the carte blanche to control the entire planet's social environments, while others inherited inferior genes and would therefore "naturally" wither away (or should best be exterminated — or yoked?). It was thought that attempting to rescue or save these "inferiors" was tantamount to defying the laws of nature, the laws of the Divine Providence.

This ideology of social Darwinism was not only sexist and racist, it was also classist. Even among themselves in the so-called New World, the Euroancestrals™ began to draw barriers based on their very own religious leanings and geographical areas. As economic power shifted from the shores of the Mediterranean to the Atlantic coast, the more northerly and westerly the better, and so White Anglo-Saxon Protestants moved to the top of the ladder. Struggling in order to survive was the "natural" way of life in the cold northern climate, but social Darwinists turned this upside down and identified struggle and survival as the natural tools for improving the genetic characteristic of humankind.

---

14 Spencer is often quoted out of context, for in reality he stressed "positive beneficence" and humankind's evolving "moral faculty" that seems all but lost in today's predator capitalism.

This theory soon gained a following in other fields of science as well. In economics, the market was construed as a giant "independent" organism by the likes of Adam Smith. Here the idea was (is) that the market's "natural laws" would evolve to give "economically deficient" people a wide berth in which to wither away while prospering the "economically progressive" people.

By the 19th century the Euroancestral™ world, having accumulated military and other technological might, set out to solidify not only their claim to "racial superiority" but to establish power over the entire planet. Nations sharing a common boundary, language, culture and physical appearance became — falsely — a "race," as in the "German race" or "British race." Religious or spiritual, intellectual and moral characteristics, even technology, became "racial" heredities, compounding the classification. By the 20th century, at the Berlin Conference and later at the Treaty of Versailles, pure brawn — military might — was the benchmark of racial superiority. "Higher" races killed or even exterminated other human beings, who had only themselves to blame for having inherited inferior genes that had failed to give them the desire to amass the technological tools needed to kill people. The massacred or the subjugated were simply "lower" creatures, or plain old "primitive." Further, the notion was propagated that the dominant and prosperous groups should produce more children at a high rate while the poor groups, being less successful, were to be discouraged or even be prevented from having children at a similarly high rate. Unfortunately it turned out that the rich wanted more riches and fewer children (or else their fertility, chemically thwarted for too long, in the end decided to adopt "sleep mode" — permanently). The poor on the other hand saw the production of children as their only "economic" resources and so their reproduction rose.

In addition, social Darwinism did away with the idea of morality somewhere along the road. Only the economically and militarily strong were to inherit the earth, not the meek. "Might" was verily "right."

Despite Darwin's promise of the survival of the fittest, yuppies were destined to grow old and retire. Another fork in the road had to be engineered. Eugenics, or biological engineering, is an idea that had proved its worth in the selective breeding of domestic animals. It was time to ease it down on humankind. Bible-thumpers will tell you that the Good Book instructs us to go out and subjugate the world; to some, other segments of humankind form part of that "world." Yet selectively, indeed! In North America, the social Darwinists and eugenicists took aim at immigrant communities. Those coming from "poorer Europe" such as eastern, southern and central Europe were "inferior" to those of Nordic, British or Germanic "stock." The presence of the "inferiors" threatened to water down the "racial" pedigree. Anti-Asian laws were passed by both Canada and the United States, erecting social and political walls against their immigration. Riots and public pressure induced British Columbia, in western Canada, to erect laws restricting the immigration from India.

The United States is supposed to be the ideal immigrants' destination. But not every ethnic group gets in easily. Efforts are made to separate the chaff from the wheat. Recently the US immigration politics aim at making the country Euroancestral, or, to use the common artificial label, "white." But even these "whites" are sub-graded. The Star-Spangled Banner Order, a secret anti-Catholic immigration organization soon dubbed the "Know-Nothing" Party, was founded around 1849. Later that century, Chinese were not allowed entry at all. By the beginning of the 20th century there were 76 million citizens of the US, the majority Euroancestrals. The biggest losers were the Native Americans who, although numbering between 10 to 20 million people, were not even considered US citizens until 1920. Between 1892 and 1924 more than 16 million immigrants arrived. Each year brought another million and the US Euroancestrals began to debate whether there were too many of the "wrong" kind coming in (the Irish, Russian Jews, Poles and people from the south of Italy). So science was brought into the debate in the form of eugenics, whose leading proponents were Madison Grant and Charles Davenport. The superiority of the Nordic race was to be proved "scientifically" by the Eugenics Record Office. Grant gave warning against mass immigration of "the weak and mentally sick races from the Mediterranean region, the Balkan and the inferior Polish ghettos." The right stock came from Britain and Scandinavia. The US Congress passed the Immigration Restriction Act which stipulated high proportions for the "Nordic" people and lower quotas for southern and eastern Europeans. Coupled with the worldwide economic crisis, this measure nearly stopped all immigration, which only picked up again after the Second World War, and with fewer Europeans coming in.

By the 1960s, only 1.1% of the 3.3 million immigrants came from Europe and 1.7% from South America. Of the estimated 950,000 immigrants who came to the US in 2004, only 128,000 were Europeans, half of them from the Ukraine, Bosnia, Poland and Russia. The majority of immigrants — 175,000 — came from Mexico, followed by India, the Philippines and China.

But as the world becomes a village, even the mighty have to rub shoulders with the meek. Today the Green Card, the precursor to citizenship in the US, is given out following the dictates of the employers seeking employees, through selective grants of asylum, and the so-called Green Card Lottery. But even more amazing is the fact that the government of the United States, under George W. Bush, employed thousands of foreign nationals to fight for the US in Iraq. At least several hundred of them have been granted US citizenship as part of their "compensation." For the US immigration lottery, the rule of thumb is that the country whose citizens *least* want to emigrate (relatively prosperous, educated Euroancestrals) to the US gets the *highest* quota.

The globalizers are today blaming the African woman for having too many children while they at the same time criticize her Western sister for not producing enough children. Meanwhile the Western woman is pitched into a life-and-death fight against her Asian sweatshop-worker sister who has "stolen" her job by working for half a dollar an hour while ruining her health, sixteen hours a day. But the Western sister is more than glad to pay $24 for jeans produced by her "disposable" Asian sister. The globalizers are turning everybody against everybody else. There is no solidarity, no reciprocity, and we identify with things instead of with fellow human beings. The employee is set against his own trade union (where any union still exists) and his fellow employees. The employers are against the social safety nets the governments want to erect for their citizens, employed or unemployed. Citizens are alienated from the governments that are leaving them in the fangs of globalizers. The governments and parliaments on the other hand become subservient recruits and must preach the dictates of capitalism to the electorate if they want to keep their jobs or win the next election.

Might has shifted from parliaments to corporate conference rooms.

CHAPTER 4: ELEMENTS INHUMAN I

> *[The] differential mortality from epidemic diseases in tradi-*
> *tional European societies had little to do with intelligence, and*
> *instead involved genetic resistance dependent on details of body*
> *chemistry. For example, people with blood group B or O have a*
> *greater resistance to smallpox than do people with blood group*
> *A. That is, natural selection promoting genes for intelligence has*
> *probably been far more ruthless in New Guinea than in more*
> *densely populated, politically complex societies, where natu-*
> *ral selection for body chemistry was instead more potent.*

JARED DIAMOND, *Guns, Germs and Steel* (1997 p. 21)

Charles Dickens put it a lot simpler: It's hell to be poor.

Natural selection promotes genes of intelligence or talent where the environ-ment and culture weed out those who are not adequately equipped to survive in challenging circumstances.

In trying to define the source of inequality in present-day human fortunes, arguing that they cannot be assigned to human ethnic groups or their physical characteristics, the American scholar and winner of the Rhone-Poulenc Science Book Prize, Jared Diamond, disputes "the hypothesis that intellectual differences underlie technological differences," and says that "tests of cognitive ability (like IQ tests) tend to measure cultural learning and not pure innate intelligence, whatever that is. Because of those undoubted effects of childhood environment and learned knowledge on IQ test results, the psychologist's efforts to date have not succeeded in convincingly establishing the postulated genetic deficiency in IQs of nonwhite peoples."[15]

---

15 Diamond,, Jaeed, *Guns, Germs and Steel*, Vintage, London, 1998, p. 20

When I read this I remembered the family historical accounts of Kenyans of African descent under British colonialism. Groups of people such as the Maasai hardly lasted a day in prison cells. Robbed of the vast savannah as their abode and the African sky, blue by day and star-studded by night, as the roof under which they could spend hours standing on one leg or sleeping to the lullaby of the African night sounds, confinement meant the grave to them. They simply folded up in a heap and stopped breathing. Indeed I can vividly imagine how a pygmy from Central Africa, used to the same star-studded African sky, would die of heart failure if he were to suddenly find himself in the middle of downtown Las Vegas. A Euroancestral professor or nano-engineer would not fare much better if he found himself in the jungle in the dark, surrounded by animal stirrings and no ready-made shelter in sight. And when day broke, he would not know which of the dazzlingly colorful blossoms must not be smelled, let alone touched. The most highly-decorated military general wouldn't find his way to the neighbor's abode by studying the shadows of birds in flight nor make his way there without disturbing a single blade of grass en route or leaving his human scent on the tiniest leaf or liana.

From information gathered in various improved scientific disciplines (i.e., those disciplines which *do not* rely on data such as how heavily one sweats, or the width of the mouth and flatness of the female posterior in ancient Greek sculptures), more tangible and demonstrable reliability has been created. The more notable of such disciplines include genetics, biogeography, behavioral ecology, molecular biology, epidemiology of human diseases, some archaeological studies, linguistics and other diversified disciplines like evolutionary biology and geology. The history and prehistory of all human ethnic groups must, in the context of such disciplines, be synthesized in both substance as well as in the sense of combining ideas, facts and experiences to create the most viable impression.

The modern space-age civilization was not simply picked up from thin air by certain human societies any more than bipedalism was the result of a blitz idea generated during an ape-council brainstorming session. The first farmer did not consciously choose "farming" one rainy afternoon, since he had not seen any other farmers using the combination of rain and crop cultivation. But once one part of a continent began intentional food production, neighboring hunter-gatherers could observe the result and consciously adopt it, either wholesale or partially, or reject it altogether.

Benefiting from conditions on the one continuous landmass stretching from East Asia to Europe, it was easy for Europeans to adopt new food production techniques wholesale from the Asian mainland (the Fertile Crescent), while it would have happened very slowly and piecemeal in Japan, for instance. In southeastern and central Europe, food production techniques were probably taken on board rapidly because this offered a far more efficient mode of life than that of the hunter-gatherer. In southern France, Spain and Italy food production practices were adopted piecemeal, with domesticated sheep arriving first and cultivation of cereals later. In the Americas, the Native Americans domesticated local plants and developed trade connections; Mexicans developed such crops as corn and beans, but some populations abandoned food production to return to hunting-gathering. In southern Sweden the hunter-gatherers adopted farming around 3000 BC, based on Southwest Asian crops, but about three centuries later they reverted to hunting-gathering for the next 40 centuries before returning to farming again. This adopting and abandoning of one lifestyle or another demonstrates that people *consciously* chose alternative strategies, competing with each other and responding no doubt to climate changes. Unfortunately, this ability can be destroyed; and this is the most worrying threat facing Africa.

There are now several consecutive generations in the continent who have known nothing but starvation. They are herded together in camps, like dispossessed domestic animals, waiting for a kinder destiny to rain down on them grains from the sky and drinking water from a convoy of lorries — if the lorries are not ambushed by young people and children toting guns. Even where the wars in several African states stopped and the climate was favorable, whole generations of Africans have forgotten not only what plant to grow and how, they have even forgotten how to hunt, gather or herd. A majority of them have known nothing but the sound, feel and fatal power of weapons and death all around them for close to forty years. They are even rapidly forgetting that humankind bury their dead. Furthermore, the fighting spirit and the tenacity that equipped Africans to free their continent from colonialism has long since imploded, and this at a time when they need these most.

In a typical TV interview President Obasanjo of Nigeria gave his own view of just how much an African life is worth. He was being questioned on the hundreds of Nigerians who had lost their lives in the clash between Muslims and Christians in northern Nigeria. His Excellency The President began by stating that the population of Nigeria is more than 100 million; in other words, he apparently felt there were enough of them that a few hundred individuals were inconsequential. That, from a man who had sworn an oath to serve the Nigerian people.

Oaths seem to be sworn in Africa because this exotic modern ritual links them somehow to the Queen's Prime Minister and the President of the United States of America — not because one really takes it to heart as a binding pledge. Africans love rituals and ceremonies, and best of all when they have the trimmings of top brass Euroancestrals. This is an expression of the self-hate mentioned in the Introduction. And for a few, there is no ethos outside of power and the exercise of power. For many African leaders there is no unified common rule to be imposed with a commonly held idea, a unifying common outlook.

Continental Africans are the only ethnic group on the planet who seem to be thoroughly convinced that everybody else deserves it but we, as Africans, do not deserve any happiness whatsoever. This seems to be the reason why any great difference between the old Organization of African Unity and the new African Union remains obscure.

The most audacious and unimaginable things happen in Africa.

Back in 1973, secret British documents revealed that there were plans to overthrow the government of Equatorial Guinea under Macias Nguema, another Excellency of the day. He was succeeded by his nephew, Obiang Nguema, who not only murdered his uncle but is also known to be only several degrees above his uncle in human compassion. He rules by torture and death like nearly all his fellow "excellencies" in Africa, with the West's heavyweight support to fall back on. When Etonian and ex-SAS (Special Air Service — a group of highly trained British soldiers working on secret or difficult military operations) man Simon Mann teamed with Sir Mark Thatcher in March 2004 to overthrow Obiang's little kingdom of 28,049 square kilometers, Obiang turned to the West, not the African Union. Obiang did not turn to a single fellow African. He also has brought foreigners and oil companies of the West into his little country, currently earning close to $7 billion a year from oil. The country has other natural resources including natural gas. But do a little mathematics and divide this oil fortune among the population of Equatorial Guinea annually — a population of approximately 500,000, whose land earns $7 billion a year on oil alone, in a country with an area of around 28,000 square kilometers! When Obiang visited Washington, following the attempted putsch by the private military company, he was told: "You are a good friend and we welcome you," by Condoleezza Rice. Did he even notice that she used the tone of a person seeking to reassure a retarded child? And that is the image Africans would seem to project to the rest of the world, but especially to the US.

The US Briggs Bank was the biggest laundering house for the money stolen by Obiang and his family, friends, prebendaries and hangers-on. His Equatorial Guinea is another rich little "province" of the United States. As Paul Kennedy, a professor at Yale University, wrote about America's world domination, "Being the number one at great cost is one thing; being the world's single superpower on the cheap is astonishing."[16]

The benefits of Equatorial Guinea's resources do not go to the citizens, for whom spending even on education is less than in any other country around the globe, and for whom public health efforts are so stunted that the average citizen dies before his forty-fifth birthday. Obiang did have an exiled opponent known as Severo Moto, whom Sir Mark Thatcher and his cronies wanted to place in government as president while they ran the economy: The age-old story of post-colonial Africa. African governments always surround themselves with Western "economic advisors." Because of the old self-hate. Pink people equals prestige, equals rubbing shoulders with the deities, to most Africans. Former president of Kenya, arap Moi, for example, had his biography written by the late Princess Diana's biographer. That the man could not write his own autobiography I can understand. But there are millions of Kenyans or any other African on the entire continent who could have written his biography for him.

Ever since the 16th century, it is Africans who have assisted and made it possible for the West to accumulate its incredible wealth. And this under the cruelest and most dehumanizing conditions. It was Africans who shed their blood and lost their lives, it is still the Africans paying with their lives to keep up the wealth accumulation that has completely run amok. What's wrong with the African citizenry? Why are Africans letting themselves be dehumanized once again and this time "willingly"? This cannot be "the normal African trait" even by the benchmarks of the most benign of Gods. All members of humankind are born with innate pride, dignity, self-worth, self-esteem, protection for the self and those of one's family when there is a common enemy. And the will to fight to the death to maintain these virtues, however poor one is. So why this abject submission by the majority of Africans? After all, they are the only massively colonized continent, yet the only "natives" who managed to drive Euroancestrals out and retain their continent for themselves. Now, many parts of Africa are as good as absolute despotisms

---

16 Ziegler, Jean, *Die neuen Herrscher der Welt*, Goldmann Verlag, Munich, 2003, p. 49

with the civil law merely an elaborate jurisprudence system inherited from colonialism. The ordinary citizen has no legal defense worth the description, no redress against oppression by the government and officialdom in general.

Africans are not all lazy, by any means, but they have had role models in the last four or five decades who, combined with the ever increasing fatalism, have taught them that hard work does not pay. Here is a gem from the treasure trove of African "politician" jokes: a politician was sitting in his huge office reading a newspaper, his feet up on his massive desk. But a fly kept on buzzing around, annoying him. He folded the newspaper in order to swat it, when the fly suddenly said, "Please don't kill me, I'm a fairy fly. If you don't kill me, I'll grant you three wishes." The politician's first wish was to be having a holiday lazing on a fabulous white-sanded beach. And whoosh, he was on the beach relaxing under a magnificent sun umbrella. Next he wished for a voluptuous nubile blonde beside him, and whoosh, there she was, clad in a scanty bikini. His last wish was that he should never ever again toil, labor or work for the rest of his life. Whoosh! He was sitting in his huge office reading a newspaper, his feet up on his massive desk.

When African soldiers, militia or the police are set loose on innocent demonstrators, they seem to lose their humanity. Whether unleashed on university students or ethnic groups that have been deliberately incited to butcher each other by politicians motivated by dubious ambitions, these armed forces kill their own fellow human beings with feral abandon. It is not simply the way they have been trained; it is also their anger and frustration in having employment that regularly stock them with weapons and uniforms but does not pay them regularly and well enough to feed their families. They kill fellow human beings as if they were butchering wild animals because their superiors expect it of them, or else they may lose their jobs to a "stronger" rival. They seem to lack the human moral conscience that would make them command empathy. These armed forces are trained in and by the West since the end of colonialism. In an atmosphere where the judiciary, the legislature and the executive become dysfunctional or partially lawless, political instability is pre-programmed. And the world community is not only watching, its appropriate members are filming and photographing and reporting and writing and cataloguing along the lines of the "they/them" and the "we/us." Full stop.

Africans are more or less kept inside their countries and continent by the mere cost of a passport. This document can cost some families a year's income or sometimes even more. That is, if they finally manage to be granted the honor of possessing a passport at all. Asking for a passport in most

African countries is like asking for half of the central bank's gold reserves. Passports are being used as tools of political oppression. Anybody who escapes the continent, in the direction of that often abused and misused idea of "democracy" and the economic opportunities mistakenly pegged to it, presumably gets exposed to other ideas such as that heads of state are no demigods. That their limousine's passage does not necessary warrant clearing the streets with a convoy of police cars, presidential escort motorcade and snarling and threatening armed forces who might shoot the pedestrian who is not quick enough to sprint away from the street. Anybody who gets to this Democracyville learns that demonstrations are not elsewhere considered capital crimes punishable by summary death, nor is it considered sacrilegious to write an open letter criticizing the head of state. A passport might take one to parts of the world where one could form an organization with like-minded people, who might then shout their views and opinions loud and clear to anybody who cares to listen to them. Once granted a passport and landed in European Democracyville, one is free to call a spade a spade (excuse the pun).

In short, passports are the best way for a country to get itself troublesome, informed rebels. But democracy, even in the West, is today not always what it was in the original Greek sense — demokratia (demos meaning the people and -kratia/kratos meaning power/strength) — of rule of the people. We all still remember the voting in Florida, so African nations have, admittedly, no monopoly on political errata.

The current president of Kenya, Mwai Kibaki, was elected into office primarily because he promised the citizens that he was going to fight corruption, probably the country's worst factor that deters economic or any other form of development. But his first parliamentary debate was to discuss bloated perks and allowances for the members of parliament. This discussion lasted all of thirty minutes and was passed. Were there no opposition parliamentarians? Kenyan parliamentarians are among the best paid in the world, with a mammoth representation of 34 ministers (2 women) and 39 assistant ministers. The number keeps on growing, in a country with neoliberal economic policies that boosts the gap between the few mega rich and the tens of millions of the poor, making it one of the most unequal populations in the world. After the introduction of multipartyism, there are 54 parties in the country, 7 represented in parliament.

But the political party tradition in Kenya is peculiar. Many registered parties have no party manifestos and the few who do have had their manifestos penned down by foreigners or donors. The manifestos are never scrutinized by party members because most African political parties tend not to be based on common or united strategies, visions, ideologies, discipline, struggles, moral values or code of conduct. Party members are sycophants motivated by banal self-interests, who keep changing membership from one party to another in no time, always looking for self-aggrandizement. The Kenyan parties are lined behind powerful personalities and oligarchs, with ethnic alliances, intrigues, public attacks and insults in the media of fellow members and insecure relationships to each other. The result of such alliances (if they can be called alliances at all) is a daily political agenda of opportunism, despondency, inertia, anarchy, a culture of sycophancy, ethnicism and all manner of retrogressive characteristics.

In the November 21, 2005 referendum, Kenyans slapped their president Kibaki and his cabinet with a 3.5 million No votes. Kibaki's campaign slogan three years previously of "zero tolerance on corruption," and his pledges which included effecting a new constitution within 100 days of occupying the office, are still unfulfilled by one of the most extravagant cabinets in Africa. The new constitution was to include, among other areas, cutting down the draconian powers invested in the presidency; the appointment of the judiciary, its duties, and limitations of its privileges; defining and limiting the privileges of the legislative and the means by which parliamentarians can raise their income and power beyond what citizens regarded as realistic for the country's economy. The official extravagance manifests itself in the fact that there is only one driver for four to five official limousines. Between 2002 and 2005, the government wasted Kshs 878 million to buy luxury vehicles, clearly showing that Kibaki's agreements and promises were made to be reneged on.

After the No vote, Kibaki simply run the country solo for weeks, without a cabinet, but accompanied by the vice president, attorney general and permanent secretaries. What goes on in the head of such a person, knowing he is supposed to preserve, protect and defend the citizens and be the personification of law and order? They become liabilities instead of assets, and conduct themselves as if in the privacy of their own sitting rooms. This is an unparalleled show of contempt to Kenyans. Instead of thinking of the future he thinks about the right now, confusing politics with statecraft. There are many like him, forcing Africa to her knees, the knees that are already covered with scar tissue. And the world community is watching and shaking their heads: *Well, Africa, right?* No, there are millions of dignified Africans who behave like intelligent, responsible human beings. Something else is going on.

When he became president, Kibaki brought in a former Transparency International (Kenya) man, John Githongo, and made him Kenya's anti-corruption chief, answering only to the president. Githongo kept a detailed report and briefed the president regularly. He unearthed security contracts by government officials to non-existent companies worth as much as $1 billion. These officials started to openly and constantly threaten him with murder, Cosa Nostra style. Of course Githongo informed his boss just as constantly, which boss on the other hand was now more worried about his cronies and his government than about smoking out cabinet thugs. Finally Kibaki demoted Githongo, publicly, on television, on June 30, 2004, announcing that Githongo "had been transferred from the Office of the President to the Ministry of Justice and Constitutional Affairs." And the circus continued. Githongo writes in his 91-page report:

> I was angry because I knew I was being demoted because of doing my job by pursuing the Anglo Leasing matter relentlessly... [And when he arrived in his office on the morning of July 2, 2004, one of the cabinet ministers was already there waiting for him and told him]... the bizarre story that ... someone had surreptitiously inserted my name into the wrong place in the President's [television] speech and therefore my transfer was not meant to have happened at all. Your Excellency, I came to your office [....] I informed you of the developments and realized you were shocked by them. You then reversed the transfer. We met again the next day and explored who could have amended your statement to effect my transfer.[17]

And so on and so forth. But how on God's earth can the president of a nation announce the transfer of one of his closest and most senior staff members, who reports to him each day or even many times a day, without realizing what he is doing? Couldn't the name John Githongo alone, and the details of "Office of the President to the Ministry of Justice and Constitutional Affairs," make something click in the president's brain?

In November 2006, another episode dubbed the "Armenian Brothers Scandal" involving government officials and stolen Kenyan passports and security badges that allowed the "brothers" to walk in and out of security areas of Kenya's airports without the slightest hitch was being "investigated." It was said that the cleaning women apparently stole the passports. Where would an ordinary Kenyan cleaning woman gain contact with Armenians, get photos of the Armenians, stamp, seal and register the passports? But the poor ladies cannot defend themselves, there is no redress for the ordinary *wanainchi* against "big men"!

---

17 The full Githongo Report is on the web of the BBC in an image PDF format, a shorter version can be found under www.africafocus.org/docs06/git0602.php. Accessed on 30.11.2005

It is a scenario worthy of a Charlie Chaplin film.

The conduct of African governments as perceived by their citizens is expressed in a poignant joke told to me by a taxi driver in my home city of Kisumu. He said he first heard the joke from a Ugandan policeman, so it seems a popular continental joke. And here it is: All the presidents of the entire world died on one and the same day. They all landed in hell. Having left some unfinished business to tie up, such as last wills and saying goodbye to families and friends, they requested the devil to at least grant them one last telephone call each. The devil generously agreed. The first to telephone was, of course, the President of the US, then Russia, the United Kingdom, Germany, France and so on. When all the presidents of all the five continents were finished with their last phone calls, the devil calculated the charges. "Okay, fellows," said Old Nick, finally, "The presidents of the continents of America, Asia, Australia and Europe each pay 300 Euros or 500 US dollars, take your pick. The presidents of the African continent each pay 30 Euro cents or 50 US dollar cents, take your pick." And of course all hell broke loose about the unfairness of the charges. After all, the argument went, the Africans had talked longest, having such extended families and hangers-on. The devil finally quieted everybody down and then announced, "The African presidents made local calls."

When I first took my husband to Kenya for a holiday, we rented a car in Nairobi from a well-known international car rental firm. The manager, a Kenyan of British descent, wished us all the best with the car and hoped we wouldn't get into a fracas with "a bad policeman" in Kenya, but reassured us that all Kenyan policemen were "good" anyway. This was no surprise to me. But when I explained to my wide-eyed husband what a "good policeman" meant, his eyes got wider. A good policeman is one with whom you can sort out differences with a bit of *chai* — baksheesh, bribe, call it what you fancy. A bad policeman is that rare fellow who will book you in if you try to bribe him or her in order to get out of your differences. No wonder the latter is a rare breed indeed. I told my husband not to worry because, once the bad one books us in, we'll meet good ones at the police station and sort things out all the same.

In 2001, the UN International Investigating Committee found out the goriest methods with which human rights were/are violated in tiny Togo. The ruler, General Gnassimbé Eyadéma, is still on his throne although he even personally gave orders in recent years for students not only to be arrested but also to be handcuffed and dropped into the Atlantic Ocean from army helicopters. He has been ruling Togo since 1967. The president aside, I ask myself how those carrying out such orders, executing the actual killing, feel about themselves as accomplices to the brutal murder of fellow citizens. Any twinges in their conscience?

Guinea-Conakry has a wealth of natural resources from aluminum to bauxite to gold and diamonds to timber to everything worth being labeled natural resources. The lord of the realm, Lansana Conté, when questioned by reporters about the violation of human rights he is practicing with impunity, replied, "Human rights? I have no idea what that should be."[18] He is an ailing, aged brigadier general who came to power after a military coup in 1984. He was recently accused of interfering with judicial processes by securing the release from prison of two men being investigated for corruption. One of them is believed to be the country's richest man, Mamadou Sylla. Now Conté is under pressure to name his successor. He has responded by a curfew and by having hundreds of innocent demonstrators and their trade unionists shot dead.

The Revolutionary United Front of Sierra Leone has a boss, Fode Sankoi, who punishes citizens who do not deliver him all the diamonds they mined from the bowels of their own motherland, by having their hands and arms chopped off. This method of punishment is in fact the rule of the day in all the "blood diamond" countries of the West African Coast from Angola to Liberia. The masters of the game are dos Santos, Compaore, Taylor, Kabila; the list is long.

Some African customs and traditions are obviously obsolete in the 21st century. There is a cultural trait that would seem to be ingrained in almost every group of African people impelling them to avoid talking about *unpleasant* matters, real or imagined, as if it were taboo. The rape victims of DRCongo's Kivu Province do not talk about being raped but those who were both raped and attacked by the Ninjas do talk about how and who chopped off their arms or hands. Family and relatives do their best to look after one of their own who is crippled, but they tend not to talk to one who has been raped, let alone accept her in their midst. They believe they are saving face for all concerned. But they are avoiding a crucial interaction — the bold, logical and truthful exchange of information. Information still remains the single most valuable commodity to humankind — it played a paramount part in enabling those early Africans to trek from the continent and finally occupy Asia and Europe.

For people out of a different cultural background, playing of hide and seek with words this way comes across as dishonest and deceitful. It robs people of various African cultural groups of their desired quality of being earnest. And it robs them of the ability to practice the likes of that Japanese virtue known as *Ringi* — where suggestions are discussed openly around before compromises and decisions are made. Most Africans are consistent only when they are up in arms to defend or salvage their "modern African" image. The trouble is, most Africans

---

18 Zieger,, Jean, *Die neuen Herrscher der Welt*, Goldmann, Munich, 2003, p. 66

mistake "modern African" with "aping Euroancestrals." There is a monumental gap in between the two conceptions.

While Olive Lembe Kabila gives out T-shirts with portraits of her husband Joseph Kabila to patients in the Panzi Hospital in Bukavu, eastern DRCongo's Kivu Province, she does not even talk to the patients about their fate. Madame Kabila hands out the shirts, and then she is gone. These patients are women victims of rape. Some are young girls in their puberty. They have not simply been raped with the usual male organ, they have also been raped with rods, rifle-barrels and bayonets. As a result many of them suffer from fistula and incontinence. But to talk with rape victims or even about rape itself is still taboo in most Congolese circles. These victims have been raped by various groups. The "Ninjas" are Hutu militiamen of the infamous *Interahamwe* who specialize in chopping off the hands, arms and feet of their rape victims. Other groups include the Rwandan army and the rebels they finance, who assisted in driving Mobutu out of the then Zaire; Burundian rebels who used the bordering country as a retreat area, and are rumored to be responsible for most of the HIV infections; the local Congolese Mai-Mai fighting against the "invaders" from Rwanda, Burundi and Uganda; the Congolese army and any number of splinter groups who fought in the war between 1998 and 2002. They all not only rape but also plunder. Women in most African societies are the symbols of morality and honor, so raping them is equal to dirtying and humiliating the entire society. But the African women, especially in insecure times, are also the home-makers and breadwinners. They are the ones who work in the fields where the plunderers come to harvest both the crops and the women they need as sex and household slaves. When the kidnapped women are no longer needed, most of them are simply killed. Couldn't Madame Kabila spare a few minutes even to merely listen to the worries of these women and show some sympathy? Madame Kabila is not alone. Most wives of Africa's "excellencies" avoid spending time with ordinary citizens. They spend time in the salons of Paris talking to Bulgari, Chopard or Cartier designers for their latest custom-made diamond and platinum necklaces for the next reception at the Ritz.

British troops stationed in Kenya (whom one should expect to have an inkling of the meaning of the word discipline, and who would never do such a thing on British soil without facing dismissal and severe charges) made a profession of mass raping the local women and girls. Of course the women were blamed, made pariahs in their own society by their own people. But the Kenyan ladies had a strength of will and unbreakable spirit reminiscent of those of the ancient daughters of Africa. They joined together and founded their own village with their children. No man is allowed in the village unless as the occasional carpenter or repairman. The women are self-reliant and live from working their land and engaging in cottage industries such as making beads, other jewellery, mats and decorative gourds for tourists who visit. They built a school for their children and teach the children themselves until the children reach secondary school level. Place Africa in the hands of the African women and the continent would leave the rest of the world way behind.

But above all, the African Union should make it their task to protect these unfortunate daughters of Africa, whether the culprits are Africans or foreigners. If such "unpleasantness" cannot be talked about in whichever African society, then they should not be allowed to happen in the first place.

In the capital city of Chad, N'Djemma, the political prisoners of President Idriss Déby are thrown for life into dungeons right under the presidential palace. Déby is simply continuing the example of his predecessor, General Hissène Habré. Habré was found guilty of violating human rights by an examining magistrate in Dakar, the capital of Senegal. Later, however, the case was simply dropped. To this day, Habré and his courtiers are living like ancient caliphs off their billions in Western financial institutions. Living like ancient caliphs in the most exclusive residential area on the Atlantic coast: Corniche, in Dakar, Senegal.

It is enough to make a rock weep.

But there are countries in the continent such as Lesotho, Mauritius, Botswana or Ghana where, by the current standards, decency, disciplined leaders, respect for human life and a sense of responsibility can be found. Comparisons with Asia in terms of corruption, human rights violations, military power, the colonial burdens and so on, are often mentioned as mitigating factors. But at least the Asiatics leave their billions and trillions circulating in and building up the Asiatic economies. Education is encouraged in all of Asia, the infrastructure developed, roads, schools and hospitals built and bridges repaired when necessary. Most African despots seem to believe that taking care of the citizens' needs and welfare is tantamount to nurturing innumerable venomous vipers within your own four walls.

On the one hand most Africans tend to accuse the Western media of intentionally perpetuating the bad image of the continent. This is not without some truth. The London-based Royal African Society, which I will come back to in a different chapter, supports this argument. The argument is that after all the West are the corruptors, the plunderers of Africa's precious natural resources from timber and oil to gold and diamonds, from bauxite to coltran, and the manufacturers and sellers of the weapons Africans are using to kill each other. All the capital flight from the corrupt leaders and the elite land in Western banks to promote not Africa's but Western economies. The West is to blame for the undernourishment, poverty, epidemics, the AIDS pandemic and a variety of evils. On the other hand Africans should well ask themselves who is responsible for the child soldiers, expulsion, displaced persons, the dreadful living standards and short lifespan of their people. They should question their own apathy in the running of their political life. Why is the world moving rapidly ahead while Africa is retreating towards archaic forms of living? Africans are the only human beings whose longevity continues to drop while all other human beings are living longer and healthier than ever before, thanks to better nourishment, advanced technology and medical science. The life expectancy of Africans is decreasing so much so that, if no great measures are taken, in a decade one in three Africans will not celebrate his fortieth birthday. I can jolly well understand the African-American Keith B. Richburg who, after traveling around in Africa in the mid-90s, wrote that he was glad that his ancestors had been enslaved in the United States.

Colonization and slavery — abhorrent enough as they were and the unbelievable damages these did — are history and should no longer be a legitimate explanation of *all* of Africa's underdevelopment in the 21st century. Strictly speaking, practically every human ethnic group in the world has been enslaved at one point or another, even if the slavery was not in the vast and inhuman proportions of the trans-Atlantic slave trade, which I do not at all condone. Asia was colonized too. Yet China has pushed Great Britain out of the 4th place as a world economic giant. India is jogging alongside both. Neither should the — granted — unfair methods of the WTO or the World Bank and IMF bear the total blame for Africa's underdevelopment. Why aren't Africans able to trade with each other, build roads and railway lines across the continent connecting them all to one another and thus dictate their own negotiating trading conditions? They have 900 million people for a market, unbelievably varied and abundant natural resources, which these people should themselves be mining, manufacturing, producing and consuming if African nations were properly governed by political leaders worth the description. The 900 million would quickly get healthier and larger and smarter. These 900 million people of Africa are a market larger than that of the whole of the European continent and more than two thirds that of China!

The lack of experts can be solved almost overnight by bringing in the experts to train the locals as well as sending Africans overseas to acquire the expertise, making sure they come back home to a decent job in a decently governed country, earn the decent salary they deserve while training more experts in the country. The Asiatics are doing it every second of the day. Despite Africa's large population in 54 different states, it is by far the world's poorest inhabited continent in terms of the wealth of the individual citizen. The nations are rich but constantly robbed in grand style. According to 2002 figures from the UNDP and the AfDB, Africa has a ratio of 0.1 millionaires (0.01%). The economy of Europe comprises about 665 million people in 48 different states, yet Europe has a ratio of 2.6 millionaires (0.3%). Europe's GDP is $13.823 trillion, Africa's $1.635 trillion.

China today is said to have at least 300,000 dollar millionaires.

Chapter 5. African Collective Psychic Damage

> *That all the claims of superiority of the whites over the blacks, on account of their color, are founded in ignorance and inhumanity.*
> — BENJAMIN RUSH (1745-1813),[19] a signatory to
> the American Declaration of Independence

Despite all that has been said or preached, I see the core of problems in Africa as being the African people themselves. Most of them are not even aware that they are their own problems. Africans are the psychologically lost branch of humankind. Not without good reason. No other group has been as physically and psychologically brutalized, and this brutalization lasted all of 500 years. Worse still, the end is not even on the horizon.

The practice of keeping a fellow human being as a slave has been implemented throughout human history and goes on even now, even between homogeneous groups of people. During the Islamic Empire, Jewish merchants brought the caliphs, sultans, maharajahs and Chinese emperors blonds and redheads (both boys and girls) from Europe while bringing Europeans silks, camphor, china, cinnamon and other desired mercantile goods from the East. As late as the end of the 16th century, Miguel de Cervantes survived five years as a slave of Barbary (Berber) pirates in Algiers.

For Africa and the Africans, after the trans-Atlantic slave trade came the colonization. This was an experience that was more traumatizing than the slave

---

19 Observations intended to favour a supposition that the Black Color (as it is called) of the Negroes is derived from Leprosy", in: *Transactions of the American Philosophical Society*, Vol.IV, No. XXXV, 1948, p. 289-297

trade. Here was a strange people who appeared out of nowhere to take the land of the African ancestors and there was no stopping them; a handful of them could kill ten thousand warriors in a matter of hours. It took a long time for Africans to recover from the paralyzing daze and think up new forms of war strategies and tactics against the victors' military might. Then, just as independence dawned on African nations, the people of Africa were latched into the toughest chains ever: dictators appointed by the ex-colonialists, imperialist and kleptocratic rulers who did not shy away from using violence of the most inhuman forms to achieve their goals. All these processes were inconsistent, abrupt, capricious, arbitrary, unpredictable and so intense that the "injuries" Africans sustained are severe and will be irreversible without concerted efforts being made to "heal" these sustained "injuries."

Finally, "globalization" is now forcing not just Africa but the entire planet to its knees, creating new ruthless forms of ethnic and gender discrimination.

In the sociological sense, Africans have emerged through all this with a collective inferiority complex affecting their entire spectrum of thousands of cultures. This is known as the *cultural cringe*. They (the kleptocratic dictators, political leaders and the elite) feel inferior to nearly all other cultures and peoples and are afflicted with a pathological desire to overcompensate by spectacularly achieving or by adopting behavior that is extremely antisocial. It assists nobody to deny the fact that Africans tend to have negative feelings of self-esteem and self-worth that fluctuates between over-evaluation (or idealization) and devaluation both of themselves and of others. Particularly African politicians and persons in responsible positions seem unable to realistically accept that, like any other human beings, they have self-limitations. These Africans see insults and slights where even radar could not detect them. They cannot deal with criticism, failures, disillusionment, setbacks and disappointments, but base their sense of self-esteem and self-worth substantially on outside events like subordination, absolutism, Swiss bank accounts, Armani suits, villas in Malibu or Florida, vast domains in England and castles all over Europe. I recently wrote a letter to the African editor-in-chief of a London monthly which I read regularly, praising many of his articles but also criticizing some as biased. He personally sent me an email indicating, rather forcefully, that if I took such a dim view then I "shouldn't read the magazine." His personal vanity was all that mattered.

Three good examples of African elites who suffer from "acquired narcissism" were Dr. Felix Houphoüet-Boigny, General Field Marshal el Haj Idi Amin and Emperor Jean Bedel Bokassa The First. Their likes — and quite a few hundred million non-elite Africans as well — are like children in the formative years trying to shield themselves from what psychologists term "the inevitable hurt and fears involved in the phase of personal development." This phase is normally evident in children aged 6 months to 6 years. By the time the subject "toddlers" I refer to above arrive at "adolescence" and "adulthood," they are drowned in infatuation and obsession with themselves to the exclusion of others. They display a chronic pursuit of personal gratification and attention, infantile verbal abuse and insulting of each other in the media and during parliamentary debates, bragging, social dominance and personal ambition, lack of empathy, insensitivity to other fellow Africans whom they devalue or annihilate senselessly, circumventing hindrances or any sense of responsibility in their daily livelihood and thoughts. Rather than progressing to maturity, they regress to the infantile-narcissistic phase. They feel omnipotent, underestimate challenges facing them and believe themselves to be almighty, misjudge their powers and the powers of their opposition. When the opposition — whether innocent citizens voicing their grievances, organizations and the civil society fighting for a humanitarian cause or political rivals gaining popularity — they simply "get rid of" such opposition. Their ability to appreciate the feelings and needs of others as well as to empathize with them rapidly deteriorates. They turn arrogant and haughty, paranoid and sadistic. The dissonance breeds the desire to keep on living in the world of fantasy, grandiosity and entitlement. Above all else they are in a perpetual feverish search for unconditional admiration which they do not deserve in the first place. Their preoccupation is their fantasy world and daydreams. And, at last, in this mode, they exploit others or pathologically envy them and become quite literally explosive. Whatever they say or do is said and done from a position of omnipotence. Hence the urge to try to Europeanize themselves and to amass castles, villas and Western bank accounts with sums of money that would feed, educate and provide adequate medical services for the entire African continent. The real world keeps on frustrating them and the frustration is acute to the point of being unbearable. Theirs is a world in which everything is either all virtue or all evil.

The federal president of Germany in 2007, Horst Kohler, was once with the Fund. He narrates how in one international venue in New York, an African leader approached him and began "ordering" the financial assistance he needed for a water project in his country. Mr. Kohler pointed out that the cost of flying, boarding, lodging, shopping sprees and maintenance for the hundred or so members of the entourage the man had brought with him to New York would be more than sufficient for several water projects. The African reverted to the over-chewed racist remarks, topped with the "you owe us — we have a right to" spearhead.

Narcissistic or not, because they devalue their fellow Africans they in effect devalue themselves along with the Africans. But unlike Michael Jackson they cannot become "white" in complexion. Failing this, they line shelves in their castles with leather-bound Encyclopaedia Britannica, the pages of which they will never turn. Their walls hug Brueghels and Correggios which mean nothing to them except that very rich Euroancestrals like Queen Elizabeth buy them with the same kind of fortune, even if not nicked directly from the country's central bank or the citizenry's services budgets.

Meanwhile the public collections of priceless Africa art have been plundered and the objects sold to Westerners for a song. Africans, let alone just the rich kleptocrats or the elite, do not value what is their own, what is truly African. And whatever is still in the African museum is gathering dust. Africans have an insatiable need for attention to regulate their fragile and fluctuating sense of self-worth, and most of them have a narcissism that is garnished with the largest dose of paranoia. They cannot develop a sense of security. The former president of Kenya, Daniel arap Moi, used to attend services in as many as five churches every Sunday — not because he was a devout God-fearing Christian, but to make sure nothing was being preached against him.

The African psyche is their worst ailment. But how did they catch the contagion?

Four hundred years of slavery brought the Africans to culture a mentality of self-negation. It taught them, even in the Bible once their majority were converted to Christianity, that the color of their skin destined them to slavery and slavery was the prerequisite for their skin color. They saw their monarchs, their nobility, rulers, leaders, religious and military dignitaries overwhelmed by a military superiority they were powerless against. A military superiority that ordered these monarchs, aristocrats, military nobility, and religious dignitaries to be publicly chained, whipped and dragged to the bowels of ships — by mere menials or other African slaves. These pillars of their society could now protect neither their people nor themselves. And they were taken away, never to be seen again.

When it was not their monarchs and dignitaries it was their daughters, wives, mothers, husbands, sons, fathers, sisters and brothers. Those who were left behind were either weak, sick, crippled or hardly out of infancy. They did not know how long they themselves would remain free, left with no spiritual, medicinal, political or military organizations worth relying on. Those who were hauled to the Americas or the Caribbean were even more helpless and lost than those left behind to blindly roam around their vast continent in an attempt to survive. Most continental Africans thus embarked on building temporary settlements and practicing a life of mere subsistence. Not only the stranger who crossed your path but also your general merchant or your neighbor was a potential enemy and was not to be trusted. They could lure and sell you or any member of your family to slavers. Those who had cultured a settled life with central organizations before this bizarre dilemma, were forced into a nomadic life, always penetrating inland and away from the coastal areas in order to survive. They mutilated their bodies or the bodies of their children in order to look unattractive or weak to the slavers. Personalities could not thrive where mistrust had such vast grazing pasture. And the worst inter-human relationships took root and became a giant obstructing oak: the defeated African always met the victor European in an attitude of self-negation, subservience, self-effacing and inferiority. To this minute, when African leaders sit with Euroancestral leaders on conference tables or play host to international conferences where the pink face is inevitable, the African self-doubt is a screaming aura around the Africans, thick enough to feel and visible enough to see. Most Africans' eyes and voices are instinctively lowered as if they have to take pains not to assault the civilized sensitive eyes and ears of the Euroancestrals (compared to when they are debating among themselves), their gaits become faltering, their composure labored and their carriage cramped. They exude an all-round air of being ill-at-ease, like schoolboys fearing a reprimand before the headmaster. In the presence of Euroancestrals, the explosions of cannon balls, bombs falling and guns smoking to wipe out fellow African brave warriors wielding spears, arrows and war axes, shredding these warriors to bits of flying human flesh from some incredible distance, is branded in the African collective memory and is ever-present — as soon as the pink skin is in the vicinity. The Cultural Cringe. It is the parental as well as an entire ethnic group's protection and survival strategies passed on from one generation to the next in more than five centuries: Extreme caution. Don't, if you can't stop it instantly, even sneeze wrongly before the pink people. Do as has been taught and demanded by them or otherwise face the fatal consequences. Tread only where allowed to tread or else meet the decimation of yourself and yours. Say what is expected of you or else; it will be the last time you open your mouth to utter any opinions of your own. Echo the convictions of your mentor, the pink ones, or you will never have the tongue to utter any convictions at all.

In other words, the Africans are generally not at ease in the psychological sense. And it happens involuntarily.

The triumphant European, on the other hand, always met the defeated African with an attitude of self-assertion, self-esteem, lordliness and superiority — like engineers presenting the details of an under-water tunnel they had constructed hundreds of times before. They were always the superhuman and the Africans were forever mere objects or at best subhuman. Heathen, and without their own history. Civilized Christian values, helplessly squeezed in the stranglehold of the new Euroancestral fist, had no room for an alternative in other hands.

In the embryonic Christendom that had to function with a militarily-crafted strait jacket, faith had to be juggled around with a flexible morality conducive to human greed. Even God had become too benign.

Black Military Musician in Brandenburger Court" by Peer Schenk, 1696-1701 in the State Museum, Berlin.

And this is why the straitlaced Islamic human values are a thorn in the impatient flesh of liberal capitalism. Overtly, Islam is a religion designed to be a unifying force, a fact the West cannot afford to acknowledge. Christianity admits that even Christ came not to unite but to divide, even child from parent, husband from wife. Islam is the only major world religion whose scripture clearly condemns all forms of racism and not only proclaims but teaches that all humankind are equal before God regardless of the color of the skin. The Prophet, having had the advantage of studying the Old Testament (culled out of the Jewish Talmud) and the New Testament with the teachings of Christ, carefully sifted both in order to come up with the Koran. Christianity on the other hand has the tortured tale of Noah and his three sons to make the demarcation of humankind between good, better and best. In my opinion, if one has to go by today's so-called "new world order," the *good* have become bad, the *better* worse and the *best* worst.

Let us revert, then, to the allegedly defeated Africans. As if enough damage had not been done by slavery, colonialism dovetailed smoothly with the inhuman practice and perpetuated the African trauma. Every last vestiges of African systems of governance, education, art, music, dance, sculpture, architecture, mode of dress, religion and even the culinary and the linguistic was forcefully wiped out and forbidden by colonial laws. The colonial administrations and their handymen, the missionaries, began an aggressive campaign for the internalization of the "virtues" of European values and religion versus the "worthlessness" as well as "heathenness" of African values and religions. The fact that Europeans had never come up with a world religion and that Christianity had been appropriated by them from the Afro-Orient was not common knowledge among the Africans, even to this day. Before colonialism there were still about 10,000 African kingdoms, which Europeans then reduced to 40 colonies dictated over and looted by the power of military might. King Leopold II of Belgium, for example, owned the entire Democratic Republic of Congo as his own personal and private land, promising France that if he ever would want to sell the vast country, France would have first option. An African country that is 666,350 times bigger than Belgium, was the private property of a single European king of no great influence; this shows just how superhuman Euroancestrals felt and still feel against Afroancestrals.

African kings were reduced to "paramount chiefs" or "chiefs" or "headmen" and the ethnic groups to "tribes" — at gunpoint. To quote John Iliffe, writing on the colonial experience, "Europeans believed Africans belonged to tribes; Africans built tribes to belong to..." And these "tribes" were taught that they were collectively belonging to a group of humankind known as "blacks." Not only Christianity (which Egypt and Eastern Africa had already adopted long before the religion reached Rome) but also European culture was introduced in the educational and other spheres of everyday African life. Even inland African schoolchildren who had never heard of the trans-Atlantic slave trade and all its gory details had in their curriculum or syllabus the entire madness as part of "Africa history." It was a systematic psychological mass murder. Also included were characters like Oliver Cromwell, Christopher Columbus, or occurrences like the Industrial and French Revolutions, the American slave system and Civil War, Max Muller & Associates and their human classification, Social Darwinism and their superior "Aryan Race" theories — the lot. A systematic identity-genocide. Children in Sunday School were listening to stories like *Cinderella* and *Beauty and the Beast*, then singing *London's Burning...Look Yonder...!* And *Frère Jacques, dormez-vous ? Sonnez les matines...*to boot. As the German expression puts it: *wenn schon, denn schon* — whatever must be must be!

Africans had to know who the master was and who the cultureless, history-less subspecies of humankind. They had to know who were the descendants of Japheth and who descended from the cursed branch of Ham. They had to dance the waltz and listen to the Blue Danube (their own dancing was banned as "animalistic prurience," but see how Shakira is raking in millions with this "animalistic prurience" today!), they had to stop killing their abundant African wild game to feed themselves but had to scout for, watch the killing and then carry the "games" the Europeans had shot for trophies, now acting as the human means of transportation. They were forbidden to drink alcohol but to serve it to their European masters. Their local alcoholic brews were declared illegal and the distilleries destroyed by fire their own fellow Africans were ordered to set. They had to wear shirts and shorts instead of robes. Their entire existence was completely dominated through colonialists' Dos and Don'ts. Psychologically, they never recovered from these dehumanizing "injuries." Instead they made sure their offspring inherited this dehumanization as a form of protection mechanism against a foreign handful of people who could kill tens of thousands of Africans as if swatting a single fly or stamping a single cockroach.

It was the rule of terror.

When Africans finally took over the governing of their countries following independence, they obediently continued the dovetailing and stepped into the only system (psychologically as well as physically) they had known for five hundred years: terror, oppression and denial coupled with inhuman violence. Whereas the colonial rulers had tied religious conversion with cultural conversion, the new rulers tied political/party hegemony with ethnic hegemony. Whereas colonial powers had had separate laws for the colonists and those for the "natives," Africa's new rulers and the elite now had laws (with a judiciary as good as non-functioning) for the ordinary citizen who had no redress against them anyway, but practically none for themselves. They had learnt from perfect role models how to be above humane laws and were out to surpass the lessons of their mentors. The African elite and rulers were practically all above the law.

The process is being carried on today by globalization, where the richest African countries are being held ransom indefinitely and their elites share the loot with the equally insatiable transnationals while the rest of the population who have nothing to gain and much less to give, are strapped with astronomical national debts and left to starve to death. Seeing what the transnational giants are practicing without any sense of human ethics or regard for Christian or any other religious doctrines, the African elites have no qualms about "bad governance" when they can reap billions as beneficiaries by simply playing the handymen of the transnationals. Their billions are after all safe in "stable economies" in Europe and America.

And the so-called world community is watching because capital has become too mighty. Capital is delighted that somebody serves the purpose and is willingly doing magnificently well as the gatekeeper of the (artificial) bottom rung of the human ladder.

CHAPTER 6: THE SCOURGE NAMED CHARITY

> *It is by the finest tints, and most insensible gradations, that nature descends from the fairest face about St James's, to the sootiest complexion in Africa: at which tint of these, is it, that the ties of blood are to cease and how many shades must we descend lower still in the scale, 'ere Mercy 'tis to vanish with them? — but 'tis no uncommon thing, my good Sancho, for one half of the world to use the other half of it like brutes, & then endeavor to make 'em so.*
>
> LAURENCE STERNE in *Letters of Laurence Sterne*[20]

There is the old English saying that charity begins at home.

When we overlook for a moment what the Western powers are doing to keep Africa not only poor but also warring, we come to the continent's next worst enemies: the G8 and NGOs. Sir Robert Frederick Zenon Geldof has been knighted and has a firm hold on a gold mine without even joining the Anglo-American company de Beers in Congo, South Africa and just about the entire Atlantic coast of Africa. The whole world makes a fortune in Africa except the ordinary Africans themselves. Mining in Tanzania is conducted today by Vietnamese excavator drivers while Africans, wearing rags, are the washers separating the precious stones from mud and muck, and Europeans sit at desks sorting and grading the stones for the world market. How is this different from strict colonialism?

If a Western film- or pop star finds his or her star fading, all he or she needs to do is make a quick flight to Africa, get filmed and photographed holding starving babies surrounded by starving people in Darfur or Ethiopia, or toadying dancers in southern Africa, and their stars will twinkle again for the next couple of years.

---

20 Sterne, Laurence, *Letters of Laurence Sterne*, ed. Lewis Parry Curtis, Oxford/Clarendon Press, 1965 p. 170

For a lifetime's publicity with the world media stalking them night and day, all these Western "stars" have to do is another quick flight to Africa to adopt a poor African child in record time. Africa is not the only continent with poor children. Yet the African child's future cultural and ethnic traumas, from which money will never protect him, are of no consequence. Even pension-journalists whom none of today's carnivorous media would employ instantly find work if they go to Africa and concentrate on the wildlife and natural phenomena such as Mount Kilimanjaro, baobab trees or Victoria Falls. If they include people, then the focus should be on people living in huts shorter than they are and, squatting before their huts, eating grilled pupae from a calabash. The colorful African market is a great place — if there are whole coal-black roasted monkeys hanging on wooden hooks for sale. Africa has a unique fascination for the Westerners who have worked so hard through the centuries to polish this patina one way or the other. All that matters is the powerful cultivated image of "us" and "them."

Euroancestral politicians are another media-addicted clan who use the magical name "Africa" to get themselves a personal image and attention. The Federal President of Germany, an ex-IMF man, Horst Kohler, started a project he baptized "Partnership With Africa" in 2005. I wrote to him and suggested a very detailed sustainable program that would be of political and sociological assistance to rural Africans. The majority of these Africans are illiterate and cannot quite grasp the true meaning of "democracy." They thus get conned time and again into voting the wrong candidates into office. He wrote back to tell me that his "Partnership With Africa" is only engaged in "dialogue." Dialogue, I thought. Alright. I wrote again and asked whether I could join the panel in their next discussions in November 2006. Sorry, was the reply, the arrangements had been completed and sealed. It turned out that the next "dialogue" took place in Ghana, Kohler accompanied (among others) by dozens of young Germans from the age of eighteen, who are supposed to work in Africa as volunteers in "development programs." The crux of the matter is that these young people will be sponsored by their government to work in Africa — because there are virtually no training vacancies in Germany anymore for ordinary young school-leavers, with the exception of the super intelligent from elite schools. Does the African Union (never mind individual African countries) ever think of sending contingents of African school-leaving youth to acquire some practical knowledge in the West because these have no training facilities in Africa?

And if they did, would the West accept such African youth?

Predatory fast-food Western reporters roam the African landscape and come up with articles and books that would curl a horse's hooves. Their richly imaginative concoctions of African "tribes" and their "primitive" or even "cannibalistic" traditions create new waves of fantasy misinformation. Africa "experts" like Germany's Peter Scholl-Latour has even managed to give Kenya two non-existent ethnic groups: the *Schamba* and the *Kalendje* "tribes" [21], the latter proclaimed by him as the ethnic group of former Kenyan president arap Moi.

The NGOs and the G8 summits in Gleneagles in July 2005 and in St Petersburg in July 2006 have not brought Africa even a glint of hope. The Gleneagles summit was a giant failure that was (un)luckily overwhelmed by the 7/7 bombings in London. Gleneagles was a naked reminder that the G8 members do not have any vested interest in "ending poverty" in Africa. The so-called communiqué at Gleneagles was, as such documents always tend to be when Africa is involved, a forked-tongued serpent.

> The commitments of the G8 and other donors will lead to an increase in official development assistance to Africa of $25 billion a year by 2010, more than doubling aid to Africa compared to 2004.... As we confront the development challenges in Africa, we recognize there is a global development challenge facing the world as a whole. On the basis of donor commitments and other relevant factors, the OECD estimates that official development assistance from the G8 and other donors to all developing countries will now increase by around $50 billion a year by 2010 compared to 2004.

Development Aid Payments (2005) in billion $
(source: OECD)

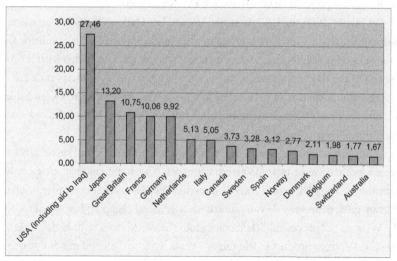

Such ambiguities, intentional or not, are irritating. What is Africa's share — $25 billion a year or $25 billion plus an unknown amount contained in the "all developing countries" package of $50 billion a year? Or is Africa's $25 bil-

---

21 Scholl-Latour, *Afrikanische Totenklage*, C. Bertelsmann, Munich, 2001 p. 147 & p. 150

lion already deducted from the $50 billion? Furthermore, the lump sum is not segmented into specific sums for each year up to 2010. Why not? How does this financial mystification mesh with the expectation that African governments lay out their plans for the utilization of the money? Is this a back door for the likes of Laurent Kabila of DRCongo and Omar Hassan Ahmad al-Bashir of the Sudan, open for "special concessions"?

On the touted goal of debt cancellation the communiqué further mystifies:

> The G8 has agreed a proposal to cancel 100% of outstanding debts of eligible Heavily Indebted Poor Countries (HIPC) to the IMF, IDA [International Development Association, which is a subsidiary of the World Bank] and African Development Fund, and to provide additional resources to ensure that the financing capacity of the IFIs is not reduced. These substantial extra resources will be focused on countries where they will make a difference, to accelerate progress towards the achievement of the Millennium Goals, and help us to achieve the objectives set out in this statement. We will focus aid on low income countries which are committed to growth and poverty reduction; to democracy, accountable and transparent government, and to sound public financial management, although aid is also important to respond to humanitarian crises and countries affected by or at risk of conflict.[22]

Who counts as eligible and who determines who is or is not eligible? How can one cancel 100% of debts that by any stretch of the imagination would never be repaid anyway?

But global public relations is always a Western gem.

On July 14, 2005 the US Treasury made an about face on the G8 discussions, maintaining that, "This isn't a proposal we could support. While conditionalizing debt relief seems attractive on its face, there are clear problems with it." At the end of the day, it means that debt cancellation to poor countries translates into the reintroduction of IMF conditions — conditions that were swept aside because they had failed all along the line. And it only takes 15% of the votes on the IMF to block a deal.

If Africa is to end her (artificial) impoverishment, then she had better rely on herself, not the G8 or other Western countries. The argument that Africa only contributes 3% of the world trade is nonsense. The fact is that the coffee, cocoa, coltran, gold, diamonds — you name it — is grabbed cheap and whisked off to the West to be "processed," then comes into the world market, at higher valuations, as Western products. Belgium or Britain have no diamond mines but they are world leaders in the diamond trade. Those British soldiers storming into warring Sierra Leone to stop the diversion of the so-called blood diamonds to finance

---

22 G8 Gleneagles 2005, Gleneagles Communiqué on Africa, Climate Change, Energy and Sustainable Development. http://www.fco.gov.uk/Files/kfile/PostG8_Gleneagles_Communique,0.pdf. Accessed 04.4.2006

the war did not do so out of philanthropic sentiment — there was an "interest" to be protected, and that interest was by no means Sierra Leone's. Africa is the only continent in the world whose natural wealth still brings not improved welfare but peril to its citizens.

Now let us take a look at the NGOs. While the per capita GDP in Sub-Saharan African countries continues to drop, the NGOs are proliferating. They now constitute a prominent part of the so-called "development machinery." In actual fact they are organized bodies of official scholars, agencies, consultants, practitioners and a plethora of miscellaneous presumed experts who are supposed to be producing and consuming knowledge about the so-called developing world. The result of it all is that after over five decades of independence, Africa is more in debt than ever before.

Yet through hundreds of years, Africa had more or less the same climatic conditions, i.e., floods and droughts, the occasional natural catastrophes like locust invasions and the ever present wild animals destroying harvests, or diseases that decimate livestock. But there was always the internal social network of aiding each other mutually. The name for this network in Luoland is *dhi kisuma*. This was an African system where neighbor communities whose harvests had been ruined for one reason or another had the "right" to ask for and receive help from neighbor communities who had had abundant harvests or whose herds had remained intact or even increased. Neighbors left with only cows, ewes, and nanny goats joined their herds with those who still had bulls, rams and he-goats, and vice versa. It was help and assistance with no interest attached to it except that, nature being moody, one knew not who would be next hit and would need help from the neighbor communities.

The colonialists destroyed this indigenous "NGO" system in more ways than one, all aimed at dehumanization of the African physically and psychologically. They divided vast tracts of land among themselves with utmost Megignoarrogance, not giving a single thought to the human beings living on the land. Artificial borders were created not only on the African soil but also in the African psyche in the guise of a plethora of identities, whether religious, "national" or "tribal," cultural and so on. Whole groups of people found themselves hemmed in by "strangers" who spoke different languages, had different customs and traditions. People belonging to the same ethnic group were separated with artificial borders they could not simply wander across when they needed their time-honored "NGO" assistance. Even families were separated, and the African extended family is very large and amorphous, sometimes involving several clans.

To force the Africans into a form of bondage labor, "hut taxes" were introduced which had to be paid in cash, not natural products. When the colonists went away, Africans were left with a vicious circle to deal with, that is forever slinging Africa back to the Stone Age — "development aid."

Like the African citizenry, the majority of the Western citizenry is also always fooled by the expression "development aid" to Africa. This aid is nothing more than a noose around Africa's neck. The aid comes in the form of credits, subsidies, the so-called ODA (Official Development Assistance) and grants, which force Sub-Saharan African countries to maintain a colonialist relationship with the West, thus pledging their wealth and natural resources to the donors, accepting dictated terms of both usage and repayment, and therefore robbing themselves of the chance to practice their own mode of development. The "development aid" only assists the African leaders and the elite, and above all else the donors. Of the Least Developed Countries, 34 are in Africa. In countries like Tanzania and Uganda, 50% of the national budget comes from "development aid" yet the aid industries do not engage in solving African problems if the solutions would jeopardize the industries' receiving further funds. On the contrary, the aid industries live on such problems year in and year out. Meanwhile dependence on aid has rendered African countries unable to negotiate effectively in world trade. Moreover, this dependence encourages governments to lean back and relax instead of working out viable economic strategies for their citizens. Nearly all African governments make concession deals with Western governments and multinationals, who are then happy to let these governments shoo in their own ethnic groups to various high posts in the state and the parastatal bodies, with complete disregard to meritorious considerations. Some of these high posts holders can hardly articulate themselves. The Kenyan government, for example, has meanwhile more than 80 ministers. Such "big men" together with Western bankers, raw materials industrialists, transnationals, economic advisors from the West and the "development machinery" actually only succeed in under-developing African countries. The foreign advisors work for the benefit of their own countries and the African governments have no role to play in the decision-making and are therefore weak. Aid also ruins the environment when monstrous projects are built (e.g. the Niger Delta). The citizens do not develop their own initiatives, nor marshal their innovations and creativity, and there is virtually no motivation for entrepreneurial ambitions because there is virtually no middle class — the mega-moneyed, with their disastrously fragmented psyches and inferiority complexes, go shopping in London, Paris or New York. Equally fragmented and uncoordinated projects are run parallel to each other, whereas they aim for similar goals. What Africa needs are technicians, but the aid industries heap bureaucrats on the continent. Corruption is encouraged. In 1982, the then Zaire owed the West a debt of $5 billion, while at the same time the country's President Mobutu had a private fortune of $4 billion stashed away in Western banks. Many a head of state have been assisted in oppressing the people by aid funds used to buy weapons. As long as Western "interests" remain intact, the West looks the other way or bury their heads in the sand or snigger in brisk asides.

Or there would seem to be a deliberate effort to keep Africans poor and steadfastly dying younger and younger.

It is estimated that there are 40,000 foreigners in Africa working with aid organizations. According to estimates, OECD countries have three thousand (3,000) NGOs, over one hundred (100) of which are in Britain. These organizations are as well-structured and well-run as any other profit-orientated entity. In Africa the NGOs have stepped into the shoes of colonial voluntary organizations such as missionaries. One could say they *are* the missionaries of development. The engagements of the NGOs contribute virtually nothing to the relief of poverty and improvement of health, rather they undermine the struggle of the Africans to be independent economically, socially and politically. Of course there are a handful of NGOs in Africa who assist in promoting an emancipatory agenda. But only a handful, like a handful of water in an Olympic swimming pool.

Let us look back into recent history, the history of voluntary organizations in the former British Empire, especially Kenya. The period between 1840-1930 was the much acclaimed period of "free trade." It is also the period in which organized charity began in Europe. Towards the end of the 19th century, British industrialists were making fortunes that often surpassed those of the aristocracy. On the other hand a third of the population of London, for example, was barely subsisting. The solution to this came in the form of private philanthropy, public means being too meager to cope with the problem adequately. In the colonies the government spent the minimum for the welfare of the colonized Africans and this minimum was targeted at "civilizing" the Africans. Missionaries and charitable organizations as opposed to the colonial government, endeavored to reach rural Africans where the Africans then received what little education plus health and social services. In return the Africans had to — at least outwardly — "pay back" by altering their spiritual beliefs. An important part of this "civilization" was the — to the Africans — alien trait I mentioned above with regards to the "hut taxes," of *labor for wages.* In Kenya, two organizations that exist till today, the WYWO (Maendeleo ya Wanawake Organization) and the CCK (Christian Council of Kenya), were supported by the colonial government funds so that the two could help in subverting the Mau Mau Uprising. Such "charitable" organizations were strewn across the British-ruled colonies in Africa and their main task was to assist in thwarting nationalist struggles. Curiously, these organizations remained intact and still prosper long after independence because they easily slipped into the national and international "development" endeavors. Community development existed in the colonial period but it was not until a much later era when the United States of America and international agencies came up with the adjective "underdeveloped," that automatically led to the universal desirability of "developing" the "underdeveloped." Two godheads emerged in Kenya and elsewhere across the African continent. One was the "classical" missionary and charitable organizations like the WYMO and CCK, and the other was the former "war charities" such as Save the Children, Oxfam or Plan International. Initially these organizations did humanitarian work arising from European — to give them the politically correct name — conflicts. When the struggle against colonial rule mounted, the majority of the population became mistrustful of the various missionary societies and charitable organizations because of their association with the colonial powers. Seeing themselves with one foot in the grave, these organizations changed tack. They first of all made their organizations "local" or "indigenous" by gradually replacing their Euroancestral™ staff with "educated" (read: YOU OWE ME) Afroancestral™ clergy and secular administrators. Next came the ideological makeup geared at toning down the previous overt racism with the new international discourse of "development." *Development*, on the surface, was void of racism and had a whiff of emancipation and progress for the benefit of everybody. The new organizations began to condemn racism with as much — if not even more — vigor and conviction than they had implemented in promoting racial exclusion and suppression during the colonial days.

They condemned racism except *à huis clos* — in private, or behind closed doors.

These fresh "development" NGOs were unlike their colonial counterparts, war charities free of any association with the racist governments. The intention of internationalist humanitarianism was popularly supported by their European bases. Europe, with the massive Marshall Plan of 1948 at full throttle, was no longer threatened with mass starvation and suffering. The charity organizations could therefore choose between closing their doors permanently or expanding into new activities and new expansions into activities outside the European continent. It was the best way to ensure the survival of their organizations. Although religious ideologies played an important role, the liberal internationalism of the founders was the most motivating factor. Soon "development" — suggestive of long-term effects — became more endearing than simple humanitarian relief geared to curing short-term signs of the disease.

Networking was the next step where organizations like Christian Aid, Oxfam or War on Want worked in collaboration with various UN bodies. The FAO

(Food and Agriculture Organization) demanded poverty relief through "self generating agricultural development." Originally there had been the problem of convincing Britons to spend for some exotic and adventurous regions of Her Majesty's "glorious Empire." Another presumption was that the so-called development would resolved the problem by offering not the "uncivilized" African but the "underdeveloped" one. The guilty conscious was in full swing turning the Bad Guys into Good Guys. Britain and Europe, after the burden of "civilizing" Africans, now had that of "developing" them. As was to be expected by the strategic marketing talents of the NGOs, "developing" became a bestseller. There was a wild romantic enthusiasm about "bringing development to the people" of the newly independent Africa. The boosting jargons of justice and emancipation, however, were bulldozed aside to give way to the swank of paternalism, neutrality and technical expertise which in the end made legitimate the marginalization of Africa as well as non-Westerners. Following independence in Africa and elsewhere, there was a concerted effort to block or curtail the expansion of communism that was threatening to ruin the expansion of Anglo-American capitalism.

Whatever benefits were doled out to Africa were pegged to some short-term Western interest.

In time, the 1960s and 1970s enthusiasm of the NGOs for development watered down. In the opinion of such organizations as USAID, UN and World Bank, development was the duty of the state and international NGOs remained on the edges. They conducted their projects in Africa with conditional freedom that excluded their involving themselves practically or verbally on how the state executed its power. In the Cold War years, the important task was to ascertain that the ex-colonies adopted economic and military agendas of Western powers. The NGOs concentrated their "projects" in the poor rural areas where, like their colonial predecessors, they established the old racial division. The local workers did the manual work, had low salaries and the projects were geared for the present with little hope for a rosy future. By the 1970s the world economy was hit by recession and the so-called oil crisis. Europe and America suddenly churned out finance capital for high rates return but little or no effect on the rural poor. The emergence of gene technology and microcomputers attracted investments in new areas with more substantial rates of profit. The developing countries were encouraged to take loans to assist them in "development," but this full indulgence was short-lived. By the 1980s the costs of borrowing was escalating as the American administration introduced a neo-liberal monetary policy that skyrocketed interest rates worldwide. Debtor nations had to service the interest in borrowings that swallowed the ever-increasing proportions of export earnings. The new headache was now "debt" instead of "development." The era of Thatcher and Reagan was upon the debtors as was the neo-liberalism. This strangling indebtedness offered "the multilateral lending agencies the leverage they needed to impose their neo-liberal policy prescriptions, in the spirit of universality." Supported by the bilateral aid agencies, the Bretton Woods institutions, which allegedly focuses on the policies and projects of the World Bank and IMF, were the new captains at the helm of post-colonial economies. Steering by means of the SAPs (Structural Adjustment Programs) throughout Africa, they could now dictate both the end-products of development and the means by which they are to be achieved. And thus the institutions had direct intervention on the processes of political decision-making. They soon determined to what extent the (African) state could be involved in the social sector and forced draconian economic and social measures on the state, that gave birth to rising unemployment as well as declines in the real incomes of the majority African population. The funds were available to NGOs and this had a remarkable impact on the sector.

The CRBM (Campagna per la riforma della Banca Mondiale), a Rome-based NGO monitoring international financial institutions as well as Bretton Woods of London, put it this way:

> The imposition of SAPs and associated policies led to demonstrations that finally forced the multilateral and bilateral aid agencies to review their approach in promoting development in the neo-liberal economic and social projects, without forsaking humanitarian aspects. In the 1990s this led to the famous Western-defined "good governance" and the co-opting of NGOs as well as other civil society organizations to a re-packaged programme to provide for welfare under social control. "Good governance" is another name for political pluralism, ergo multipartyism. Those African governments who adopted multipartyism were allotted welfare initiates to accompany the good governance agenda. These funds were aimed at "mitigating" the "social dimensions of adjustment." In actual fact such programmes were meant to alleviate the disease without curing it. And the disease was the stark inequalities that the SAP policies had caused. In other words African governments had been forced to "retrench" away from the social sector and then aid agencies made funds available for the "safety net" of social services. Now, with their new man at IMF, Lipsky, who has a history as a Wall Street banker and advocacy for private finance, the man suggests he will push for more open capital accounts and greater access for private finance in developing country markets.

Martin Koehler of CRBM commented, "As long as the powerful members in the IMF reject any reform of its voting structure in order to reflect the increasing importance of developing countries in the global economy, the IMF must simply be called for what it is: an unrepresentative and undemocratic organization."

The impact on the NGOs was such that in Kenya, for example, the number of international NGOs rose almost threefold to 134 between 1978-88. Overseas Development Institute reports that in 1992 NGOs distributed between 10% and

15% of all aid transfers to "developing countries." Most of the money came from private donors but a significant proportion also came from official sources. Department for International Development — Great Britain — sets aside 8% of its aid budget to NGOs, the United States on the other hand nearly 40%. Within the last two decades the official funding has increased considerably. At the beginning of the 1970s NGOs received less than 2% from official donors, but this figure had increased to 30% by mid 1990s. Between 1984-94 the British government increased NGO funding by nearly 400% to 68.7 million pounds! As if being inflated, the UK-based international NGO funding swelled as the budget of the Department for International Development was increased to 3.22 billion pounds in 2001-2, from the previous 2.33 billion pounds in 1998-99. Similar increases occurred to NGOs based in Australia, Norway, Sweden and Finland, from the 1980s onwards. With the current estimated 40,000 NGO foreign nationals working in Africa alone, I ask myself whether this whole "aid business" is a job-creation scheme for Westerners. According to a statistics report by Gary Younge in Britain's *The Guardian* (May 28, 1998), "about 75% of the money aid agencies collect is spent on the administration of their own organization." Be that as it may, NGOs working in Africa have grown out of all proportions but with little effect on the indigenous population.

In Kenya, around December 2005, 40% of the NGOs were foreign. They are regarded as the preferable channel for service provision, deliberately substituting the state, which means that international NGOs have taken over the seat that once belonged to missionaries. They are running — some dubious, some pointless — "projects" motivated by charity and pity, delivering services and doing things for people who implicitly cannot do the same for themselves. And for how long? Should the people remain helpless "children" forever? In many regions in Africa where there are the all too famous "conflicts," NGOs — without meaning to, perhaps — assist in keeping the warring parties warring.

One of the most famous humanitarian camps is Lokichokio (sometimes spelt Lokichogio or Lokichoggio), situated thirty kilometers from the Kenyan-Sudanese border, on the Kenyan side. Its western horizon borders on Uganda, the northern one on Sudan. About twenty years ago Lokichokio was a cluster of huts, two little shops, shaded resting places under fig trees and a fortified police station. Often simply called Loki, this camp is now labeled Kenya's third largest city. It houses the entire genre of NGOs from the UN's World Food Program over USAID, MS, Operation Lifeline Sudan and IRC, to just about any other NGO one can think of, from the entire planet. Forty-nine are organizations and UN offices which are part of the Operation Lifeline Sudan Program. Loki is squeaking clean and has perfectly arranged dwellings, streets, Cessna planes, tarmac airstrip and the most modern communications technology that money can buy. The NGOs are coping with crises in the neighboring countries after all.

ChevronTexaco and its subsidiary, Caltex Oil (Kenya) Ltd Global Aviation, supply the aviation fuelling facilities on site. There are about thirty-five flights leaving Loki's airstrip per day and it is the relief capital of East Africa. The jet fuel is transported by the US oil multinational from the Kenyan harbor city of Mombasa 1,000 miles (1,600 kilometers) away, who pipes the fuel 500 miles through Nairobi to the town of Eldoret from where the fuel is driven to Loki in a two-day trip, and then stored in 211,000 gallon (800,000 liter) storage tanks. These NGO fellows know how to look after themselves.

The World Food Program alone, for the Southern Sudan, spends more than a million dollars *per day!* Of this sum 75% to 80% are spent in the administration of the WFP. Kenya has a population of around 30 million, therefore the WFP here has the wherewithal to make dramatic changes in the life of every single Kenyan, in a single year! Lack of drinking water, for example, would be history in the entire country in a matter of months.

The role NGOs are playing in cementing neo-liberal hegemony around the globe may be pure coincidence. But it still leaves a margin of doubt and faint memories of the missionary societies who willingly worked hand in hand with the colonial powers. And the NGOs seem to be much more successful. Back in 1986 at the UN General Assembly, African (local-based) NGOs made a formal declaration to their Western "partners" which read: "We encourage Northern and International NGOs to recognize the linkages of many policies of their governments, corporations and multilateral institutions which their governments heavily influence and which adversely affect the quality of life and political and economic independence of African countries." International NGO workers in Africa earn dream salaries (even those termed "field workers") and it might be more than tempting under such favorable conditions not to jeopardize one's own position. In his book *Afrikanische Totenklage,* the German journalist and author I mentioned earlier, Peter Scholl-Latour, writes about a visit to the Bahr el Ghazal in Southern Sudan where he spoke to one of the international NGO workers, an Irishman stationed in Loki. To the question of how anybody could be starving in this Sudanese region, the Irishman answers that if (instead of the indigenous Nuer and Dinka people) the region were populated by the Chinese or Cambodians, they would have long since turned the swamps into rice fields and harvested enough to feed half of Africa. Now, if this NGO-Irishman knows the cure, why hasn't he started a project in which the indigenous people are taught how to grow rice in the abundant swamps? If they don't choose to eat rice, they could sell it to the rest of Africa which no doubt would be happy to eat it, and use the money to feed themselves. Scholl-Latour seems never to have posed this question to the Irishman.

It is estimated that there are more than 25,000 groups qualified as international NGOs around the world, with affiliates and programs in numerous countries. They operate at community, national and global levels as non-profit organizations. In various African countries such as Kenya where they have successfully entrenched themselves as the lifeline, their roles run from planners in ministries, supporters in WTO (World Trade Organization) negotiations and advisors in the implementation of aid funds. Without the knowledge or even information of the targeted population, NGOs are increasingly influencing government policies and are the spokespersons of poor African countries as "partners" who often negotiate single-handedly. "They influence the way knowledge is generated and utilized," writes the Kenyan journalist Michael Onyango, and, "Their selective blindness to the injustices around them makes great learning on how institutions can deliberately marginalize some poor people while claiming to foster their core agenda." It is very much like the kettle calling the pot black. The NGOs' so-called local knowledge is used as leverage in lobbying global institutions to direct their programs in specific directions and in arenas where poor African countries are excluded and the NGOs participate as the representatives of such poor countries. In total exclusion of the "beneficiary populations," NGOs now wield a power equal to those of UN agencies such as Inter Agency Standing Committee (IASC), UN humanitarian bodies based in Geneva which include the American consortium Inter Action and the European NGOs' consortium International Council of Voluntary Agencies, and the Steering Committee for Humanitarian Response (SCHR) — to name but these. As UN equal partners, international NGOs define standards and procedures in humanitarian and other development priorities in the above forums. It begs the question of whether the international NGOs are pseudo governments or surrogates of Western powers.

In Stockholm and later in Ottawa in May 2004, "Principles of Good Donorship" and the need to focus on humanitarian imperative was highly touted. It transpired that NGOs were promoted and became surrogates of their representative governments. Countries at loggerheads with Western powers such as Zimbabwe receive no aid to afflicted groups from NGOs unless NGOs were allowed to distribute it themselves as a way of cautioning such countries. But poor and needy Zimbabweans are not Robert Mugabe, so why should they be punished in his stead? Besides, whatever atrocities are taking place in Zimbabwe, they are, like those taking place in Iraq, the babies delivered by Western midwives. It is Tony Blair who reneged on the Lancaster House agreements the Thatcher government went into with Zimbabwe regarding land redistribution in the African nation. As usual whenever Western bungling turns to a fatal steamroller, everybody else under the sun is guilty except the West. In the year 2000 European NGOs lobbied against Zimbabwean companies for the "wanton destruction" of DRCongo forests. The same NGOs turned a blind eye when South African companies with influence in European consortiums became involved in the same wanton destruction of forests in DRCongo. NGOs' support for the development agenda runs along these lines: Countries whose governments are deemed difficult and cannot be collaborators, even where specific sectors of their economies merit collaboration, get short shrift. In these countries NGOs support is targeted at substitute local structures, including the potential for weakening those very structures, so that in the long term, the NGO structures become the formal structures. Under such circumstances, any resistance to the NGO agenda is met with strong advocacy strategies both at national, regional and global levels, to the extent that the affected country comes under pressure from global bodies such as the United Nations to behave differently on a given strategy. Furthermore, Western donors are unwilling to provide aid unless this is distributed by NGOs. The US Public Law 480 stipulates for example, that US Administration only finances aid activities exclusively through NGOs and related institutions. No aid is ever to be provided through local governance of recipient nations. Even "America's greatest friend of Africa," Bill Clinton, announced this publicly at the UN General Assembly. Things can be quite the opposite if American or Western "interests" would be involved. When George W. Bush took over the White House scepter by means more foul than fair, he confounded matters by separating civic and religious projects funded by Washington. A good move for "American interests," because China and Sudan's al Bashir were getting cheek-and-jowls with the oil concessions in troubled Southern Sudan, where America has been supporting SPLM/A "brother Christians" in the south of the country.

Both the European and American NGOs have been mandated to provide leadership roles in meetings conducted by ECOSOC (the UN Economic and Social Council). The NGOs plan the contents of such meetings down to how deliberations should proceed — to the exclusion of the poor nations who are supposed to be the beneficiaries of such deliberations — as it relates to the humanitarian agenda. Writes journalist Onyango in *New African* of August 2005, "The closest representation opportunity open to the poor countries is from the Red Cross Movement, which sits in the same forum." The ECOSOC is a member-state forum, so NGOs have been elevated to the status of member-states. This is where the Janus (the Roman god of doorways, passages and bridges) face of the movers-and-shakers of this world hits onlookers in the face like a raging blizzard. "States" have been plucked out of thin air, placed on higher and more powerful rungs than actual existing countries, and then plonked on seats in a UN organization. Full stop. Wielding this kind of power, the NGOs have been known to marginalize the poor countries whom they claim to assist in "development."

Countries deemed weak and ready to collaborate are the ones awash with projects that are sometimes disjointed and competing, and occasionally at variance with the long-term national development goals of the recipient countries. Often, short-termism becomes the whole preoccupation. Food insecurity is one character of such countries, and as the former US Secretary of State Henry Kissinger once put it, "It is amazing what a few grains of cereal in a pocket can do to an African leader." The food security projects supported by the NGOs, again through their intrinsic host governments, are tiny subsistence projects that have no linkages to the other sectors of the economy. Having recognized in the last ten years that they are hugely funded and encouraged by the donors, NGOs have learned to put together consortiums and are now able to respond directly in a bigger fashion. The new power of the NGOs makes them far more strategic in relation to national governments with whom they have to negotiate. The perfect smokescreens with full awareness of their roles. National policies are either ignored or done away with altogether to conform to the priorities of the NGO consortiums. As a result, recipient countries now have the enormous challenge of maintaining their basic sovereignty and territorial integrity. Yet the same NGOs are implementing agents for UN agencies who sub-contract their activities to the NGOs.

Whichever way one looks at it, the NGOs win. Or better said, Africa loses because some of the NGOs' cures are worse than the disease.

CHAPTER 7: AFRICA AND THE MIDDLE KINGDOM

> *If they know and they believe that China can sustain them and support them, and China becomes a donor country, then they don't care. And then what will happen, the United States and Britain will start ac-commodating them because they do not want them to go to China. So if anyone starts trying to change the constitution or imprisoning jour-nalists or breaching procurement rules and regulations, they'll pretend not to understand because they're afraid they'll go over to China.*

> ZAINAB BANGURA, *Sierra Leonean activist & politi-cian, in a speech to the Commission for Africa,* 2005[23]

Welcome back to Africa, Iron Curtain. The Western nations' credo for Afri-can leaders is: "You can't choose your friends freely, you have to accept whoever declares himself to be one or whoever offers you their friendship in whichever form suits them. On the other hand you cannot stop such friends turning into your enemies."

Yet Africa, solely by the virtue of the continent's wealth and history, should be ruling the world. Africa has humankind's oldest libraries and universities, palaces and mansions, funerary complexes and walled cities, toilets and sewage systems, several among the hundreds of the oldest monarchies in human history who had royal ministries for etiquette and protocol, ministries for astronomy with a collection of scientific texts clearly showing the planets circling the earth long before Europe's Galileo and Copernicus would come up with similar cal-

---

23 Zainab Bangura has won the following awards: Humanitarian Award - Bayard Rustin (2002), Human Rights Award — Lawyers Committee for Human Rights (New York) (2000), African International Award of Merit for Leadership — Nigeria (1999), Democracy Woman of the Year Award — Concord Times — Sierra Leone (1996)

culations and be persecuted for the audacity. Africa boasts the ruins of a 300 BC astronomical observatory which was found at Namoratunga in Kenya, and Nok art from the Nok site calculated to have existed in 4580 or 4290 BC. Africa had been mining gold on an epic scale as long ago as 43,000 years, organizing fishing expeditions 90,000 years ago. Malian sailors reached America in AD 1311, almost two centuries before Columbus, while Ethiopia minted its own coins 1,500 years ago, kept archives in mediaeval Nubian kingdoms where thousands of preserved documents discovered are written in Meroitic, Latin, Greek, Old Nubian, Coptic, Arabic and Turkish. A check for 42,000 golden dinars written in the outskirts of Ancient Ghana to a merchant in Audoghast by his partner in Sidjilmessa in AD 951 was the first check ever issued. Ancient African writings assisted the Armenians in developing their own writing and apart from *dhi kisuma* in Luoland, other Africans had a social welfare system that especially took care of the handicapped members of the society as far back as the antiquity. Africa had and still has it all.

The infant European hegemony grows from strength to strength by clambering on Africa's back as the beast of burden and source of resources. Because Africans kept tight reins on the primitive aggression that drives one to becoming ruthless predators on fellow human beings. They still do this in matters like "reconciliations," "truth commissions," that innate psychological paralysis in the presence or at the sight of non-Afroancestrals, the affection and trust in all that is exogenous while on the other hand treating all that is endogenous with disaffection and mistrust, resignation to the thuggeries of the "big men" and the self-negating fatalism. If every member of a family gives himself up, then who is going to provide encouragement and whip up everybody into believing in themselves?

The African leaders seem to have learnt the ruthless predator lesson so well that they practice the same on their political colleagues and the public at large. Following the end of the Cold War, Africa of the 1990s was all but ignored by the rest of the world. But since Africa became the final frontier of the world's supplies of energy, a lot is up for grabs. The losers, as usual, will be the majority of the African people. Most of the new oil for the world market in the next two or so decades will come from African fields, as the fields are the only substantial new ones to have been brought into production. As is always the rule when outsiders want Africa's wealth or resources for themselves, the continent has become the target of military intervention by the US, China, France and others competing to wield control over energy supplies, with the United States being the most determined. The words of Jimmy Carter in the 1980s, called the Carter Doctrine, stipulated that "any means necessary, including military force"[24] was to be engaged to ensure the free flow of the Persian Gulf oil. It has been engaged. And as Bill Clinton put it, "...in a world of growing energy demand, our nation cannot afford to rely on any single region for our energy supplies."[25]

Africa is now on, and the continent will be given enough rope to hang itself.

The former US Assistant Secretary of State for Africa Walter Kansteiner said in July 2002 in Nigeria, "African oil is of strategic national interest to us and it will increase and become more important to us as we go forward."[26] Such statements have been followed with either expanding or establishing military aid programs in Africa "and the provision of US arms, military equipment and technical assistance,"[27] writes the Director of the African Research Project in Washington DC, Daniel Volman. On the surface such aid is earmarked for internal security "enhancement" of friendly African nations. That means, in anybody's language, controlling or suppressing religious, ethnic, factional or any other such "conflicts" in the African states.

And everybody knows that the cup always spills over.

The largest US military aid to Africa goes to their two leading oil suppliers, Angola and Nigeria. In the period 2002-2004, the substantially increased amount was $300 billion. Such sums turn right around and are back in US banks with nobody batting an eyelid. Such internal security "enhancement" capabilities aid are extended to a variety of other African countries. They are purported to improve anti-terrorism actions and support international peacekeeping operations (seductively named "Enduring Freedom" while they perpetrate and perpetuate conflicts), but the techniques and skills taught, such as counter-insurgency, small unit maneuvers, light infantry operations and the like, can easily be used in the suppression of religious, sectarian and ethnic disagreements. Professional military training of the African soldiers is provided by the US both in the US and in Africa, by the International Military Education and Training (IMET) program. Observers claim that Washington has used a multi-facetted security assistance programs, including sales, acquisition of bases in strategic African countries and training exercises to improve its military influence in Africa. The arms sales to Africa through the Foreign Military Sales (FMS) rose from $25.5 million in 2004 to $61.5 million in 2005, the main recipients being Djibouti and Kenya. Others are Botswana, Eritrea, Ethiopia, Nigeria and Uganda. The US govern-

---

24 *New African*, London, No. 453, July 2006, "The Scramble for African Oil".
25 Ibid.
26 Ibid.
27 Volman, Daniel, *Oil, Arms and Violence in Africa*, Report: African Security Research Project, Washington DC, February 2003

ment has also approved sales directly from American companies through the Commercial Sales program, monitored by the State Department, to Angola, Botswana, Kenya, Nigeria, Senegal, South Africa and Uganda. Some of these countries are far from being labeled internally secure. Yet the US increasingly pour more oil into the fire.

In May 2003 there was an indication by the NATO supreme commander, General Jones, that the US Navy will spend less time around the Mediterranean Sea and "...they will spend half the time going down the west coast of Africa."[28] At the maritime security conference of the US European Command (EURCOM) in Naples in October 2004, the three-day event included naval leaders from Gabon, Ghana, Guinea, Equatorial Guinea, Angola, Nigeria, Benin, Cameroon, Congo Brazzaville, Sao Tomé and Togo. The Western personnel representation came from the US, France, Italy, Netherlands, Portugal, Spain and the United Kingdom. Three months later the US deployed the *USS Emory* with about 1,400 sailors and marines along the Gulf of Guinea. Washington prefers a less visible and thereby provocative presence on African soil. It is also deemed easier for the US to conduct military intervention from off-shore naval fleets which could be rushed to oil-rich African regions at short notice. Wealth, greed and power-mania is watching over Africa's wealth for themselves like they have always done throughout history. Might is right. Meanwhile their African stooges are opening new foreign accounts in the West, where their money is safe from the next African Fing Fang Long Fingers leadership.

In 1972, before the oil crisis of 1974, the Arab world's most powerful men, especially the Kuwaiti oil minister, loudly questioned why they should sell their oil — the source of their daily bread and butter — for some invisible paper money. They soon demanded that the US should stop supporting Israel, they reduced their oil production and hiked the oil price up. The world economy took a nose dive into a crisis. This is a strategy oil-rich African countries should adopt. For their own good.

The African Union energy producing countries should take this example of small and weak countries forming alliances to stand up to more powerful countries. Even a country like Iran, who has the second largest gas reserves as well as the second largest oil resources in the world, has powerful global friends take their side when the West begins to apply the thumbscrews. Friends, not Albert Schweitzers ("I'm your brother, but your *big* brother)."

---

28 *New African*, London, No. 453, July 2006 in the article: "The Scramble for African Oil".

There is a new world power in town, joining the growing crowd who are making a fortune on Africa's natural resources without addressing the African people's poverty: the Middle Kingdom, better known as China. China was until the 1980s by far the largest non-capitalist country. Now China has dramatically changed its economic policies and as a result receives nearly 50% of the foreign direct investment formerly channeled to developing countries. Prior to the 1980s China had blocked all foreign investment.

Africa is practically teeming with the Chinese. I first made acquaintance with them in Guinea (Conakry), then in Sierra Leone, then in Angola. The Chinese have found the perfect formula for trading with African governments — they demand no good governance, adherence to human rights, an end to corruption, environmental rules and they are the last on God's planet to preach to anybody about democracy. In the last case, they have smartly circumvented the hypocritical approach of the US. The Chinese come to Africa, not looking for their son of a bitch but posing convincingly as equals, with no colonial hangover, no complex relationship of resentment, no outward show of hegemonic clout. China wants to buy; Africa has something to sell. If African governments could respond in a way which would channel some of the new wealth to the African citizens, then China might provide an opportunity which Europe and America have failed to provide. But I doubt that this will be the case under the present *modus operandi* in Africa.

Looking at China's investment in Africa, one sees a gradual and steady increase. It is reported that Africa now has 450 Chinese-owned investments projects, out of which 46% are in manufacturing, 40% in services and only 9% in resource-related industries. Between 1990-1997, Chinese investment into Africa came to about $20 million, and between 1998-2002 it had increased six-fold to $120 million. Around 20% of the amount came into South Africa. China is not out to invest only in "safe harbors" in Africa. Although the extractive and resource-related projects yield a share of 28% in terms of value, 64% of Chinese investment value in Africa is in the manufacturing sector. The belligerent Western policies towards many African countries also push such countries to look East. In August 2005, Kenya's President Kibaki visited Beijing and came back with $8 million in grants as well as a loan of $27 million for Nairobi's power distribution. Not only that. President Kibaki also signed a contract with Huawei Technologies Company, the giant who leads the scores of Chinese companies in Nairobi, and Kenya Airways now has landing rights in Hong Kong and Guangzhou. The University of Nairobi now boasts a Confucius Institute. The game is opened. The International Monetary Fund and the World Bank kept on stretching the yardstick for

Kenya over the years, so that in the 2006 budget Kenya did not include donor support. So other Asian countries — Japan, Thailand and Indonesia — were also welcome aboard. The former prerogatives of the UK and the US in Kenya's lucrative "orders" for defense, telecommunications, medical, construction and so on have now been awarded to the Asian giants. Just in the last two years of Kibaki's presidency, China and Kenya have signed 12 bilateral agreements in the fields of technology, economy, health, media, energy, tourism, aviation, archaeology and education. Being the central gateway to central, landlocked east and the horn of Africa, Kenya is strategic for the 400 million market of the East African Community (EAC) and the Common Market for Southern and Eastern Africa (COMESA). This country is now the single largest recipient of assistance from the Far East.

There is one thing the Chinese now share with the US and (lately adopted by) the EU — the word INTEREST. Like Americans combing the whole world in the name of American interests, the rapidly industrializing Chinese are out for Chinese interests. And therefore Bush is again wide awake and out wooing India like a repentant unfaithful husband and keeping Pakistan on a short leash even if he has to make quite a figure of himself attempting to play cricket. China's emerging capitalists are the most openly voracious in Africa and expanding with the speed of light. Up until the 1980s Africa, the Chinese faces could only be seen in their embassies or Chinese restaurants. Now, they are part of Africa's landscape — negotiating and engaged in joint businesses in South Africa, building the new State House in Uganda, and, most significantly, establishing themselves in countries with natural resources. Chinese companies are involved in mining, timber, fishing and precious stones, according to Lindsey Hilsum in *Capitalism Magazine*. Above all, they are involved in oil. China is on the rise, and this big time. This nation has a practically endless supply of low-cost laborers who will work seven days a week, 14 hours a day, for less than $100 per month. The Chinese now make around 60% of the world's mobile telephones, half of the world's shoes and most of the world's video games and TV sets. An estimated 81% of children's toys sold in the US are made in China, while every major US furniture manufacturer has a factory in China. It is now using 55% of the world's cement to lay down roads. Whereas in 1989 China had only 170 miles of motorway, by 2003 this had increased to 18,500 miles of expressways costing the Chinese government $42 billion. And they have only just began. The plan is to achieve 51,000 miles of motorways by 2008 (the US has 46,500 miles of interstates in place at the moment). *The Wall Street Journal Barron's* wrote at the end of 2006: "[China is] in the middle of expanding and electrifying its railways, irrigating the north with water from the Yangtze River, and doing a construction for the 2008 Beijing Olympic Games. It's also undertaking several major energy projects, including a 3,900-kilometer gas pipeline."

Second only to the United States in its oil consumption, China needs Africa's resources to fuel its own phenomenal growth. In oil-rich countries like Angola, Chad, Nigeria and Sudan, the influence of former colonial plunderers like Portugal, Britain or France is waning. The Chinese government imposes no political conditions on African governments before signing contracts for exploration, extraction or production. No Chinese pressure groups lobby Chinese oil companies about "transparency" or environmental damage, which is not to say that such measures are always successfully carried out. Often, all concerned ignore everything or use such lobbying as smokescreens. Not surprisingly, African governments welcome these undemanding new "brothers in investments."

In the Sudan, the Chinese investment has changed dramatically and many still remember the recent Chinese veto threat in the UN Security Council on embargoes to the Sudan for the country's mass killing derring-dos in Darfur, where Sudan also grossly violate human rights. But with befitting kowtows at the Sudanese energy ministry, one can have a look in video archives, of Chinese activities in the oil sector. These Chinese are not in Armani suits and do not wear Cartier wristwatches. These are earnest seismologists on their knees tapping the dry, brown African desert for the latest oil coup. You peek at the Sudanese President, Omar al-Bashir, and the head of the African division of the Chinese National Petroleum Corporation (CNPC) at a ribbon cutting ceremony for the new oil *refinery* at Al Jaily, north of Khartoum. Driving around, you glimpse billboards across the capital showing smiling Sudanese and Chinese oil workers in yellow hard hats shaking hands. CNPC: YOUR CLOSE FRIEND AND FAITHFUL PARTNER, the legend proclaims in Chinese, Arabic and English.

It is like a new scramble for Africa. The trade between China and Africa doubles each year. Sixty percent of Sudan's oil goes to China and twelve percent of China's oil comes from the Sudan. No wonder the Sudanese government is untroubled by the oil sanctions which prevent American investment. With the Chinese, interference in the Sudanese government's traditions, politics, beliefs or behaviors is not even in the horizon. There is no other business like the resources business — with China as the negotiating partner.

In 2004, when Britain and the US pushed for a punitive UN Security Council resolution against Sudan for the mass killing of civilians in Darfur,

China's threatening veto made the Security Council decline itself back to the weaker resolution which passed with Chinese approval but had little impact. Chinese companies have built three small-arms factories near Khartoum. Most of the weapons used by government forces and militia in Darfur are manufactured there — or in China. The machetes used in the Rwanda genocide factions were also made in China. And like their colonial predecessors and their present Western competition, the Chinese perfect the game of bringing in to Africa what they can also take away back to China in the movement of a handshake.

On the other side of Africa, in Angola on the Atlantic coast, there is a sea of Chinese faces. Angola has a population of 13.5 million people in a country that spans five times the terrain of Great Britain, which has a population of 57 million people. The real Angola is a post-war (the civil war between Unita and the Marxist MPLA that raged on and off for almost thirty years) landscape with bullet-ridden ruins, destroyed roads and wrecked T-34 tanks. Large signs with *Perigo Minas!* warn of the danger of the 3 to 5 million landmines strewn all over the countryside which still maim people to this day. Two thirds of Angolans live on less than $2 per day, but some of the foreign aid machinery who know that the Angolan central bank in the capital city Luanda has reserves of about $4 billion, are questioning whether Angola still needs any foreign aid programs at all. Angola has not only oil but also large reserves of diamonds and has a huge agricultural potential. The peasantry long for plows even if most of them have forgotten how to be agriculturalists. They build their dwellings, schools and dispensaries with clay. They have no sanitation and live next to mountains of refuse. But in Luanda itself, one steps completely out of Angola, out of Africa in fact. The city is booming and like no other African capital city. House rents are at an astronomical figure of $10,000 or more per month (November 2006) while a liter of petrol costs less than a bottle of mineral water. Welcome to Africa, the continent of discrepancies. The seven richest men in the country are all in or connected to the ruling MPLA government of Eduardo dos Santos. They all grin knowingly when the West warns of "yellow colonialism" while their oil giants such as Chevron, Agip, Elf or BP are extracting as if in their own backyards. The super rich in the middle of the confused traffic jams in Luanda cannot be overlooked. They drive 4WD Humvees, Prados and Nativas of the most expensive designs and latest make. The banks, shopping malls, office and public buildings are palaces of glass and black marble. The petrol stations of the state-owned Sonangol twinkle so much that they have been likened to the temples of idols. The construction business is booming like it did in the Nigeria of the 1970s. Huge placards are cheering away, *Angola Avante!* Let's go, Angola! Forward, Angola! But the ever-present corruption is right in the middle of it all. The IMF estimates that from all the petro-dollars earned annually, $1 billion is ferried out of the country to the usual Western destinations.

As their economic interest in Africa has comparatively declined, Europe and America have gone along with calls for "good governance" and an end to human rights abuse in Africa. It is easy to moralize at regimes which you have no reason whatsoever to improve and whose citizens matter less than little to you. But such regimes will not cow to this new and racist "yellow colonialism" moralizing if China is offering practical support without conditions. Human rights workers have a new problem here. In May 2005, President Robert Mugabe — regarded as a pariah by Europe and the United States — told the crowd celebrating twenty-five years of Zimbabwe's independence: "We have turned east, where the sun rises, and given our back to the west, where the sun sets." During the period Euroancestral farmers dominated commercial agriculture in the country, Zimbabwe used to sell tobacco at international auctions. Now the auction houses in Harare are deaf, dumb and empty. The tobacco goes directly to China's 300 million smokers, as payment in kind for loans and investment from Chinese banks to Zimbabwe's bankrupt state-run companies. As Zimbabwe's agricultural sector collapses, the Chinese are taking over land the Zimbabwean government confiscated from Euroancestral farmers, and cultivating the crops China needs. China has a lot of people to feed and a strong interest to do just that — unlike most of African states. On a recent visit to Beijing, President Mugabe, who had once been armed by the Chinese during the bush war against Ian Smith's Rhodesian forces, was given an honorary professorship at the Foreign Affairs University for what was termed his remarkable contribution in the work of diplomacy and international relations. The same week, a UN report condemned Mugabe's government for demolishing 700,000 homes and businesses without any regard to the human suffering. But everybody seems to love the new kid in town, from Cape to Cairo, from Khartoum to Conakry (the Republic of Guinea, the world's second largest bauxite producer, where the Chinese are into everything, including timber and diamonds).

When I skipped from Guinea to Sierra Leone, next door, the scene was the same. (Sierra Leone, "land of the lions," with Freetown as the capital, was founded by freed slaves who once had been destined for the Americas or the so-called West Indies.) I had read and seen on television news of the senseless battles that had been fought in this small country. But even forewarned, the streets of Freetown are a rude awakening. Especially in June, the height of the rainy season. I felt a tortuous shame as my eyes swept across dozens of people in the streets without arms or legs or hands, begging while huddled in the muddy shop fronts or crouched against tree trunks. But I'll get on with the Chinese success story in Africa.

Sierra Leone evokes former British Prime Minister Tony Blair's vision of Africa as "a scar on the conscience of the world,"[29] but the other way round. It is the world knocking open scabs on the little country's conscience. I checked into the Bintumani Hotel's best rooms — the Presidential Suite. Just about everything in the rooms but the land on which the hotel stands is Chinese and apparently with Chinese clientele in mind. I'm five-foot-eleven in my stocking feet and had to stoop to get through the door. Even the toilet bowl, shower and the television are made in China. This hotel exists because, even before the civil war in Sierra Leone ended in 2002, the Chinese rebuilt it. The clocks above the reception area give the time in Beijing, Freetown, London, Paris and New York. The manager of the hotel is a Chinese called Yang Zhou; he does not speak English and therefore has a (Chinese) transla-tor. But Mr. Yang is beaming with the famed Asiatic hospitality. His transla-tor has an English first name which is the only name by which he introduces himself. "It makes communication easier with the African people and visi-tors from Europe," he explains to me. My Sierra Leonean taxi driver later in-formed me that this is the standard explanation the Chinese give to foreign journalists and that Yang Zhou does speak English, if he is so inclined! Large red lanterns are swinging on the porch. The rebuilding of the hotel had been done by the Chinese government-owned Beijing Urban Construction Group, Mr. Yang informs me in his office. He seems to do the explanations as if he does them daily to other foreigners. Like a tour guide. The walls of the office are plastered with glossy pictures of the Chinese rise to industrialization, with captions in both Chinese and English. More pictures of a graduation ceremony where young Chinese women are throwing mortar boards in the air, the Three Gorges Dam, Shanghai by night, and so on. Outside the door of the ladies' cloakroom is a striking feature of a Pippi Langstrumpf of the sticking-out pigtails. A curious Nordic underscore.

Mr. Yang thinks that Africa is not too competitive and therefore a great place on God's earth for investments. Most European companies, he informs me, turned their back on Sierra Leone ages ago. I mention the big British paw on Sierra Leonean diamonds. Mr. Yang does not want to talk politics,

---

29 The G8 Summit in Gleneagles, July 2005

he insinuates subtly. Then he mentions one of the negative African traits that I myself never stop lamenting. The typical African business partners see only difficulties (in my opinion they misinterpret their own laziness, half-heartedness and the miraculous belief that a business opened this morning should make the African businessperson a multi-millionaire by this evening as "difficulties"). The Chinese only see opportunities. A couple of things cross my mind about Mr. Yang: Philoctetes, the Trojan War hero who killed Paris, a Philistine bent on investments and having no love for the arts, culture or philology. I mention to him that, by most estimates, Sierra Leone is the world's poorest country with more than 70% of the citizens living at best in subsistence level. Mr. Yang assures me for the third time that he never discusses politics, when I question him about the favorite Africa twin conflict midwives — resources and power — whether African, Chinese or any other nation's. Politics for Mr. Yang includes the UN troops keeping the peace in Freetown, the amputees who were robbed of their limbs in the most brutal way by child soldiers who were also known as the "West Side Boys," the 60% young Sierra Leoneans who remain unemployed. Yang will not talk even about the lack of tap water and electricity in the city.

Since the China-Africa Forum of Beijing in 2000, the Chinese are now the top capitalists in Africa, doubling the Sino-Africa trade annually. In West Africa they have replaced the Lebanese who up to now had had a monopoly in all business sectors in these countries, just as East African Asians (Indians) dominate the commercial sectors of the region. In the continent itself — a continent that has forever had to come to negotiations with eyes lowered and voiceless — it is the Chinese's no-political-interference and equal-negotiating-partner strategies that smooth the Sino-African relationship so effectively. The Chinese seem very adept at not openly displaying the tedious age-old attitude of the West: I'm not only the boss and the smartest, I'm also the superior being. The Chinese companies are becoming multinationals "on the quiet, simply going global in what our country has declared the period of strategic opportunity," stresses Yuan, a young Chinese project manager with whom I talked in Conakry, Guinea. The Chinese are indeed not living in mansions with an army of African domestics. They dig, shovel, saw, clear and carry away the rubble themselves instead of standing around raving sharp orders to African workers. The trouble is, practically no African gets employed in any position whatsoever in any Chinese projects. Everybody is Chinese from the engineers to the office messengers.

Africa is China's teething ring as well as proving ground. They have built Sierra Leone a new parliament and Uganda a new State House. They are in fisheries and joint venture businesses in South Africa, including mining, in timber and precious stones. Whatever African country has significant natural resources, the Chinese are there setting themselves up. They are the first major power doing this in Africa without the power of the gun or direct monetary blackmail and pergola-structured economical slavery. And oil is top of their list whether in the Sudan or in West Africa's development of new oil resources. According to the official Chinese customs figures, the Sino-Africa trade leapt by 39% (i.e., $32.17 billion) in the first 10 months of 2005. On the other side of the scale, Africa is buying more goods made in China. The exports to Africa in those first 10 months amounted to $15.25 billion while the imports from Africa stood at $16.92 billion. It is as rare as a meteorite hitting Mt Kilimanjaro, that any nation imports more *from* Africa than it exports *to* Africa! But as a source of raw material needed for the Chinese manufacturing sector, Africa is now of significant importance to the Middle Kingdom.

In 2004 the Chinese consumption of petroleum products grew by 15% while its output only rose by 2%, although Chinese oil firms try to press more out of their wells by applying better technology. Rumor also has it that the Middle Kingdom plans to buy parts of Western oil multinationals. Being wooed are also the 11 oil producers of the OPEC cartel who are getting the red carpet treatment come rain or shine. And should one be interested in why China is against embargoes on Iran — it is because China has wrapped up an agreement to develop oil fields in Iran. Even Cuba has agreed to have its coastal oil fields explored by China. The president of the world's fifth biggest oil exporter, President Hugo Chavez of Venezuela, has not hesitated to welcome Chinese firms to join in, in operating rights to mature oil fields. All this is making the West uncomfortable, to put it mildly.

But there is the good side of the Sino-Africa cooperation. The Chinese are now the second largest petroleum products consumer in the world next to the United States as already pointed out, having overtaken the Japanese in 2003. According to the US Energy Information Administration, the Chinese accounted for 40% of the total growth in global oil demand in the last four years. Chinese companies invested $175 million in oil in Africa in the first 10 months of 2005. In the meantime 190 types of goods from 28 of the poorest African countries have been excluded from tariffs in China. Up until the beginning of the millennium, the TanZam railway built in the 1970s linking Tanzania with Zambia was China's biggest project in Africa. But since the China-Africa Forum there are a row of significant construction projects, especially in the building of infrastructure. Whether China is doing this to aid trade and the movement of goods is beside the point. The infrastructure serves the ordinary citizen as well, not the growth of a Swiss bank's reserves or the growth of the Western economy. The Chinese are also way ahead of the West with regards to oil contracts in the Sudan. And as the West limits Chinese textile exports, Chinese companies involved in clothing and textiles are turning to investing in Africa. Of course there is much discussion, if not a right royal hue and cry, about China's democratic and environmental ethics. Coming from the West, this is hypocrisy of the first order, as Ms Bangura's quoted words at the beginning of this chapter aptly put it. No Western industrialized country makes much ado about where its oil is coming from — whether it is Angola or Kazakhstan. And coming to environmental pollution, how often have countries of the West simply bribed some African so-called leader to let them dump their toxic wastes on African soil or in African rivers? Very often, and it is still an ongoing process. It is a pity that in their dealings with Africa, the West only gets halfway fair when there is non-Western competition, completely unfair when there is none.

But what Africa should consider when dealing with China is China's agenda. They should bear in mind that they are dealing with a country seriously bent on being the next world superpower and that within the shortest time. China now, for example, controls the Panama Canal — the very canal that made the US kill the then President of Panama, Omar Torrijos, because Torrijos negotiated with the Japanese to rebuild the canal, sidestepping the US Bechtel Corporation.

Africa should make sure that this agenda tallies with the African one. In the competitive world of today's savage predator capitalism, there is no fair give and take. It is take as much as possible while giving as little as possible — if giving at all. One very obvious log in the eye is the fact that the Chinese projects in Africa are practically an all-Chinese affairs down to the office messenger. Not even an African cleaning lady or sweeper is employed in the majority of these projects.

This is less than undesirable and should be discouraged by all means. Whatever level of "expertise" is readily available in the African countries must be utilized in the projects. Furthermore, the Chinese experts should be requested to act as mentors to African trainees. Africa does not need a Chinese bricklayer or ironing person; there are more than enough Africans for such unskilled and semi-skilled work, and they have families to feed, house and clothe.

Dave O'Reilly of ChevronTexaco has expressed his worries about a "bidding war for Middle Eastern Oil between east and west,"[30] and a former United States ambassador to China, James Lilley, said "the Chinese are on an aggressive quest to increase their supply of oil all around the world."[31] The West is gaping with an open mouth as China ventures into their "territory," but Africa is simply enchanted. Responsible African countries will know how to

30China's global hunt for oil, Mary Hennock for BBC News, 9 March 2005
31 Ibid.

utilize this bargaining leverage they now have again, following the doldrums years of post Cold War, and use it wisely for the benefit of their countries. It is said that some African governments trust China because, contrary to the G8 club members, the Chinese managed to get 400 million of its people out of poverty in 20 years, and that the poor ones of Africa can afford to buy the Chinese products on the African market. When one is poor, hungry and struggling for subsistence by the hour, this sounds like a good argument. It is estimated that China uses 43% of its oil in their industry and 34% in cars. In 2005 China used 7.2 million barrels a day and the demand for that year rose by 9%. China's rapid industrial growth gets up to 12% of its oil needs from the Sudan, the country in which they built their first oil refinery outside Chinese borders.

But it is a foolish African government indeed who indiscriminately chases its citizens out of their land and villages to make way for foreign-contracted oilfields without giving the citizens an alternative home. The oilfields belong to the citizens, not to their government and the foreigners. Here is one area where the African Union can show its determination to advise African leaders and finally unite the countries rich in resources to form their own cartels and stand their ground.

CHAPTER 8: SLAVERY THEN, GLOBALIZATION NOW:
A NEW BRAND OF CHAINS

> *I speak of Africa and golden joys...*
> *SHAKESPEARE in Henry IV*

> *Strangely enough, it was the Germans who made Russia Abyssinian-conscious. At the end of the seventeenth century a strenuous effort was made by the small German dukedom of Saxe-Gotha, a center of ecumenical thinking, to evoke Russia's interest in Abyssinia. This country, at the time terra incognita to the Russians, was to become at a later date, along with Egypt, the chief target of Russian ambition in Africa. The aim of the plan was to create an anti-Turkish league comprising of Russia, Abyssinia, and Western Europe. This early liaison between Moscow and Abyssinia was to be based on three pillars: similarity of religion, common enmity toward the growing strength of the Mohammedan Turks, and the seductive wealth, reputed or actual, of this African land.*

> — SERGIUS YAKOBSON[32]

During the West Africa Exhibition which took place in 2003 — and remained open for six months — at the Smithsonian's African-American history museum in Washington, there was a huge discussion on the trans-Atlantic slavery. It was correctly labeled "dehumanizing." All through the human history, slavery was part of everyday life and dehumanizing in various degrees. But it was never necessarily based on "race," whether in Africa or in any other part of the world. The Egyptians, Greeks and Romans all had slavery as did the Incas and the Aztecs. The above-mentioned exhibition stated: "Because the economies of Africa did

---

32 Yakobson, Sergius, "Russia and Africa" in *Russian Foreign Policy. Essays in Historical Perspective*, ed. I. J. Lederer, Yale University Press, New Haven, 1962 p. 453-487

not depend on slave labor, the number of enslaved people was small until European traders arrived." The Middle Eastern Arabs traded with and had African, Arab, and European slaves. But the Africans too traded with and had African, Arab and European slaves. The West always makes the mistake of assuming that all Arabs are light-skinned, in the same way they assume that Iranians are Arabs. Most of the "famous" Janjaweeds terrorizing the victims of Darfur in Sudan are in the majority darker than their East African fellow citizens.

Africans still enslave human beings today in Mauritania and the Sudan. In the former it is widely claimed that the relationship between slave and master is a form of kinship. The fact still remains that the slaves (known as Haratin) are mostly dark-skinned Africans and the slave owners (known as Bidan) would seem to have more Berber and Arab African blood. But both slave and master remain members of the same clan, where there are cases of the dark-skinned people being the leaders. It is not unusual for some slaves to be far richer than their masters, or for some to refer to themselves as slaves although they have never been any other person's possession. They are as free as any other citizen of the country and share a common culture. Africa is forever full of intoxicating discrepancies. Both Haratin and Bidan often live together in equally ragged tents in the desert and even the wealthier ones intermarry. This age-old African slave system is a far cry from what happened to the Africans enslaved in the Americas. Despite being a minority, Haratin enjoy fair representation in the government. One of them was Mauritania's representative in the United Nations, despite referring to himself as Haratin. Mauritania practiced slavery for 700 years and only abolished it "officially" in 1980. But the practice continues and not all cases are as harmonious as described above. Owing to poverty, some Mauritanians voluntarily offer themselves as slaves who work merely for food and clothing. The country's economy depends on iron ore whose price keeps on falling, and fisheries which have been drastically depleted by international fishing fleets. The per capita income is less than $500 and life expectancy is estimated at forty-one years. The 1980 law banning slavery is not being enforced by the government and the compensation they promised to pay the slave owners was never paid, so that privately slaves are still being bought, sold and bred. In the hope that the government will some day honor their pledge, released slaves are "reacquired." In the Sudan the authorities themselves organize militias who routinely raid villages and kill the men while carrying off the women and children. The male children end up being forced to harsh manual labor while the females become household servants and concubines.

The sensitive issue of slavery in Africa and in America even in the 21st century was good reason for staging the West African Exhibition in the US. It is true that slavery hardly ran for two generations in most inner African cases, not to even think of several centuries. That is to say, when one disregards the fact that Egyptians — Africans — kept Hebrews in bondage for 400 years. Americans have their own historical experience with slavery and a very dehumanizing slavery at that, and therefore have an aversion to slavery in Mauritania and the Sudan. So does any human being in his right mind.

Yet slavery goes on and not just in the two African countries mentioned above. The "accusing" of America began as long ago as the 17th century with the Mayflower Compact of 1620, which emphasized the importance of a government as a covenant between "man and man," and for it to be legitimate it had to be based on the consent of the governed. A government was legitimate only if it was chosen by those it purported to govern. But even at this time, Native Americans were being deliberately massacred. Children were snatched from their parents to be "civilized" in Euroancestral schools, with the disastrous outcome (as also happened to all of Africa) that an entire people lost touch with their culture while at the same time not quite knowing how to grapple with the Euroancestral culture. Meanwhile, America today has strayed far from that early definition of good government. Democracy is a relative notion.

In effect, slavery has appeared throughout history in various forms. Since the fall of the Berlin Wall, girls and young women from Eastern Europe and the Balkan region are ferried illegally into the West and forced into prostitution. This 21st century slavery is subtle but very effective.

In Africa today, slavery still endures not only in Mauritania and the Sudan but also in many West African countries, where poor parents send off their children from one country to another or to neighbors who are apparently better off. The children are practically turned into slaves in a sort of labor-for-upkeep-and-education program. This is in continuation of an old non-slavery tradition of African solidarity. But this old tradition, like so many of the old African social traditions, is no longer acceptable, because Africans have become "capitalists." Most of the children receive no education whatsoever, but the worst upkeep and plenty of abuse.

Often slavery is hinged on traditions that make it part and parcel of the culture. In India it is the agricultural system known as *koliya*, where workers forsake their freedom of movement for a kilo of rice or wheat a day and a plot of land where they in exchange grow other food for which they have to borrow money for seeds and fertilizer. The landowner makes sure that the bonded laborers never have enough money to run away but accumulate debts that are passed on generation after generation. When the government lends such a bonded laborer any money, the money is paid to the landowner and the bonded laborer owes a

debt to the government. The Pakistanis have another centuries old slavery system called *peshgi*. The 7,000 kilns in Pakistan producing hand made bricks uses
750,000 people including children. The kiln owner gives a family a small advance
payment for them to settle, buy tools and food. The family loses their freedom
and labors for a season, where in a good week they could make enough bricks
to earn them 800 rupees ($15) to keep them alive on rice and vegetables. In case
of sickness, marriage, floods or drought, the family has to borrow from the kiln
owner and slip into debt bondage passed on from generation to generation, and
be completely dependent on the kiln owner. It is not unusual for the kiln owner
and his henchmen to regularly abuse the wives and daughters, and all marriages
have to take place only with his approval. Any troublemaker gets his or her foot
singed in the kiln, with all the other bonded laborers gathered to watch the torture. A fraction of 0.5% of the population owns a third of the farmland and rural
unemployment has produced more than 15 million landless peasants.

Thailand, and not Africa or any single African country, has the highest HIV
rate. Some rural areas have as much as 60% HIV positive villagers. The locomo-
tive is sex tourism. Alone in Bangkok there are over one million prostitutes. Poor
villagers sell their children to brokers for $2,000 and the broker sells the child
to the brothel owner for double that price. The brothel owner "breaks in" the
child — male or female — to submission by repeated rapings and beatings. Then
the child has to have sex with 300 or more men a month just to pay the rent of
$1,200. When the children, male or female, run away and are recaptured by the
police, the law enforcers bring them back to the brothel keeper — for a price,
which price is added on to the child's "debt." The same goes for refugees from
neighboring Laos or Burma who work as prostitutes in Bangkok — when they
get caught at the border after deportation, the police make arrangements to sell
them to brothel owners. Thai women are exotic hot exports as prostitutes in
Japan, Europe or the US. Kevin Bale, in his book *Disposable People: New Slavery in
the Global Economy*[33], mentions a New York brothel owner who paid $6,000-
$15,000 for 30 Thai women held captive in her brothel.

In the mushrooming cities of Brazil, huge slums called *favelas* sprouted in
the 1960s and 1970s. Yet in the state of Mato Grosso do Sul, the government
practically gave away vast forest areas to transnationals such as Nestlé and
Volkswagen who offset these against taxes. It was planned that the companies cut down the forests, replant them with eucalyptus trees and send
the wood to a government paper mill which was never constructed. The
companies now use *empreitoros* (subcontractors) to clear the forests to make

33 Bale, Kevin, *Disposable People: New Slavery in the Global Economy*, California, University
of California Press, 1999

charcoal for steel mills. *Gatos*, meaning cats, who did not shy from using child labor until the government outlawed it in 1996, are employed to make profits from the charcoal ovens by exploiting the poor, who are recruited and used as isolated bonded laborers. They are tricked into accumulating debts — the families are given cash advances before the workers leave, in part to buy food to bring along, pay for transportation to the work places, and so on. Their identity and labor cards taken away, the penniless imprisoned laborers are soon exhausted, burnt, scarred by the work, and at risk of lung disease.

And that is what the gilded chimera of globalization represents. Globalization is forcing the world back even further than pre-historic barbarism. It is estimated that globalization exploits and keeps more than 27 million people worldwide against their will, in places like Thailand, India, Pakistan, Brazil and even in the Western countries. To these tens of millions of people, globalization is a curse. Liberalized world trade will not guarantee freedom; trading and exchanging businesses will not naturally create a community of interests. Globalizing the financial markets will not unite the planet and globalization will only benefit a handful of the world's already rich people. There will never be a global village and, despite nearly every country in the world having signed the Declaration of Human Rights' "Right of Emigration," the rich North has long since built a fortress so that the poor South remains imprisoned in its poorhouse.

But the rich North travels all over the face of the earth, and as long as these are not found within their own borders, the rich North loves armed conflicts, wars and despots. Globalization is doing away with the civilization that humankind has taken tens of thousands of years to achieve. It is not parasitic, it is cannibalistic and its hunger is insatiable. The mother of neo-liberalism, Margaret Thatcher, once said that there is no society, there are simply individual people. She must have meant the globalizers

Globalization is demarcating and fragmenting the world and its people, rather than unifying it. It is rendering parliaments and government systems obsolete, by threatening economic ruin. If their terms are not met, "global" companies can always take their business, and jobs, someplace else where they will be allowed to accumulate more profits while returning less in the form of pay and benefits to employees and tax to the community. This pits one city and nation against others in a downward competitive spiral. Or the oligarchs simply install their own stooges as legislators and heads of states, and thereby "legitimately" rule those states behind the scenes.

The Bush administration is an oil-and-military administration. Its leaders and advisors come from Texan transnationals who drill, process and transport oil, while the CIA and the Pentagon are busy developing biological and toxic weapons. Up to now about 143 nations have signed and ratified the international agreement forbidding these nations to develop biological and toxic weapons. But unlike the agreement on chemical weapons, there is no verification on observable evidence. There was an international conference in the Palais des Nations in Geneva in 2001 to work out a supplemental agreement to close this loophole. The conference failed because the US (on behalf of behind-the-scenes powerbrokers) refused to sign and ratify it. And this same so-called superpower has the Megignoarrogance to claim to be in the lead on the fight against development, production and distribution of such weapons, accusing countries like Sudan, Iran, North Korea, Syria and Iraq of breaking the agreement.

Also in 2001 George W. Bush pulled out of the Kyoto agreement meant to control environmental pollution, when the US alone spits 24% of the poisonous gases into the environment. The required reduction would put financial demands on the petroleum companies and car-manufacturers. The US has also pulled out of the antiballistic missile agreement. Two months after 9/11, in an effort to convince the Congress to accept the law on Trade Promotion Authority, Bush used the curious argument that the World Trade Center had been attacked — and to defeat the terrorists, world trade must be expanded. The concept was that free trade was not only a question of economic efficiency but also promoted the values of freedom. The voices of the powerbrokers giving commands behind the scenes were loud and clear.

The hypocrisy is abundant but the rest of the world pretends not to see it for fear of provoking the wrath of the world oligarchs. The OECD nations have for years worked on ways to control the tax oases known as off-shore centers, where huge flows of capital escape taxation, and money laundering is rampant. The Bush administration refused to sign the OECD agreement, hobbling the fight against corruption practices.

For the African continent, it has been said that globalization is a new order of marginalization and recolonization in a "neo-neo-colonial fashion." Even the Indonesian Minister of Development and Infrastructure is quoted as having uttered as long ago as September 1994 that, "Nobody can resist globalization. In the field of infrastructure globalization is a kind of war: kill or be killed." This phenomenon is capital gone insane.

For Sub-Saharan African countries, globalization is a new colonial nightmare. The West is once again marching on to conquer and subject the African continent and her people culturally, economically and technologically. The only thing missing this time is the Bible. Instead of the colonizers' appropriated God, the globalizers are wielding Capital.

From the end of the 15th century, Europe began a systematic looting and plundering of their newly "discovered" territories, the first steps leading to the accumulation of today's Western capital. Author Jean Ziegler[34] writes that in 1773-74 there were more than 200,000 slaves in Jamaica spread over 775 plantations. A single medium-sized plantation engaged 200 Afroancestrals on 600 hectares, out of which 250 hectares were planted with sugarcane. In 1773 England made a net profit of more than £1.5 million. In four centuries roughly 20 million Africans were abducted from their homes, hauled across the ocean, and forced into slave labor. The importation of slaves was abolished before 1850 but slavery as an institution was not officially abolished in the US until the Emancipation Proclamation (1863) of President Abraham Lincoln, and that could not be enforced until Union victory in 1865. The wealth stripped from the colonial territories enabled Europe to turn the peasants into workers in the new industries. Edgar Pisari remarked that the interlocking of rural exodus with industrial growth built the foundation of the development model which accounts for Europe's present strength.

The people of the periphery countries are therefore doubly victims. Because of the devastations suffered in the past and the inequality of development between their societies and those of the colonial metropolis of the northern hemisphere, they are today — in the time of globalization as the only model for economy and mentality — unable to resist the new assaults of the transcontinental capital. The countries of Africa, Asia, Latin America and the Caribbean are bled to death by barter trade, triangular businesses through established subsidiaries, colonial occupation, plunder and exploitation. In other words globalization hits with full force a social body that is already starkly weakened.

Africa regards globalization with skepticism if not with downright abhorrence. And Africa is not alone. Globalization has been on the rise for more than 30 years, and Africa has been systematically derailed from both socio-political and socio-economic development, not to mention the environmental and cultural destruction. Globalization has its sights on *Africa* but is less and less interested in *Africans*. There is no "trickle-down" in economics; it is a chrome bowl with not a single hole. Whatever is poured into it remains contained in it. Most Africans have no buying power worth seducing, and those Africans who have — the African oligarchs — do their shopping elsewhere, for everything from weapons to wristwatches.

---

34 Ziegler, Jean, *Die neuen Herrscher der Welt*, Munich: Goldmann Verlag, 2005 p. 24 ff.

The Africans are victims of environmental pollution, but without having enjoyed the fruits that the perpetrators in the industrialized world enjoy. Being "passive recipients of globalization," as Martin Khor, the Director of *Third World Network* in Kuala Lumpur puts it, the developing countries and Africa in particular are left wide open to the merciless vagaries of globalization which, like the Indian deities, have dozens of arms in the form of institutions such as the International Monetary Fund and the World Bank with their annihilating SAP (Structural Adjustment Programs) or the revived London-based Bretton Woods institution.

The primary goal of the IMF and the World Bank is the issue of global capital. For Africa, globalization comes down to polarization of the few groups and countries who profit from it and the many countries and social groups who are the losers. According to Khor, globalization, polarization, concentration of wealth in fewer and fewer hands, and marginalization of the rest, are processes that are linked by the intensification of political, economical, social and cultural relations worldwide. National economies are increasingly linked in their breadth, width and depth into a global market offering goods and services, but above all capital.

There are 223 children born every minute, 173 of them in 122 "Third World" countries. Jean Ziegler writes that in the year 2025, the world population will be 8 billion, that of Africa 1.3 billion or 16% of the world population. In 1997, the worldwide ratio of births was 24 to 1,000, that of Africa 40 to 1,000. In that year 15% of humans born were Africans. In 2025 this African figure will rise to 22%.

Presently, nearly 40% of Africans live in urban areas. By 2025 the percentage will rise to over 50%. Africa's perennial wars are regurgitating displaced persons; and Malthusianism is not Africa's strongest point. The forests are being decimated by timber marauders for mere chopsticks; the Sahara is widening and deepening; the oil and natural gas are being pumped off to the gigantic storage reservoirs of Western petroleum companies and other natural resources are being whisked out of Africa. State public services are being privatized and thus are beyond the ordinary citizens' means; health and education are perpetually under-funded; central banks are turned into personal banks of dictators; arms are pouring in for the perennial wars; toxic waste from the West is being dumped on the continent; young Africans are unable to work their fields and are dependent on food donations, no longer sure just what they are eating. Pasture is being taken over by transnationals to produce pineapples and cash crops while the megalopolis is bursting at the seams and millions of people eke out a living choking in the rubbish dumps.

Enter the IMF and World Bank to save the day. When they strapped Kenya with their famous SAP, for example, the then president of Kenya, arap Moi — instead of trimming down an oversized cabinet — sacked around 80,000 schoolteachers. This created overnight a new group of poor and jobless, and the younger generation suffered irreparable harm. But the likes of Moi do not send their children to school in Kenya. And as long as subsidized French peanut oil in West Africa costs less than the local peanut oil, or the subsidized German sugar in Uganda made from sugar-beet costs much less than Uganda's indigenous cane sugar, which is healthier, there is not much international outcry.

The West and their globalization muscle men know that the woman is the backbone of most of the hundreds of millions of poor homes in Africa. She is wife, mother, organizer, governor, economist, crisis manageress, breadwinner and governess. Yet she is discriminated against especially in terms of education and opportunities in the employment market, rendered helpless with traditional shackles in terms of inheritance, divorce, paternity suits and so on. Still, she remains the strongest and most independent woman on the planet. The Senegalese filmmaker Ousmane Sembène often portrays African women as the heroines and maintains that this is because he knows women better, having been brought up exclusively by women. Most Africans are brought up by women alone. Regardless of her faith, the African woman ignores that part of the Christian culture that puts men in the center from street names to the Sistine Chapel, whereas in most African cultures the two basic symbols are female and male. The Luo woman controls her man by giving him the illusion of being superior to her. She has no time to waste in haggling with a husband. The African woman, as a rule, doesn't need a strong muscular arm to hold onto for a walk down the street or while standing in a queue before the theatre — to demonstrate ownership and demarcate territory.

The African daughter may have a husband chosen for her but the families are more likely to choose a better match than a computer dating program. If falling in love guaranteed a successful marriage, divorces in the so-called "free societies" would be decreasing instead of increasing. In the West, one falls in love with anybody and everybody all the time. This is not to say that hundreds of millions of African women do not marry out of love.

The African woman has formidable courage and tenacity, from those few who hold doctorates to the many whose street smarts and home-taught home economic skills give them the savvy to run the market stalls throughout the continent. African women with their extraordinary innovation and energy sell local products from greengroceries to textiles. They run more than 80% of the continent's informal economy, produce 70% of its food and are the principal labor force. They have managed to force even the African Union into enshrining gender parity — a parity of fifty-fifty female and male African Union Commissioners, and the AU's SDGEA (Sacred Declaration of Gender Equality in Africa). Liberia, Mozambique, Rwanda and South Africa have women in top level political positions of their governments. Of the estimated 316 million Africans who have too much to die from and too little to live on, all owe whatever lives they live to the African woman.

And yet this family backbone is being broken by the IMF/World Bank SAP and by globalization. These sharks are not interested in survivalist economies. The African market lady with her stall of textiles, rice and palm oil is buried alive complete with her trading goods.

Populations Living on Less Than $1 per Day (%)
(the diagram shows that the number of the poor is decreasing — but not in Sub-Saharan Africa) (source: World Bank 2006)

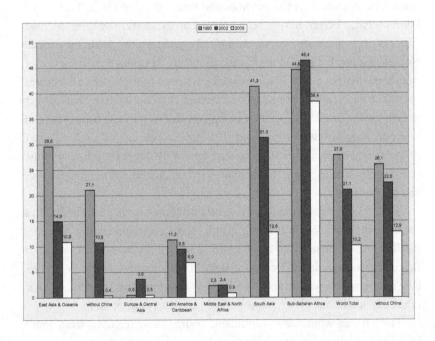

The African Union's first head, Alpha Oumar Konaré, stressed that the AU's goal is integration in the age of globalization. This is easier said than done, even if the qualities we have in common as human beings far outweigh those that separate us. This is something fundamental, but a fact that globalization will never accept, any more than colonization accepted the equality of all humankind. Already there is abundant evidence in how the Bank and the Fund see wrong only in the policies of African governments and supremely ignore the fact that those policies, from import substitution to export orientation to privatization, bear their hand-written directives and signatures. Their intellectual dishonesty is fostered by ongoing ideological brainwashing that prevents them from seeing the links between globalization and the poverty in Africa. Both the Bank and the Fund lack strong ethical evaluation and the keen analysis that would arm them with the creation of viable alternatives.

Because they work for the globalizers.

At the conference on "Land and Globalization in Africa" in Lusaka, Zambia, and in his article *Globalization: Implications for Africa* of 12 January 1998, Peter J. Henriot, S.J., describes two variations of globalization: the *natural* order such as the El Nino which affects the entire globe, causing droughts here and floods on the other place as a result of the interdependence of diverse activities taking place across the planet, and what he describes as the artificial, human-made order of globalization in the economic, political and cultural spheres of life. To understand the significance of globalization in the African context, Henriot laid stress on two factors. The first sought to explain globalization as "the fourth stage of outside penetration of Africa by forces which have negative social consequences for the African people's integral development," stating that the first foreign penetration was (once again!) the period of slavery which drained the continent of its "most precious resources, African women and men [who] were stolen away by global traders, slavers, working for the benefit of Arab, European and North American countries." The second was the period of colonialism, the third neo-colonialism which Pope Paul VI termed "the form of political pressures and economic suzerainty aimed at maintaining or acquiring dominance." Even after independence, the future of African states were still firmly chained onto outside influences, who manipulated and bartered African countries and the continent's resources during the Cold War, throwing many of the continent's states into (much or less desired by the West) armed conflicts which devastated the not-so-precious (to the West) human resources but abundantly loosened avalanches of natural resources to be whisked away in exchange for a single military tank. President Eisenhower directly ordered the murder of Lumumba, of

DRCongo,[35] for more or less the same reasons that made Fidel Castro a pariah in the West: both Lumumba and Castro asked for US assistance, were turned down, and then looked to the Soviet Union.

Now the globe is being artificially conceived as a free market. It is far from it. It is a market fuelled by profit motivations or private enterprises who want to do away with national boundaries and local allegiances (except among themselves even if in their famous *hostile takeover*), leaving Africa wide open to the most minimal influence and maximum dire consequences.

The second factor Henriot describes as "an obvious but not always acknowledged fact: globalization is not working for the benefit of the majority of Africans today." Disparities and inequalities in Africa's economic growth and development have increased. Nearly three quarters of the world's Least Developed Countries are in Africa, the continent has the highest debt to export ratio, the exported primary commodity prices keep on falling, and the FDI (Foreign Direct Investment) are small.

For young Africans, following global communication systems, globalization taunts them with the wealth and way of life in the West. This has led not only to brain drain but also to the mass migration from South to North. The migrants do not think twice about risking their lives on the uncertain journey to the wealthy West. Pregnant mothers risk the journey, in the hope that the child may be born in the West and therefore become automatically a "passport Westerner." If the mother succeeds, these children lose their cultural society, undergo a double-edged pseudo-acculturation and grow up in a society that at best "tolerates" them. The lucky few, very few lately, of these migrants who manage to set foot in the West are prepared to do the dirtiest and most physically taxing jobs, almost always at the lowest wages, and to endure psychological abuse along the line. And this meager earning has to be, in accordance with African cultural traditions, shared by the entire extended family and relatives back in the continent. Without this traditional burden these few "lucky" ones might have made it to a life of reasonable welfare or even climbed up to middle class status in the West. But with the burden of egalitarian ethics of the African tradition, the person is doomed to labor for a lifetime and still only manage to live from hand to mouth, just as the extended family also will somehow manage. I do not criticize this and similar African solidarity which is always a stronger backbone than that of individualism. It is an excellently humanistic tradition that should indeed be held

---

35 The details of this bloody fact have been written by none other than the former Chief of Station at the time, Larry Devlin, in his book *Chief of Station — Fighting the Cold War in a Hot Zone*, London:Public Affairs, 2007.

above the egoistic yuppie model. But at the very least African governments should scrap the exorbitant "commissions" African banks charge recipients for the money transferred from abroad by family members to their families back in Africa.

Globalization reverses this African cultural ethic and demands behavior that is not sanctioned in most African societies — competition for self-aggrandizement, African Fing Fang Long Finger despots notwithstanding. Whether this should be seen as good or bad, what the Africans find "threatening" in globalization is the process' negation and/or devaluation of cultural mores and conceptions of the world and humankind. There are question marks on Western concepts of "the virtue of material acquisition" and values of "private property." Neither do I quite believe that the Westerner comprehends the logic involved in sacking a Western corporate manager and then sending him on his way with a double figure million compensation instead of a three months' salary in lieu and letting him head for the labor office and queue like everybody else — or take his grievances to the industrial tribunal.

Africa has not yet got over the shock and pain of having lost a great deal of its solidarity conception of the world and humankind. Africans are not as "ready to be freed" from their traditions as Westerners are. In Africa, most traveled intellectuals are of the opinion that the West is on a rapid course of socio-cultural and spiritual degeneration. Africans generally place great value — *ceteris paribus* — on "obedience" to and respect for parents/grandparents, elders/ancestors, topped with and as part of religious piety. Freedom in the sense of its Western interpretation is for most ordinary Africans the height of disintegration and the passport to the foulest decadence in a human environment.

Confronted by expressions of "personal liberty" that run to pornography and voluntary involvement in bizarre sexual activities, Africans may ask, "Have they written their own new Bible or are they still using the usual one?" Told that what the popular German lingo calls *Media-Geilheit* — media lechery — is seen as an exercise of "free will," they can only wonder, "Has that free will rendered them brainless animals?"

For most Africans, globalization has not yet transformed their fundamental beliefs and values. Children are born, raised with these fundamental beliefs and values, become proud and dignified grownups and independently start their own families. Aunts and uncles, grandmothers and grandfathers contribute to their upbringing. They do not regress to mindlessness but progress to become dignified members of the human society with values to pass on. The universal homogenization (meaning Europeanization in the global sense) of cultures, values, ideas and living conduct is beyond their grasp. But — even if not consciously — they are already netted in the villagization or deterioration of the planet by capital's "blood-sucking principles."

Kenya is one of the African countries firmly caught in the pinch of neo-liberalization, privatization, commercialization and (what I consider good news) property-based democratization. Except that too often it is not a question of who should rightfully own the property and who actually owns and utilizes it. The Kenyan government printing having been privatized, the education ministry changes school curricula yearly — after being bribed by publishers so that new books have to be published. Globalization is touted to be a tool for removing administrative barriers and shooing in the "virtues" of liberalization and international movement of labor. Greater openness and participation in competitive international trade is apparently supposed to increase employment, primarily of skilled labor in the tradable goods sectors. And where are these sectors in Africa? Further, it is taken for granted that with the expansion of such sectors, unskilled labor has found increased employment opportunities in the non-tradable sectors such as construction and transportation. If that were the case, I ask why Africans risking their lives trying to migrate to Europe to offer their labor in whatever labor market that would be granted to them, drown in the Atlantic or get sent back to Africa. Is the global economy not supposed to work on terms of functioning independently of national boundaries and domestic economic considerations? From the time Europeans expropriated fireworks powder from the Chinese and turned it to gunpowder, the West has always addressed the rest of the world with the forked tongue of a snake. In truth the preached global economy and international division of labor really means that equal-level economies continue to trade and exchange labor with one another — all in the tradition of the "one-arm banditry and ethos capitalism" whose expansion is rooted on parasitical and cannibalistic processes. For African economies, this amounts to the age-old expropriation of resources and the post-independence capital flight. Furthermore, the end of the Cold War in 1990 also marked the end of making compromises from the West's front, in any negotiation. Former public-owned enterprises in African countries are being privatized to attract capital from developed countries, but finally ownership of such privatized enterprises reverts as well to citizens not of Africa but of developed countries. Globalization terrifies even the developed countries (decreased national control on internal economies and the labor market, for example); it renders the African political, social, economic and cultural values as extradites without validated crimes. It wipes out the indigenous cultural and psychological composition. The notion that Africa "needs to be globalized" is as sound as the notion that it "needed to be civilized and Christianized," notwithstanding that parts of Africa were Christianized long before the Christianization of Europe.

An ever expanding share of the world's GDP is generated by direct or indirect linkages to international trade. Capital flows are primarily powered by the considerations of risk and return and it is preached by the IMF that individual countries all over the world should liberalize their exchange and trade policies as the best approach for growth and development. Africa's share of the international trade has decreased from 3.1% in 1955 to the current estimated 1.2%. What Africa desperately lacks in this age of globalization is what the Deputy Managing Director of the IMF, in the Southern Africa Economic Summit in Harare in 1997 termed, "the revolution in communication and transportation technology and the much improved availability of information [which allows] individuals and firms to base their economic choices more on the quality of the economic environment in different countries. As a result, economic success in today's world is less a question of relative resource endowments or geographical location than it used to be in the past. Now, it is more a question of the market perception of the orientation and predictability of economic policy."

Cross-border financial flows, particularly of private equity and portfolio investment, have recently seen a staggering growth. Here, Africa is still not even to be glimpsed on the horizon. The initial prerequisites of globalization are trade and financial linkages between involved countries, expansion and diversification. But in the North-South transactions, multilateral tariff reduction and trade liberalization are efforts that turn to an unequal tug-of-war whose winners are predestined to win. It may be true that the non-industrialized world practices protectionism with higher tariffs and greater tariff escalation that bring about more antidumping actions; the same protectionism measures in the industrialized world render their proclamations in favor of free trade unabashedly hypocritical and empty. The agricultural exports protection of the industrialized countries against the industrializing world is 4-7 times higher than that against the latter's manufacturing exports. According to Martin Tupy in *Trade Liberalization and Poverty Reduction in Sub-Saharan Africa*, "Tariffs of up to 500 percent are sometimes applied by the United States, European Union, Japan, and Canada on products that include beef, dairy products, vegetables, fresh and dried fruit, cereals, sugar, prepared fruit and vegetables, wine, spirits, and tobacco ... the African Growth and Opportunity Act (AGOA), a preferential trade agreement between the United States and 37 countries in SSA, exclude dairy products, soft drinks, cocoa, coffee, tea, tobacco, nuts, and many types of fabrics. Researchers at the World Bank, the International Monetary Fund, and the University of Maryland found that AGOA stands to yield only 19 to 26 percent of benefits that it could have yielded if it were comprehensive and unconditional." Not to mention the generous government support or subsidies for agricultural products that undercut competition from cheaper products coming from the developing countries. More importantly, not all developing world countries "are equally able to make use of the opportunities arising out of increased access to markets in the developed world."[36]

The industrialized nations' protectionism restricts growth of exports from the developing countries, which for the latter accounts for 73% of citizens living in rural areas, dependent on agricultural goods and constitute 60% of the labor force whose income is solely from agriculture. This sector, agriculture and agro-related services, generate about 40% of the GDP in developing countries. Of the global price distortions in agricultural commodities, 80% is caused by the industrialized world. The EU's Common Agricultural Policy causes annual losses of $20 billion in poor countries. Increasing trade may have indeed given consumers and producers a wide choice of low-cost goods and/or advanced technologies that facilitate a more efficient use of global resources. But all these, when it comes to Sub-Saharan African countries, are lopsided. The fact that "rapid increase in capital and private investment flows has raised the resources available to countries able to attract them, and accelerate the pace of their development beyond what they could otherwise have achieved" may be true of the so-called advanced emerging markets, it is not for the Sub-Saharan region. Economies that have benefited from globalization, according to IMF's World Economic Outlook, have their success linked to a) achieving and preserving macroeconomic stability; b) promoting openness to trade and capital flows; and c) limiting government intervention to areas of genuine market failure and to the provision of necessary social and economic infrastructure. Try it in Sub-Saharan Africa and see how successful it all would be! Creating confidence as a valued and trusted partner of private economic agents is not the African "big man's" cup of tea. The Fund's Alessane D. Ouattara explains the foregoing as follows:

> Macroeconomic stability, embodied in low inflation, appropriate real exchange rates and a prudent fiscal stance, is essential for expanding domestic activity, and is a precondition for benefiting from and sustaining private capital flows.
>
> Openness, in the resolute pursuit of policies to rationalize and liberalize the exchange and trade regimes, is vital in international competition.

---

36 CATO Instute paper No. 557, December 6, 2005.

This forces the economy to fully exploit its comparative advantage through trade.

And finally, the primary role of the government should be the creation of an enabling environment that encourages foreign and domestic investment, and of a solid infrastructure to support an expanding economy. The government must also implement policies that eliminate the structural weakness that would be exposed by the heightened international competition. Not surprisingly, these elements are generally central to the policy dialogue between the International Monetary Fund and its members.[37]

The IMF, globalization-mongers and the entity known as the world community may, during dinner, bandy about with words and phrases like "etiquette" about takeover proposals, "national security," "revival of beggar-thy-neighbor policies," "the ebbing spirit of internationalism" or "diminishing multilateral dialogue." Africa remains caught in a viselike clinch. It is desirable to establish public policies that will maximize the potential benefits of globalization while minimizing the downside risks of destabilization or marginalization or even both, and African countries have made substantial progress towards the stability of their macroeconomic institutions. But so far there is little to show for it. Little emphasis is given to policies that would encourage more sustainable reforms for economic flexibility, the reduction of vulnerability to exogenous shocks and diversification. The maneuvering margins for African domestic policies could be sacrificed at the altar of the speedy flow of information with no time for correcting them. Increased capital mobility, according to IMF's Ouattara, brings the risk of destabilizing flows and heightened exchange rate volatility, in cases where domestic macroeconomic policies are inappropriate. On the other hand non-participation in the integration trend presents the risk of being left behind.

Ouattara, being an IMF person, also maintains that it is not necessary for some countries to lose in order to have others gain. It is a question of adopting the right policies. To benefit the most from globalization, economies have to open and integrate themselves to trade and capital flows "on a free and fair basis" and be able to attract international capital. But the premium on good macroeconomic policies, I'm afraid, still remains the ability to respond quickly and appropriately to changes in the international landscape. This landscape is more likely to exclude rather than include Sub-Saharan African economies as they are currently structured. The lost credibility of their economic policies is indeed difficult to regain even if their perception of markets is that economic policy formulation and implementation should be consistent and predictable. Institutions that are

---

37 Ouattara, *The Challenges of Globalization for Africa*, Address given at the Southern Africa Economic Summit sponsored by the World Economic Forum, Harare, May 21, 1997.

well-governed or nations practicing transparency in governance are extremely rare in the current Sub-Saharan Africa.

But the biggest evildoers are in the US and the rest of the West. Yet by some quirk of schizophrenia, they twist facts around so that the innocent are the evildoers, the perpetrators the victims. Interviewed by Amy Goodman for *Democracy Now!* about how closely he worked with the World Bank, John Perkins, author of *Confessions of an Economic Hit Man*, replied:

> "Very, very closely with the World Bank. The World Bank provides most of the money that's used by economic hit men, it and the IMF. But when 9/11 struck, I had a change of heart. I knew the story had to be told because what happened at 9/11 is a direct result of what the economic hit men are doing. And the only way that we're going to feel secure in this country again and that we're going to feel good about ourselves is if we use these systems we've put into place to create positive change around the world. I really believe we can do that. I believe the World Bank and other institutions can be turned around and do what they were originally intended to do, which is help reconstruct devastated parts of the world. Help — genuinely help poor people. There are twenty-four thousand people starving to death every day. We can change that."[38]

And why were people in his line of profession called economic hit men? Again Perkins' reply is:

> "Yeah, it was a tongue-in-cheek term that we called ourselves. Officially, I was a chief economist. We called ourselves e.h.m.'s. It was tongue-in-cheek. It was like, nobody will believe us if we say this, you know? And, so, we went to Saudi Arabia in the early 1970s. We knew Saudi Arabia was the key to dropping our dependency, or to controlling the situation. And we worked out this deal whereby the Royal House of Saud agreed to send most of their petro-dollars back to the United States and invest them in US government securities. The Treasury Department would use the interest from these securities to hire U.S. companies to build Saudi Arabia new cities, new infrastructure which we've done. And the House of Saud would agree to maintain the price of oil within acceptable limits to us, which they've done all of these years, and we would agree to keep the House of Saud in power as long as they did this, which we've done, which is one of the reasons we went to war with Iraq in the first place. And in Iraq we tried to implement the same policy that was so successful in Saudi Arabia, but Saddam Hussein didn't buy. When the economic hit men fail in this scenario, the next step is what we call the jackals. Jackals are CIA-sanctioned people that come in and try to foment a coup or revolution. If that doesn't work, they perform assassinations. Or try to. In the case of Iraq, they weren't able to get through to Saddam Hussein. He had... His bodyguards were too good. He had doubles. They couldn't get through to him. So the third line of defense, if the economic hit men and the jackals fail, the next line of defense is our young men and women, who are sent in to die and kill, which is what we've obviously done in Iraq."

---

38 Perkins interwiew in *Democracy Now!* by the commentator and activist Amy Goodman, on 11 November 2004.

For those interested in knowing, the so-called "Royal House of Saud" is quite a recent construction in the poverty-stricken Arabia that was run by mainly absentee Ottoman viceroys of the 18th century.

It happened that in 1744, one Mohammed bin Abdul Wahhab founded that branch of Islam (today's Wahhabis), where veneration of saints, ostentation in worship, mode of dress, behavior or architecture, pilgrimage to any other site than Mecca, dancing, wine, music, hashish, wearing charms and practicing magic was forbidden, and the head-to-foot veil was mandatory for women. Wahhab teamed up with a powerful Arab clan headed by Mohammed bin Saud and together they gathered strength and willing followers of the new fundamentalist sect. The Wahhabi-Sauds then stormed into the holy Shiite city of Karbala in Iraq, maintaining that Shiites were heretics, and destroyed the mosques and holy places while pillaging and making off with every valuable thing they could carry. By 1803 the Wahhabis had captured Mecca and Medina and laid the first foundations of the first Saud state by destroying the Shiite and Sufi shrines that were dedicated to saints, including the tomb shrine of Fatima (the daughter of the Prophet). There were decades of local wars with the Ottoman viceroys in Egypt and surrounding regions that led to the control of Qatar and Bahrain and by 1811 the progeny of the Wahhabi-Saud alliance controlled all of Arabia but Yemen. The pillaging Egyptian troops and their Ottoman lords, who were famed for mismanagement and corruption, were finally defeated and gradually Riyadh was established as the seat of the clan chiefs before being defeated by the Turks — using British battlefield tactics — in 1904.

Europeans had entered the scene and now tactics changed. Turks became German allies in World War One and the British (who had been a dominant power in the Persian Gulf for over a century, being the world's only superpower) gave the Sauds protection after a "friendship" treaty was signed to the effect that the British would watch over the Sauds' foreign policy. At the end of the war, Sharif Hussein, an al-Rashid, proclaimed himself "King of the Hejaz" appointed by no lesser being than Allah. The European and Middle East politics being complex at the time, Hussein was acknowledged internationally as a "monarch" of western Arabia. The British, playing both fields depending on political considerations, assisted the Sauds with weapons and a monthly stipend of 500 pounds to finally defeat the al-Rashids. Turkey became a republic (as opposed to an "Islamic republic") in 1924. "King Hussein of the Hejaz" was sent packing to Cyprus and a Saud descendant named Abdul Aziz, assisted by the British, proclaimed himself "King of the Hejaz," making local conquests until by 1932, when Abdul Aziz declared himself king of the "Saudi" Arabia. Six years later the Americans found oil for him and Abdul Aziz and the Wahhabis were in paradise on earth.

The poverty-stricken Arabia of the Ottomans was gone. By then the British and the French had staked out their spheres of influence: France in Syria and Lebanon, Britain in Iraq, Kuwait, Jordan and Palestine. These two European powers, seeing no united Arab states between Turkey and Arabia, picked "kings" for Iraq, Syria and Jordan out of which only the Hashemite Kingdom of Jordan still survives today. In Africa, on the other hand, kingdoms were deleted and great kings of centuries-old dynasties were demoted to "chiefs" or "headmen." The pigmentation construction was already long in the making. The West moves and shakes the rest of the world for their often murky interests.

And of course Saudi Arabia, of Abdul Aziz's self-proclaimed "kingdom of the Saud," whose descendants today are the rulers of Saudi Arabia and great "friends" of America. This "friendship" is what feeds terrorists like Al-Qaeda's recruits. Other fonts of Islamic terrorism spring from wider complications going back to the partition of India to Muslim Pakistan and the rest of the subcontinent. And Europe's slotting their "rejected" Jews into Palestine to form the state of Israel. But the West has not only deliberately ignored this fact, they have also successfully schooled the rest of the world to believe that they are "good" and the non-Westerners are "evil." All the way to the war on Iraq, with "smart bombs" — one of the US's greatest blunders, but sold to the world as "a great success". The West and some of its citizenry seem to believe that violence, misstatements about who has what weapons, and exploitation of religious belief are effective and acceptable tools to use in sorting out differences in every sphere from politics to natural resources pricing. And the rest of the world looks on with (or without) critical remarks, outrage or condemnation.

Pakistan and India now both have nuclear weapons and George W. Bush goes over to them for a bit of cricket practice. North Korea defies the powers that be and tests nuclear weapons as and when it deems it necessary, so the Western movers and shakers more or less say: Let's talk, North Korea. What a message for the rest of the wannabe nuclear powers! Nuclear weapons are a bad idea, irrespective of in whose hands those weapons are. But Iran, who supposedly claims to aim at developing nuclear energy for domestic civil use, is being threatened with the thumbscrews. What's the West's message to the rest of the world? When you have nuclear power, we talk. When you don't, we attack and effect embargoes.

Back to the interview with the economic hit man. What made Perkins have a change of heart and go public with his knowledge? He told Amy Goodman:

> "I felt guilty throughout the whole time, but I was seduced. The power of these drugs, sex, power, and money, was extremely strong for me. And,

of course, I was doing things I was being patted on the back for. I was chief economist. I was doing things that Robert McNamara liked and so on....

"Omar Torrijos, the President of Panama. Omar Torrijos had signed the Canal Treaty with Carter — and, you know, it passed our congress by only one vote. It was a highly contended issue. And Torrijos then also went ahead and negotiated with the Japanese to build a sea-level canal. The Japanese wanted to finance and construct a sea-level canal in Panama. Torrijos talked to them about this which very much upset Bechtel Corporation, whose president was George Shultz and senior council was Casper Weinberger. When Carter was thrown out (and that's an interesting story — how that actually happened), when he lost the election, and Reagan came in and Shultz came in as Secretary of State from Bechtel, and Weinberger came from Bechtel to be Secretary of Defense, they were extremely angry at Torrijos — tried to get him to renegotiate the Canal Treaty and not to talk to the Japanese. He adamantly refused. He was a very principled man. He had his problems, but he was a very principled man. He was an amazing man, Torrijos. And so, he died in a fiery airplane crash, which was connected to a tape recorder with explosives in it, which — I was there. I had been working with him. I knew that we economic hit men had failed. I knew the jackals were closing in on him, and the next thing, his plane exploded with a tape recorder with a bomb in it. There's no question in my mind that it was CIA sanctioned, and most — many Latin American investigators have come to the same conclusion. Of course, we never heard about that in our country."

And this is supposed to be God's own country.

It is not just the African governments and the African elite who are corrupt and lack any sense of ethics. It is not just the African politicians who murder their political opponents and practice economic nepotism. The Africans have simply learnt from the perfect role models, from the masters of the game, and they too put their money where their mouth is. Corruption, especially political corruption, is firmly entrenched in the West. That's where the axis of evil may well be grazing, and that very voraciously.

CHAPTER 9. SUB-SAHARAN AFRICA'S FINANCIAL SECTORS

> *[T]echnological advancement [s]... which were to be defining ac-*
> *complishments in the rise of the West...were gunpowder, the formula*
> *for which the Arabs had long before obtained from the Chinese...*
> *improved and transmitted to Europe...in the late 13th century [which]*
> *Westerners put to good effect in bronze cannon in the early 16th*
> *century for ship-board use.... Sailing ships with greater ocean-going*
> *capability...guns and ships... by the Venetians in the late 15th century*
> *added to expanding markets, increased availability of investment*
> *capital and the newly designed banking and insurance safeguards*
> *enabled maritime nations of the West to profit directly from the*
> *treasures of the East while in the main cutting out Arab middlemen.*

— RODNEY COLLOMB[39]

I had a savings account in Kenya, in the beginning of the 1980s, with the Kenya Commercial Bank, Shankardass Savings Branch, Account No. 140122006, into which I regularly deposited money. At some stage I noticed that the bank was deducting 10% every quarter as a "commission." A commission for a savings account — which should be paying interest, instead? I wrote to the chairman of Kenya Commercial Bank, who wrote back to tell me he had contacted the Shankardass Branch manager to sort the matter out. Nothing was sorted out. Eventually I had occasion to visit the bank in person, but nobody could explain the phenomenon to me. If I commenced legal proceedings I would need to remain in the country for several years, as they all knew, so I had no choice but to close the account and fly back to Europe, making myself an accomplice to the fraud by default.

39Collomb, *The Rise and Fall of the Arab Empire*, Gloucestershire: Spellmount Limited, 2006, p. 138

The operating environment of Sub-Saharan African financial institutions is often too poisoned even for money to breathe in. The most lethal of the viruses are the legal and the institutional frameworks, especially because banks are the dominant actors in SSA financial sectors. The banks in Africa are there to serve the handful of rich people, governments and the formal sector. Widespread poverty makes it possible for only 10% of Sub-Saharan Africa's households to save, thus limiting both the supply and the demand for savings facilities. In the industrialized nations, 90% of the households have savings accounts. The IMF's African Department think tank maintains that access to the savings and loans financial services is lower in SSA than in other developing regions, and thus the share of the population having a formal savings account is strongly correlated with poverty rates and per capita income. A vicious circle is then generated where poor people have little sums to save, which in turn limits banks' economic opportunities due to the high costs of maintaining small accounts. The banks then revert to charging for opening and maintaining a deposit account, which in turn makes access to bank services more difficult for small-scale savers. These are the biggest losers in the globalization village. The African policymakers should indeed face the *new challenges that reflect the nascent globalization of African financial markets*, and this means reforming not only the banks but also developing new markets and institutions as well as the operating environment. Other drawbacks such as the minimum deposit rates (which are fairly high for the ordinary citizen), the structural constraints with concentration in the urban areas, and the small branch networks making it hard for the majority of the population to access banks.

There is a causal and economically important effect of financial development on volatility. Sectors with larger liquidity needs are more volatile and experience deeper crises in financially underdeveloped countries. It has been proved that at the macroeconomic level, the results indicate that changes in financial development can generate important differences in aggregate volatility. Three new evidences in this regard are that:

1. Financial development affects volatility mainly through the intensive margin (output per company).
2. Both the quality of information generated by companies, and the development of financial intermediaries have independent effects on sectoral volatility.
3. The development of financial intermediaries is more important than the development of equity markets for the reduction of volatility.

Sub-Saharan Africa's financial sector is rated to be among the least developed in the world. This is primarily because Africa's amazing wealth, monetary or natural, have but a very temporary turnaround time in the continent's financial sectors. IMF Advisor Anne-Marie Gulde and the senior economist Catherine Pattillo write in an article:

> Sustained improvement in growth is contingent on the establishment of a supportive financial infrastructure. Sound, deep, and efficient financial sectors are critical for improving the business climate and creating the conditions for the private sector to be the engine of growth... The range of institutions is narrow, and most of the countries' assets are smaller than those held by a single medium-sized bank in an industrial country. Most people do not have access to even basic payment services or savings accounts, and the largest part of the productive sector cannot obtain credit. Limited finance lowers welfare and hinders poverty alleviation, and a lack of credit to the economy impedes growth. In addition, implementing monetary policy in the context of shallow markets is costly and inefficient. To date, the region's efforts to address these challenges have borne little fruit.[40]

The Commonwealth HIPC conference should have devoted less time to sorting out how the ESF funds should be disbursed, where, and to whom and for what, and should have laid emphasis instead on discussing whether ESF are of any use to the shocked countries in Sub-Saharan Africa *without* adequate financial sector reforms. Such reforms are long overdue. No Western financial institute would be hoarding corruption money, for example, if no African financial institute or central bank transferred the money to the West in the first place. Yet the ordinary SSA citizens who would fulfill the vacuum that exists in small and medium-sized businesses have no access to financing at all. I remember another visit to a bank in Kenya in 1997, where a man wanted to open an account. The fellow was asked to pay an initial deposit of *three thousand* Kenyan Shillings in order to open an account. I was standing before the counter next to the man and he turned to me, and cried, "What is this now, do I have to be a millionaire in order to save?" I could very well understand the man's shock. In Germany, this man could have opened an account with no more than his identification card or driving license and not a single cent. I arranged for him to get the 3,000 shillings from my account there and then. To him, it was an unbelievable amount of money; to me it was about 35 Euros. This example shows just how much wider the gap between the haves and the have-nots has become. In the mid-1970s to early 1980s Kenya, 3,000 shillings was a good monthly salary for an administrator or management secretary. One US dollar at the time was between 5 to 7 Kenyan shillings. In the late 1990s the dollar reached 39 shillings and today (2007) the dollar is nearly 100 shillings.

Sub-Saharan Africa could build on its efforts to increase financial support through financial sector reforms. The financial sectors should effectively mobilize and pool savings as well as producing information on possible investments

---

[40]Anne-Marie Gulde and Catherine Pattilo for the IMF in their article, *Adding Depth* — *Finance & Development,* Ju ne 2006.

so that resources can be channeled to their most productive use. Next is the monitoring of the use of funds, then the facilitating of the trading, diversification, and management of risk. Lastly, the easing of the exchange of goods and services. Because SSA is a high-risk environment exposed to terms of trade shocks and a volatile climate, it would benefit from greater risk-sharing through portfolio diversification, consumption smoothing, and insurance, which are facilitated by financial development.

This simple knowledge is probably not even known to those who should know it, but banking is the most developed part of the financial sector in low-income SSA countries and accounts for more than 80 percent of the assets. Insurance, the few stock markets, non-bank financial intermediaries, and microfinance are all small sectors, although the latter two are supposed to be growing rapidly. By contrast, the few middle-income SSA countries, whose performance is considerably better, have larger and more diversified financial sectors. The middle-income countries in SSA which include Angola, Botswana, Cape Verde, Equatorial Guinea, Gabon, Mauritius, Namibia, Seychelles, South Africa and Swaziland, have much larger financial sectors and broader institutional coverage than the low-income countries. Gulde and Pattillo assert that these countries' key indicators of financial depth are comparable to, or higher than, those in other middle-income countries though this outcome is partly due to South Africa's far more mature financial sector. Botswana, Mauritius, and Namibia also compare favorably with other developing regions.

More sizable financial sectors in middle-income SSA countries have given their populations greater access to financial services than those in low-income countries. But banking in oil producers like Angola, Gabon, and Equatorial Guinea is different from banking in the other middle-income countries. Lending to the private sector is limited, and branch network density and access are even lower than in most low-income SSA countries. The number of banks in these countries is low in relation to the size of the economy, reflecting limited lending opportunities in the non-oil economy.

Sub-Saharan Africa's banking systems have come a long way since the 1990s, the two authors maintain, if only because the region experienced a number of crises. The politically motivated lending to public enterprises and political insiders, as well as a blind eye from supervisors, created the problem of rampant non-performing loans, insolvent banking systems, and financial crises. Now, most of the region's banking systems are, on average, adequately capitalized and highly liquid. However, some countries' financial systems and many individual banks are still weak, with many banks failing to meet tests of basic capital adequacy, a sign of persistent problems in banking supervision. This is not a wonder when one again calculates that average non-performing loans in 2004 stood at 15%. Less diversified countries are more vulnerable to credit risk; a big shock to the major export sector could turn most of their banking loans absolutely rotten to the core. To reflect this risk, SSA countries need higher capital-adequacy ratios, although few set their minimum ratios above the standard 8%. Some frequently violate other prudential ratios, such as those limiting banks' exposures to a single client or sector, because of the alleged shortage of bankable customers. Yet a hoard of ordinary Africans are lining up in order to offer their meager savings to the banks. And get treated like trash. These are the customers — in a developing country who should be encouraging its citizens to save and borrow! These are the customers who should be assisted on their way to become the carrying middle class economy. Having rules on the books that everyone knows cannot be met, given the economies' structures, can unintentionally create a culture of non-compliance. Once again, is it the alleged SSA *non compos mentis* management and governance?

Although concentrated, SSA banking systems nevertheless show signs of becoming more competitive. Some concentration is inevitable because institutions must achieve economies of scale and scope. Many SSA economies can support only a small number of banks. Although the number of competitors in a banking market rises with the population and the economy's size, a number of SSA countries are hedged out. Ethiopia — a populous country with one dominant commercial bank — is the most striking case. In contrast, Cameroon, Ghana, and Senegal have a large number of banks in relation to their population and income. SSA concentration ratios are said to be generally moving in the right direction because they have declined in the wake of recent bank restructurings and privatizations. The growing presence of foreign banks — which represent a larger share of banking systems than in other low-income countries — also indicates some market contestability.

But the banking sectors of low-income SSA countries are not becoming more efficient. For all SSA banks, including foreign-owned institutions, low efficiency is reflected in high overhead costs and higher net interest margins than those prevailing in other low-income countries. Net interest margins are used as an efficiency indicator, albeit an imperfect one, since banks with high operating costs need a high spread — the gap between what banks can charge borrowers and what they pay savers — to cover those costs. Cross-country research has found that high inflation, corruption, and concentration reduce bank efficiency. Despite high overhead costs, SSA banks are profitable. Their main source of income is interest-related items. Given non-competitive market structures, banks can charge high interest margins and remain profitable even in a difficult operating environment.

SSA banks are less efficient than banks elsewhere, but profitable. (percentage of assets)					
	Net interest margin		Overhead		Profit before tax	
	1996-99	2000-03	1996-99	2003-03	1996-99	2000-03
SSA	8.0	8.2	7.4	7.4	3.0	3.0
Other low-middle-income countries	7.1	6.6	7.0	7.1	0.2	1.1
SSA low-income countries	8.2	8.5	7.6	7.7	3.3	3.2
Other low-income countries	5.5	4.9	5.3	5.3	1.1	1.1
Source: IMF staff calculations.						

Another setback is that the economies are still cash based. Consumers in many parts of the world are increasingly using debit and credit cards and electronic banking, but cash transactions are still dominant in SSA, and Africa has made less progress than other regions in moving to non-cash forms of money. Banks' core business of financial intermediation, i.e. mobilizing deposits and lending them on to borrowers, is less pronounced in SSA than in other low-income countries. Bank deposits in low-income SSA in 2004 were only 19% of GDP, compared with 38% on average in other regions, and private sector loans were only 13% of GDP. There are many reasons for the sluggish growth in banking activities. In addition to legal and institutional weaknesses, the after-effects of banking crises which often caused banking activity to grind to a halt, also appear to have played a part. For example, following the sharp contraction in the banking crises of the late 1980s, private deposits and credit in the CFA franc countries have been stagnant.

For the economy to function, most financial sector activities take place between financial institutions, promoting market efficiency and risk-trading. Deepening inter-bank markets are signs of maturing financial systems. But most SSA countries use inter-bank markets infrequently and trade in small amounts. One reason is that banks in many SSA countries have excess liquidity in the form of cash holdings that exceed the prudential reserves required by the central bank, often because they do not find enough attractive projects to finance and therefore have no need to borrow short-term funds from other banks. Other reasons are the lack of instruments that can be used as collateral and the lack of mutual trust among banks as well as between banks and the citizenry in general. The banks are nearly always convinced that the citizen's only collateral is his need. This mistrust is caused by the lack of transparency as guideline information on financially weak banks.

Many countries are trying to improve their financial market infrastructure — the "plumbing" of the financial system — but have not yet achieved greater financial market activity. For example, the West African Economic and Monetary Union (WAEMU) and the Central African Economic and Monetary Community (CEMAC) have either recently put in place or are implementing state-of-the-art real-time gross settlement and retail payment systems to speed up check clearances. Most SSA countries that have introduced treasury bills are moving from paper-based securities to more modern, book-entry systems. Once the remaining technical problems are resolved, the availability of these systems should facilitate further developments.

Financial experts have repeatedly pointed out the factors that impede financial development and economic growth, as well as suggesting remedies. Several factors, such as the operating environment, impede progress in developing stronger financial sectors in the continent. Legal and institutional frameworks are generally poor, and improvements have been slow. Legal systems are underfunded, and the public often has little confidence that legal proceedings are objective and will take a reasonable amount of time. A credit information index measuring the ability of financial institutions to obtain information on client creditworthiness, and a legal framework index, rate the SSA lower than other low-income countries. Studies have shown that improvements in these indices are strongly associated with higher shares of private loans to GDP.

Weak property rights and poor contract enforceability constrain financial market activity. Financial institutions are reluctant to lend because of the difficulty of securing collateral and seizing assets if loans default. Borrowers often have difficulty presenting collateral because of unclear land titles as a result of inadequate documentation and overlapping systems of rights and ownership. Registering titles of movable property (such as cars and other durable goods) is also problematic. For example, when borrowers in Rwanda and Senegal use movable property as collateral, they must often physically surrender it for the duration of the loan. SSA businesses are ranked the lowest in the world on indicators necessary for efficient financial system operation: registering property, getting credit, protecting investors, and enforcing contracts. On average, to enforce a commercial contract through the courts, creditors must go through 35 steps, wait 15 months, and pay a sum equal to 43% of the country's average annual per capita income before receiving payment. Banks' concerns about credit guarantees seem natural in such an environment.

In a big stride forward, SSA countries have brought many regulatory and supervisory requirements into line with international norms. But the actual supervision is often constrained. Supervisors tend to be subject to political pressure and thus have little power to demand "prompt corrective actions." They also tend to exhibit substantial tolerance for violations of prudential rules. This forbearance often reflects underlying pressures, such as banks' inability to meet the requirements (for example, on loan concentration), given structural features of the economy (limited lending opportunities) that are slow to change. Politically influenced supervisors also sometimes worry about the possible fiscal costs of bank restructuring. Resource constraints in supervisory agencies and the generally weak accounting and auditing systems in place also hamper supervision.

Reserve ratios in SSA are high and have been climbing since the mid-1990s. In 2004, the average reserve ratio was 11.3% and ranged from 0% in the Central African Republic to about 50% in Zimbabwe. Increases in required reserves reflect the continent's heightened focus on stabilizing inflation and maintaining financial system stability. Yet rule-based monetary policy instruments force unpopular costs down the throats of banks. With many SSA countries only partially remunerating required reserves, if at all, this instrument amounts to a heavy tax on banks. Because of the lack of remuneration, banks do not have the incentive to seek deposits or to develop products against which they must hold reserves. And empirical studies find that high reserve requirements contribute to high interest rate spreads. Despite increases in required reserves over the past years, most SSA banking systems hold significant unremunerated excess liquidity amounting to more than 13% of total deposits, on average. Why do banks hold these funds if they are not required to and receive no return on them? In some countries, persistent excess liquidity is linked to growing oil and aid inflows. Capital controls, structural problems in financial systems (such as interest rate restrictions, perceived limited and risky lending opportunities, and asymmetric information), and underdeveloped government securities and inter-bank markets also play a role. Excess liquidity is both higher and more volatile in oil-producing countries and is higher than the SSA average in the CEMAC and the WAEMU zones.

Many suggestions have been put across the table on how SSA countries could make more rapid progress in their financial sectors so that the improved economic performance can be sustained. While many countries are taking measures to address some of the challenges — through promotion of microfinance and efforts to enhance enterprises financing and improve the operating environment — these efforts have yielded only partial results. Some priority actions have been identified, such as a harmonized approach to regulation in the context of low restrictions to market entry, which would allow financial firms to benefit from economies of scale and scope in larger markets. An elimination of distortions, such as the forbearance practice of bank supervisors, could improve banking soundness and facilitate greater inter-bank activities. Similarly, reducing the excessive use of costly monetary instruments (high reserve requirements) could spur development of the banking sector.

Nearly all financially underdeveloped countries partially protect themselves from volatility by concentrating less output in sectors with large liquidity needs, but such insulation mechanism seems insufficient in reversing the effects of financial underdevelopment on the so-called within-sector volatility. SSA countries could benefit from alternative instruments (such as leasing) or alternatives to collateralization (for example, group guarantees, reversible equity stakes) to overcome bottlenecks created by weak property rights. While governments' interest in promoting access to finance is well founded, new specialized state institutions should generally be avoided. Finally, even-handed application of the legal framework, which is important for improving lending to the private sector, could benefit from development of commercial courts and, in some cases, specialized judges.

The latest analyses come from the December 2006 IMF Finance & Development report. The IMF African financial sector think tank of independent experts such as the assistant director Anne-Marie Gulde, senior economist Catherine Pattillo and the economists Jakob Christensen and Amadou Sy recommend that the new reform efforts provide financial sectors with market-based incentives to increase their engagement with the private sector and address the pressures from the starting globalization of African financial markets. The action priorities they list include freeing the financial sectors from excessive restrictions such as fees, charges and state direction; bolstering the information base on which financial decisions depend; increasing market size to enable the new markets and institutions to flourish; tackling regulatory obstacles pertaining to the registration and seizure of collateral including those created by unclear land and property rights; and reviewing macroeconomic policies for the integration into the global financial system.

Equally limited in loans services of commercial banks are enterprises and agriculture, although agriculture employs the majority of the workforce in Africa. Banks tend to lend to export and import firms as well as the government. Four main aspects have been identified as causing low private sector credit: 1) This lending, under weak institutional and legal environments, becomes a risky business because enforcing commercial contracts through the courts is more difficult in SSA than it is in other regions. It takes as much as going through 35 steps, waiting 15 months and paying a fee equal to 43% of the country's annual per capita income before payments are received. 2) Loans are costly due to high real lending interest rates. In the developed countries the average lending rate is 3.5%, in low- and middle-income countries 8% and in SSA countries, where bank credits are the only option, it is 13%. 3) Since most lending is attached to collateral, the weak property rights and deficient land title system or other movable property such as vehicles in SSA limit the use of such assets as collateral and therefore constrain financial intermediation. 4) Many SSA banks increasingly lend to governments or buy government or central bank debt instruments, as this proves more lucrative to them than credit to the private sector.

Skewed Lending

The agriculture sector accounts for nearly 32 percent of GDP but receives less than 12 percent of bank loans. (percent, 2005)

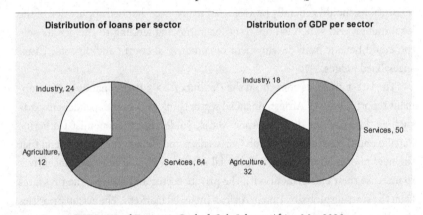

Distribution of loans per sector   **Distribution of GDP per sector**

Industry, 24
Agriculture, 12
Services, 64

Industry, 18
Services, 50
Agriculture, 32

Source: IMF Regional Economic Outlook Sub-Saharan Africa, May 2006

Note: Agriculture includes forestry, and fishing; industry includes manufacturing, mining, utilities, and construction; Services include government.

Shallow financial sectors are inefficient; therefore reforms should aim at increasing the financial institutions that would serve the poor, small and medium enterprises, and strengthen the overall operating environment. Where commercial banks fail, the increasing number of microfinance institutions (MFIs) should be encouraged. Since the average member savings in these MFIs amount to less than half the average per capita income and are even smaller than the average savings accounts in banks, they reach a larger spectrum of the population. The MFI account outreach is on the average less than 2 out of 100 people in most countries, with assets reliant on small-scale savings and loans amounting to only 1.3% of GDP compared to commercial bank assets averaging 6% of GDP. Due to high costs, however, and despite client repayment rates being generally good, the real lending rate of MFIs (which averages 43%) is often in excess of the banks' lending.

Another suggestion to deepen the financial sector diversification are the nonbank financial institutions (NBIs), who provide products and services not offered by banks. These NBIs include postal savings banks, pension funds, mortgage finance, consumer credit, insurance and finance and leasing companies. Currently this sector is much smaller than the banking sector in nearly all SSA countries and has assets of about 10% of the total financial system. Few examples such as insurance sectors (predominant in Gabon and Kenya) and pension funds (predominant in Rwanda and Botswana), according to the Finance & Development report of December 2006, are exceptions.

Sprucing up the legal challenges has to include the modernization of banking and business laws and the central banks, to create a greater role for markets. Factors impeding on financial sector reforms, which urgently need to be streamlined, include the judicial systems, accounting practices and the enforceability of contracts. Despite the many positive changes, the stumbling blocks still remain the legal and regulatory frameworks, weak institutional setting and shallow markets. Well over half of all SSA countries have replaced direct borrowing from central banks by governments and instead introduced treasury bill markets — an important step for better fiscal management likely to enhance the development of the financial market. Such bills assist in establishing "interest rate benchmarks for other commercial paper and their use as collateral. Low-risk government debt can also help offset the high risks of private sector lending, allowing it to increase within prudential limits on risk-weighted capital asset ratios. Most treasury bill markets in SSA are immature. The average size of a set of key markets was only about 14 percent of GDP in 2005. The instruments offered on these markets are generally short term, and the investor base is narrow, consisting mainly of commercial banks. Secondary markets are nonexistent or small, except in Nigeria, South Africa and Uganda."[41]

Another report by Amadou Sy in 2006 contends that 8 members of WAEMU (Benin, Burkina Faso, Côte d'Ivoire, Guinea-Bissau, Mali, Niger, Senegal and Togo) set up a regional treasury bill market as an alternative. All countries issue securities, which has made this treasury bill market grow rapidly from about CFAF 55 billion in 2002 (when it replaced the direct lending of regional central bank to national treasuries) to about CFAF 290 billion in 2005, with interest rates falling. The demand for treasury bills mirrors better fiscal positions but additional incentives have apparently come from excess

---

41 IMF African Department, *Regional Economic Outlook Sub-Saharan Africa*, May 2006.

banking liquidity, allowable refinancing at the regional central bank and tax exemption and zero risk weighting of interest earnings. The report states that better regional financial integration accelerated cross-border treasury bill sales, making more than 50% of the bills issued being purchased by banks in another WAEMU country between 2004-2005. The bills can assist "financial deepening if they are used for market-based pricing for government debt, collateral for interbank deals, and a pricing benchmark for other commercial debt issues."[42] With a market of around 900,000 people, African governments would be well advised to give serious thought to the cross-border treasury bill market.

Countries such as Gabon are implementing development banks to channel credit to priority sectors, while Rwanda and Burundi have adopted realignments of the time limits for filing appeals on commercial disputes, with Burundi cutting off as much as three months on the time required to recover debt. Rwanda is said to have "expanded the scope of public registries' credit reports and even made them available online in 2004."

Member countries of WAEMU are forming specialized state-owned banks to enable certain sectors to gain access to relevant finance — with little success because of the high risk factors. Nevertheless the Organization for the Harmonization of Business Law in Africa, formed in 1963 by 16 African countries, has so far successfully standardized a wide range of commercial laws. Still other problems arise in the failure in many countries, of the export credit agencies subsidizing access, and financing through the stock markets. The ailments of the SSA stock markets are "little turnover and market capitalization due in part to inadequate informational and disclosure rules and supervisory frameworks" and "the stock markets tend to be more efficient and deliver economic benefits when basic financial sector infrastructure and well-functioning banking system are in place," says the September 2006 report.

Politely put, but it is quite obvious what is meant.

---

42 Sy, Amadou, *Financial Integration in the West African Economic and Monetary Union*, IMF Working Paper 06/214; September 1, 2006.

"Moor girl under the magic tree," by an unknown painter, 1944

The African woman, in Euroancestral eyes, is always a seductress with her mysterious sexuality.

"Heinrich Carl Baron of Schimmelmann," by Lorenz Lönberg, ca. 1773
National Historical Museum, Denmark

The ladies and gentlemen of the nobility took to bleaching and powdering themselves white and acquiring African children as companions to set off their "whiteness." The "blacker" the child, the better.

*"The Garden of Lust" by Hieronymus Bosch, ca. 1500, oil on wood
Prado Museum, Madrid*

Notice the color polarization!

"Moor and Peasant in a dance" Nuremberg City Library
Anti-American Propaganda Placard, Italy, Boccasile, ca. 1942

PART TWO — DARKEST EUROPE

Ascending the line of gradation, we come at last to the white European; who being most removed from the brute creation, may, on that account, be considered as the most beautiful of the human race. No one will doubt his superiority in intellectual powers; and I believe it will be found that his capacity is naturally superior to that of every other man. Where shall we find, unless in the European, that nobly arched head, containing such a quantity of brain, and supported by a hollow conical pillar, entering its centre? Where the perpendicular face, the prominent nose, and round projecting chin? Where that variety of features, and fullness of expression; those long, flowing, graceful ringlets; that majestic beard, those rosy cheeks and coral lips? Where that erect posture of the body and noble gait? In what other quarter of the globe shall we find the blush that overspreads gentle features of the beautiful women of Europe, that emblem of modesty, of delicate feelings, and of sense? Where that nice expression of the amiable and softer passion in the countenance; and that general elegance of features and complexion? Where, except on the bosom of the European woman, two such plump and snowy white hemispheres, tipt with vermillion?

— CHARLES WHITE[43]

43 White, Charles, *An Account of the Regular Gradation of Man, and in Different Animals and Vegetables; and from the Former to the Latter* London, 1799, p.134 f.

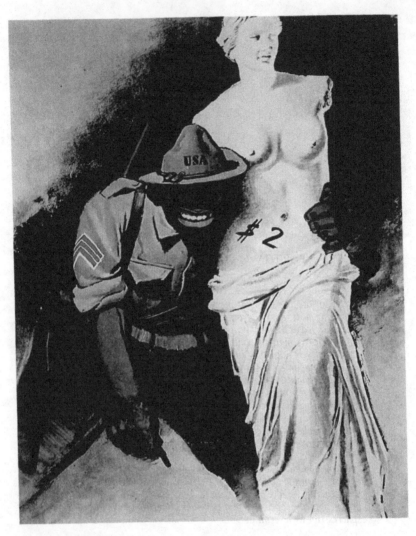

Anti-American Propaganda Placard, Italy, Boccasile, ca. 1942

CHAPTER 10. DARKEST EUROPE AND AFRICA'S NIGHTMARE

The Aryans left their homes... on the 1st of March. This settles the question of the climate of their original home. Had their homes been situated in a moderate zone, the Aryans would never, of their own free will, have made their exodus so early; they would have delayed it, if not until May, at any rate until the middle of April.

RUDOLPH VON IHERING, 1897[44]

One of the presumably paramount delusions in the Euroancestral's™ psyche is that of calling themselves "whites." Even the Kiswahili word *mzungu* (singular) and *wazungu* (plural) — which the likes of Kuki Gallman, Barbara Wood, Corinne Hofmann, the remarkably inventive Frank Coates and a plethora of the so-called Africa experts or romancers of Euroancestral descent perpetually spell wrongly as *misungu* or *musungu* et cetera — actually means "European." But look at all the glossaries of Euroancestral writers and the word is always translated as "white." For those who care to know, "white" in Kiswahili is: *-eupe*, so that the feminine and masculine singular adjectives become *mweupe*, and the neuter *kiupe* or *nyeupe*.

Euroancestrals are leeches on the word "white," a star-studded sword of purity. Unfortunately the word is applied for the darkest impurity that ever evolved from the caveman, endowed with amazing degrees of the Push and the Pull factors.

John Perkins, the author of *Confessions of an Economic Hit Man*, is a mainstream Puller with elements of the Pusher in him, too. George W. Bush is a benchmark mainstream Pusher with elements of the Puller as well. The evolved caveman is

---

44 Mallory, *In Search of the Indo-Europeans*, London: Thames & Hudson, p. 222

not a Janus, he is a Hydra. This is a human society with sanctioned *Capi di tutti Capi*. Killing is still what The Family (the West) does best. Dialogue is strictly an internal affair. Even Berlin is at last snuggled close to Washington's feet on the hearth rug while London's head is being patted on Washington's lap. But for walks in the wood, Washington still prefers London because when Washington throws the stick, London eagerly runs after it to bring the stick back to Washington.

When applying trickery, coercion, threat, blackmail, cooperation under duress and finally death, Euroancestrals all stick together. Look at their trail in Africa, North and South America, Australia, New Zealand, the Caribbean, Asia. The deaths of a few heads of state demonstrate: 1952, Mohammad Mossadegh of Iran; 1961, Patrice Lumumba of Congo (present DRCongo); 1961, the mysterious plane crash killing the Swedish UN Secretary-General Dag Hammarskjöld while he was trying to secure peace in (DR)Congo; 1963, Ngo Dinh Diem of Vietnam; 1965, Ahmed Sukarno of Indonesia; 1966 Kwame Nkrumah of Ghana; 1973, Salvador Allende of Chile; 1981, a double hit in South America eliminating first Jaime Roldo of Ecuador and then Omar Torrijos of Panama; 1994, Juvenal Habryarimana of Rwanda (setting the Rwanda genocide in motion); 2005 Slobodan Milosevic of Yugoslavia; 2006 Saddam Hussein of Iraq. Not to mention failed "hits" such as the ones on Abdul Qassem of Iraq and Muammar Gaddafi of Libya. The fireman sets the fire so that his fire brigade can come in to extinguish the flames. Even Saddam Hussein, once their malleable "man of the hour" finally had to be "silenced." He could not be allowed fair trial at the permanent International Criminal Court in The Hague for his crimes against humanity (crimes that the Global Policeman had assisted him in and practically encouraged him to commit). He could not be tried at the International Criminal Court in The Hague because, as is well known, this court does not have a death penalty provision.

George W. Bush hailed Saddam Hussein's death as an important milestone.

That is not really far from the caveman. And very incompatible with humanity. Civilization has nothing to do with one man's passion, and the last thing the world community needs in this millennium is a lone rancher bent on authoritarianism, regarding dominance of one nation over the world, attenuating other nations en mass, as some kind of historical social Darwinism and therefore to be accepted as the natural course of events. That is barbaric. Robert Fantina in *Desertation and the American Soldier* succinctly illuminates the barbaric attitude of many in the United States: war is the answer, war is a way to solve problems. Fantina quotes a Gulf War deserter, Erik Larson, repeating "some chants he'd learned as a Marine":

Rape the town and kill the people;
That's the thing we love to do;
Rape the town and kill the people
That's the only thing to do,
Throw some napalm on the schoolhouse;
Watch the kiddies scream and shout;
Rape the town and kill the people;
That's the thing we love to do;
Napalm, napalm;
Sticks like glue....[45]

A few paragraphs on Saddam's liaison with the West should be in order. It began in the 1950s when Washington wanted a change in Iraq and so toppled the leader of the country, General Abdul Qassem. Qassem's crime was that he had breached the US-initiated anti-Soviet Baghdad Pact, in that he nationalized eight foreign-owned oil companies in Iraq. A failed assassination-*cum*-coup against Qassem was carried out in October 1959 under President John F. Kennedy. Saddam, aged 22, received a leg injury during this scuffle and fled to Egypt where he remained for four years before the CIA rigged a successful coup that whipped up the Ba'ath Party (at the time headed by Ahmed Hassam Al-Bakr) and Saddam returned from Egypt to take up the post of chief of the secret service in Iraq. By 1979 he was president of the Ba'ath Party and chairman of the Revolutionary Council, when Al-Bakr bowed out. In 1980 the US was bristling at the long-bearded ones in Iran. And Washington's man Saddam Hussein was funded to the hilt to arm himself to attack his neighbor. One million people died on both sides; the US gave support to Iraq. Then Saddam seemed to need cutting down to size again, so he was induced to attack Kuwait in August 1990. That provided Washington the excuse to give him a lesson in January 1991.

In Mark Curtis' book, *Web of Deceit – Britain's Role in the World*, the author reveals that, "Before the country became an Official Enemy by invading Kuwait in 1990, Western policy had been to support Saddam's Iraq since it served two useful functions: first, fighting the new Ayatollah's regime in Iran, and second, brutally suppressing Kurds in Iraq. London has always opposed full self-determination or statehood for the Kurds for fear of destabilizing its allies in the region, principally Turkey and Iraq. From 1980 to 1990, Britain

---

45 Fantina, Robert, *Desertion and the American Soldier*. Fantina is himself quoting from Jeff Syrop, 1991. The New Order. http://www.zenhell.com/GetEnlightened/stories/neworder/neworder.htm. Accessed October 11, 2005

provided £3.5bn in trade credits to Baghdad — critical economic support that had the effect of freeing up resources for the Iraqi military. British ministerial trade missions were regular throughout the war years and continued as Iraq used poison gas against the Iranians in 1983-4."[46]

The UK-Iraq trade talks in 1987 extended the export credits and London's Department of Trade and Industry "noted that 'the new facilities amounted to an expression of confidence in UK-Iraq commercial relations'." Curtis continues, "One of the absurdities of the current crisis is that London and Washington are attacking Iraq supposedly on the basis of the latter's development of weapons of mass destruction aided by London and Washington." He then lists exports from Britain as including three tons of sodium cyanide and sodium sulfide that can be used as nerve gas antidotes, delivered in April 1989, and plutonium zirconium, thorium oxide and gas spectrometers, all of which are essential for nuclear technology. The drug pralidoxine which is also an antidote to nerve gas was sold to Iraq later in March 1992. Furthermore, the trade continued throughout the 1980s when Saddam destroyed 3,000 Kurdish villages — "the same Kurds we now are 'defending' out of our natural humanitarianism," Curtis adds ironically. "A key date is March 1988, when Iraqi forces used poison gas at the town of Halabja killing 5,000 Kurds, an event now invoked to show that the Saddam regime is the personification of evil."

Retaining the irony, Curtis writes that London continued deepening its military support for Saddam after Halabja and the "British government expressed its outrage over the use of chemical weapons by doubling export credits to Baghdad, which rose from £175m in 1987 to £340m in 1988." The Department of Trade and Industry referred to the doubling of support: "this substantial increase reflects the confidence of the British government in the long-term strength of the Iraqi economy and the opportunities for an increased level of trade between our two countries..." Foreign Office minister William Waldegrave in October 1989, "I doubt if there is any future market of such a scale anywhere where the UK is potentially so well-placed."

Washington supplied Saddam with chemical warfare-agent precursors, drawings, chemical warfare-filing equipment, biological warfare-related materials, missile fabrication equipment and missile system guidance equipment. After the "quick and successful" war in Iraq in 2003 and still going on, and obviously to curtail Saddam's chances of a trial at The Hague, the US newspaper *International Herald Tribune* revealed that, "The US government

---

46 Curtis, Mark, *Web of Deceit — Britain's Real Role in the World*, London: Vintage, 2003

spent more than $128m building the courthouse, exhuming mass graves, gathering evidence and training Iraqi judges," and that "hundreds of American lawyers, investigators and prosecutors played a crucial role in securing conviction [of Saddam Hussein]."

The West does unto others what they never do unto their own. If crimes against humanity have to be punished one way or another, then why were the befittingly named savage reptile *Groot Krokodil* (Great Crocodile), P. W. Botha of South Africa (deceased), and Zimbabwe's Ian Smith, who between 1965 and 1979 committed serious crimes against humanity, never brought before any court? But Robert Mugabe, the man who initiated the spirit of national reconciliation in Africa, is of course a right royal rogue, the very personification of evil. Even if Tony Blair reneged on the Lancaster House agreements, Mugabe should have dutifully tucked his tail under like a good boy despite the suffering and the pressure from Afroancestral Zimbabweans! That the civilized and humane spirit of reconciliation and transformation Mugabe brought to life (despite the bitterness of the Afroancestral Zimbabweans) influenced the likes of Nelson Mandela or the Namibians to follow suit is of little or no consequence. That the United Kingdom reneged on agreements they had made with Mugabe regarding the land issues is of even lesser consequence.

The pendant of "Darling of the West" is now glued on Kufuor of Ghana and especially on Museveni of Uganda. Uganda is now touted to be booming in economic development. Indeed it is. Museveni is a liberally generous host. The Ugandan construction industry alone is groaning under the weight of contracts; there are excellent new roads stretching through the country; buildings going up, up and away. But whose economy is actually booming while Uganda is groaning under the weight of accumulative foreign debt? Uganda is strategically important, because the bordering countries are elegantly wobbly but wealthy physical giants of Africa trembling on the brink of (or actually entrenched in) "conflicts" — the Sudan and DRCongo. Perhaps the West, in this era of Hot Wars, will need a base for quick military sorties.

It's the Push and the Pull factors all over the place.

Turkey, once pivotal to the theory of the roots of the "Aryan race" and the home of ancient Troy, endeavors to get into Europe as a member of the European Union. The door is slammed in Turkey's face. According to Germany's Angela Merkel and those who brought her to power, Turkey is welcome as "a privileged partner" in the EU. At the start, Merkel wanted Turkey to be "a tolerated partner." But not a *member* of the EU. Maybe I've got it all wrong: is it Turkey who should "privilege" and "tolerate" Germany and the European Union? The German-Turks form a pillar in the country's economy that Germany cannot do without.

Germans have trouble accepting that somebody of my pigmentation is a German. I don't encounter such assumptions in France, Belgium, the Netherlands, the UK, Ireland or the US. In these countries I'm "innocent until proved guilty." In Germany, I'm "not a German," full stop. Months prior to the Football World Cup Championships, a media concern shoved the campaign *Du bist Deutschland* — you are Germany — down the throats of the German citizenry. Very popular, as all things shouldered by the media turn out to be. The models were well-known celebrities of the country in all the colors of the rainbow, prodded into action for a use-and-discard polemic. This was supposed to promote a friendly atmosphere for the championships, since some politicians were already establishing high profiles by declaring certain parts of the country as "no-go areas" (yes, in the English phrase!) which dark-skinned visitors to the World Cup should avoid lest they get into fatal confrontations with neo-Nazis. Being a history junkie, I had read about the fascists using this very slogan to agitate Germans against non-Germans and get them to take up arms against Jews and non-Germans (read: "non-Aryan"). This was as far back as 1935 in the city of Ludwigshafen. DENN DU BIST DEUTSCHLAND, it proclaimed then, with a placard of Hitler's head towering over the words.

Lately, German politics is trying a different tack because, glued to their history no matter what, they have a huge problem with calling every German citizen a German. We are "foreigners," whether born in the country or not, are a whole range of entities from *ausländische MitbürgerInnen* (foreign fellow citizens), XYth generation of *Gastarbeiter* (guest worker) descendants, *Ausländer mit deutschem Pass* (foreigners with a German Passport), *Personen mit deutschem Pass* (Persons with German Passports), or whatever land of origin, such as *Kenianer mit deutschem Pass* (Kenyan with a German Passport), *Deutsch-Libanese* (German-Lebanese) and so on. We simply cannot get away with being Germans per se. The very latest tack in the Federal Republic is that we are citizens with *Migrationshintergrund* (emigrational background). These attributes are imperative. The wheat has to be sorted from the chaff.

But now, a look at a section of the African past which is too often swept under the carpet. Africa is always used as the barometer of the whole humankind to uplift anybody who might think that his/her lot is rotten — because this lot is always portrayed as "better than that of the African." *That* African of the Western media who makes you feel good because you are not at the bottom of the human ladder, like him. *That* African whose — if you trust the cameraman and his lighting — ash-grey or blue-black naked feet are covered with crawling maggots, which he/she is shaking off the fish-heads drying in the sun. The fish filets have of course been exported as Victoria tilapia to richer tables abroad.

This is taken for granted even by the Africans themselves, not only the Westerners, as the natural order of things. If the African lets himself get so dehumanized, then it is his own fault. If he believes that poverty and misery are his condition, well then, he is welcome to it. Touché. Remember *humanitarian* Gilbert Murray's blatant assertion?

> There is in the world a hierarchy of races...those nations which eat more, claim more, and get higher wages, will direct and rule the others, and the lower work of the world will tend in the long run to be done by lower breeds of men. This much we of the ruling colour will no doubt accept as obvious.[47]

From the beginning of the 13th century a certain Wolfram von Eschenbach of Germany created the image of the so-called noble Moor as a knight full of virtues, courage and a ripe fruit of faithfulness. With such famous institutions of learning like Timbuktu, the Moor's education was touted to be beyond any other; pure and brave in battle he was, too. No other knight before him was so gentle for he knew no injustice, according to von Eschenbach. In Peter Martin's book *Schwarze Teufel, edle Mohren,*[48] the author delves into a few details about this Africa's and Africans' light hidden under a bushel by the calculating West.

From as early as the Carolingian period — 7th to 8th century — African warriors were fighting in Europe under the banner of the lion, the shield and the half moon in order to bring the "true faith," Christianity or Islam, to Europe. Europeans at the time were in the majority heathen and did everything in their power to remain heathen. From the start of the Hegira in Egypt and Nubia, leagues of African soldiers, later referred to with great respect as "Allah's Black Ravens," played an important role in the army that defeated North Africa and finally crossed the Strait of Gibraltar to conquer Spain in the 7th century.

They then continued storming northwards up to Burgundy.

---

47 Murray, Gilbert, *Liberality and Civilizations: Lectures Given at the Invitation of the Hibbert Trustees in the Universities of Bristol, Glasgow, and Birmingham in October an November 1937*, London: Allen & Unwin 1938.
48 Martin, Peter, *Schwarze Teufel, edle Mohren*, Hamburg: Hamburg Institut für Sozialforschung, 1993, Junius Verlag, p. 81-112.

Parallel to that, a second column of these soldiers marched into Sicily and built a long-lasting kingdom there before they continued their conquests into upper Italy "like a swarm of bees," as a cleric wrote in the 11th century. Africans were part of Saladin's troops who defeated the Crusaders and captured Acre, Jerusalem and Ashkelon. They were generals of Saladin's armies as he fought Richard I of England and Philip II of France during the Third Crusade. These were still virginally self-confident Africans with the proud blood of their ancestors coursing through their veins. Christians of Eastern Africa and Egypt, who had adopted the religion since the first century AD, also fought in the Crusades on the side of European Christendom, who were the newcomers into the Faith. The Africans concentrated on the battle for defending their Christian faith; the Europeans glanced right, left and center, mentally mapping out advantages and strategies for conquest. Since the times of the Crusades when Africans fought on both the Christian and the Islamic fronts, some of the Africans made it as far north as the Alps and settled there. But in two to three generations their complexion and other "African" characteristics disappeared.

Those were the days before Africans were classified as "heathen" and "black."

At the turn of the 10th century in central Europe the world was suddenly divided into two: Christendom and Islam. The conflicts of these two worlds influenced to a great extent the presence of Africans in Europe, and always with that double-headed Janus of the Threatening and the Desirable embodied in it. The ever ringing melody of the primitive "race" and the cultured one, the pre-logic and the rational, the savage and the civilized, the superstitious and the enlightened, the primitive art and the prime art, and so on, not to forget, finally the Christian and the heathen. It didn't and doesn't matter that Euro-Christianity is based on and entwined with Euro-heathen religious cults.

During the Renaissance Africans were representative of the envied "oriental" culture and thus the privileged rank. Then the African went from the superior military adversary to the desired courtier/servant. As the colonization of the non-European world began, this image changed drastically. Out of the cultured oriental "Ethiopian" (with regard to the trans-Atlantic slave trade and the far-reaching economic, social and psychological processes of change in Europe) emerged the "primitive Negro."

At this point the African was still not yet referred to as "Black" owing to his complexion. His so-called decline began at the end of the Crusades, at the time the old Euro-Christian cosmology folded up. In 1486, when the Benin

Empire was flourishing, Timbuktu in Mali was an international trading center and the Empire exchanged ambassadors with Portugal, the then leading
European sea-voyaging nation. Ambassadors in those days were picked from
the ruling nobility, there being no governments with civil servants. It seems
that the liaison between Africa and Portugal would later mingle African
blood with nearly every European ruling noble family from Portugal up to
Germany and the English monarchy, in the person of Queen Charlotte, wife
of George III.[49] The couple had 15 children, nine boys and six girls.

*Sophie Charlotte zu Mecklenburg-Stre-
litz aka Queen Charlotte, portrait by Es-
ther Denner, 1761*

*Queen Sophie Charlotte, portrait by Allan
Ramsey, 1744,*

Emperors and kings of Europe as well as merchants were very interested in
Africans and spent a great deal of time with them. In 1638 an Ethiopian ambassador of the Negus, the Ethiopian Emperor, had spent many years in the courts
of Europe's central powers as a learned and cultured friend. He was a favorite of
Cardinal Richelieu of France. All through this same time an impressive bust of
the Holy Gregorius Maurus wearing majestic Roman-Baroque vestments was
displayed in Cologne's St Gereon Church. Ordinary European folk looked at Africans with curious astonishment. The people of Africa have left their traces in

---

49 The Blurred Racial Lines of Famous Families http:www.pbs.org/wgbh/pages/
frontline/shows/secret/famous/royalfamily.html Accessed: July 2007

European philosophy, art, theology, myths, music and literature. In these inter-actions there arose no problems until the time when European powers set about promoting a certain social order, and scientists, statesmen, scribes and artists as well as the common people began to apply metaphors to Africans.

An image then emerged that reflected the Europeans' new view. All through the centuries that followed, the nature of the African would be variously com-prehended and represented but would always mirror the problems and way of thinking of the Europeans — not the reality. This explains why Africans are of-ten viewed as objects rather than subjects by Euroancestrals and as such Africans are depicted in Euroancestral™ art, literature, science and folklore as strange, as "other" and impersonal.

The significance of Africans tends to increase whenever a deep-rooted change takes place in the Euroancestral™ society such as during the Crusades, the Reformation or the pre-revolution phase of the 18th century. Africans become symbols of Euroancestral™ intentions and thereby cultivate defense or fear in the Euroancestrals.

Throughout their captivity as slaves and then during colonial days, Africans remained chattels being captured and whipped in the plantations by Euroances-tral overseers, or hearing degrading remarks about them and their people while meekly serving the gentry at the dinner table in silence. From this phase of his-torical interactions, the Africans always had to swallow their anger and dignity, and accept their degradation as "the natural law of things." When there were rebellions or uprisings, the Afroancestrals themselves were incited by the Eu-roancestrals to fall upon and massacre their own for the welfare of their oppres-sors. The physicians to cure this psychological warp are long overdue, but their efforts are thwarted by the patients themselves who reject the medicine when it is offered.

These distorted relations wiped out the history of respectful relations. The fragmented knowledge of specific Africans ever since the Roman Expansion in the 3rd century seems to have been erased, and texts in the Bible where Ethiopia (at the time representative for all of Africa south of the Sahara) is mentioned, Africans are given a mythological image.

About mid 17th century when the language of philosophy began re-arranging the world order, the "Negro" began sliding down the ladder of humankind to-wards the rung next to animals. The African finally was turned over to "primi-tivism," made an object through which progressive minds could judge how far general knowledge of humankind could go. Eurocentricism (an acquired taste) and Western pre-eminence throughout the world had begun in earnest. Around 1830, the image of the African was completed. Africans were unutterably strange and demonic, impulsive and depraved, cultureless, lacking both common sense and history, imbued with animalistic body-build and childish conduct.

Since the era of the manufacturing society and the beginning of modern colonization (from about 1830) this image of the African has remained in all its basic nuances. And it began taking on new social functions: from this period onwards, it legitimized the oppression, colonization and exploitation of the African and the continent's natural resources. It legitimized physically and violently forcing the African to deny his religion and culture. Any traces left in Europe today of the 3rd century, when Europeans interacted with Africans who were Rome's generals, soldiers and mercenaries, are vague and hard to find. European scholars of history and religion are the only ones who seem aware of such facts — and they also seem to have conspired to keep quiet on these topics.

At the beginning of the 17th century there had been long years of social upheavals in the aristocracy and merchant classes in nations of northwestern Europe, especially the Netherlands and England. The upheavals flowed over into politics. These northwestern nations began to question the Atlantic monopoly of Spain and Portugal which had began in the 15th century. By 1644 it was necessary to negotiate peace in Munster, Germany, ending the Thirty Years War. The French ambassador came to the negotiations with a retinue of at least 140 Africans. In those days the significance of the ruling classes was also measured by the splendor of their African attendants. These attendants were regarded as courtier employees, not slaves. They were advisors, having had interaction with all manner of European as well as Arab nations and knowing how each respective nation "ticked." But the African assimilation of such knowledge, similar to the Arab adaptation of the Roman and Persian bureaucracies, was passive. When the French ambassador and his African retinue attended religious services in Munster's cathedral, the Spanish delegation were outshined by the French and brusquely left the cathedral.

Three hundred and sixty-one years later, Spain is actually turning African refugees back to Morocco, the Atlantic Ocean, and the African desert.

Paradoxically "freedom of the seas" in those Atlantic-jostling days also became the bane of the Africans. Instead of the old days when they came to Europe via caravans of the Sahara, the Mediterranean Sea and the Alps, Africans now came directly over the sea route from West Africa or the roundabout route from the Americas or the Caribbean islands. This was the moment Europeans now came to acquaint themselves with an altogether different breed of Africans. The "Oriental Moors" or the "Cultured Ethiopians" had been dark-skinned people but they had represented a culture far superior to that of the Europeans. Because Christ came from their corner of the world, they had embraced Christianity at a time when the religion was struggling to take root in Greece and Rome. These Africans had been richly clothed and bejeweled, well-educated and cultured in conduct. Armed, the Moor or Ethiopian had threatened the European on his — the European's — ancestral land. The initial interaction between Africans and Europeans had been initiated by the Africans coming to Europe and not the Europeans going to Africa.

But now European nations were aggressively competing with each other on the Guinea Coast, where they discovered a breed of Africans inferior to them both economically and "spiritually." The social and cultural achievements of Muslims and Coptic Christians which Europeans had so admired was not alien on the Guinea Coast. But Europeans conveniently closed their eyes to the fact, and deliberately assigned the development level of these West African people to be representative of all of Africa. Today, the warp still firmly in place, almost all Afroancenstrals think that all light-skinned people, the pinker the more so, are representative of a higher degree of humankind — even among their own kith and kin.

The Arab conquest of North Africa occurred between AD 639-708. Before this period all of Africa including the north was Afroancestral. All the pyramids and monuments were the works of continental Africans, such as the Pharaoh Djoser, ruling in the Third Dynasty between BC 5018-4989. Djoser built the Funerary Complex in Saqqara that still pulls in crowds to Ethiopia's Temple of Almaqah that goes back 2,500 years ago.

No ethnic group of humankind has ever had the privilege of possessing a uniformity of the skin shade. Even family members differ in the degree of their shade in coloration. The shades of African skins differed then and now, but no more than the shades of the skins of Asians from Uzbekistan to the Philippines or Europeans from Iceland to Sicily.

Be that as it may, the miraculous world of the Ethiopian Priester John which had cemented itself in European minds in connection with Africa was smashed at the Guinea Coast. Priester John and his King Solomon's Mines was relocated farther south, somewhere, where Europeans still had no knowledge. European fantasies began to operate in overdrive. They began to write about and draw Africa and Africans. Even Ethiopia and Nubia were dragged through the mud while Egypt and the rest of North Africa were artificially cut off from Africa and joined to the Middle East. Psychologically, the Guinea Coast Africans gave Europeans the weapon with which to revenge themselves for the agonizing feelings of inferiority to Africans that had distressed them for centuries. And the noble Moor became a Negro whose "black" complexion was suggestive of barbaric primitives.

Europeans, pink- to light-brown-skinned as they may be, are struck by a person's skin color, and even that, only in a superficial way. Since the Roman days, Europeans tend to see a uniform "black" in all Africans, even those sired by and born of them. And those of mixed heritage inexplicably find it easier to wiggle over to the Afroancestral turf where skin color "tags" are much more liberal and thus human. Afroancestrals place more weight on the blood that trails back to revered ancestors, rather than on outward appearances.

The terms Ethiopian, Moor, or the Latin word *niger*, were generally used to describe a dark-skinned person of African descent, including the North African and Middle East population. Around 1170, a story was told in the West of two rich kings from Africa: "One was Carthaginian, the other Ethiopian...they were black and evil..."

The Crusades were raging at the time.

But it was in the 15th century, with the frequent contact with the Oriental and North African worlds, when the Europeans began to differentiate between the "Orientals" and the "Africans." The terms began to switch from Moor to "black Moor." Before this, European scholars regarded dark-skinned people as Africans coming from the three regions of the world known to Europeans since the Middle Ages in accordance with the Bible story of the Flood and Noah's three sons. But no European from Middle Europe ever set foot in Africa. They did not even know for certain how enormous the continent was, except for scanty passages in the Bible and from the scribes of antiquity. All such passages, as already mentioned, only helped to mystify Africa and the Africans to the Europeans. First, Africa was treated as a mythological place whose significance was not grasped in a geographic-ethnologic context, but in a military-theological one. The Saracen army from Africa was known as "the Devil's troops" and their dark-skinned allies were "the Devil's children." Ethiopia, the land they came from, was accordingly an "accursed land." As long as the devil was depicted in the darkest colors, Good had to be symbolized by the color white. The antique, Christian and Germanic symbols of black and white had conditioned Europeans to arrange the universe in those terms, later making it easy to identify dark-skinned Africans with the devil. In the Scriptures the devil is for the first time referred to as "the black one" meaning "the evil one," and not "the Negroid one." There is no anthropological meaning to connect it with Africans. Until the so-called "Arabic danger" turned the devil into an African. And as the devil became an African, an African became "the devil."

The Spanish-Portuguese word "Negro" for the first time replaced the "noble Moor" in a shipping register in 1606. Twelve years later, in 1618, the word "Negro" was used for the second time by the Lutheran Gaspar Ens, a Protestant vicar.

And so it progressed until the end of the 17th century when "Negro" replaced the 400-year-old word "Moor" altogether for dark-skinned Africans.

Even more important is the rapid sinking of the Africans' status from the image of the Queen of Sheba and the Holy Mauritius to the half-animal nigger. But then, as Immanuel Kant philosophized: "We see things not as they are but as we are."

There were European merchants and travelers who wrote unbiased accounts on Africa's civilization of those very Guinea Coast days. Filippo Pigafetta's *History of the Kingdom of Kongo* was published in 1591 and stated that the circumference of the kingdom was 1,685 miles divided into 6 administrative provinces, with the capital city Mbaza Kongo having a population of 10,000 people. The people were "a swarming crowd dressed in silk and velvet ... well-ordered, and down to the most minute details, powerful rulers, flourishing industries — civilized to the marrow of their bones..." [50] In the Gulf of Guinea "...the captains were astonished to find streets well laid out, bordered on either side for several leagues by two rows of trees; for days they traveled in a country of magnificent fields inhabited by men clad in richly colored garments of their own weaving!" Earlier still, a Portuguese friar called Francisco Alvarez visited Ethiopia and feared that if he wrote the truth of what he saw and experienced by way of African culture, nobody in Europe would believe him. After all, he had been sent there to turn Coptic Christians into good Roman Catholics! The embittered hypocrites and rapacious merchants proved him right. Alvarez's reports about the Ethiopian city of Lalibela were published in 1542. "I swear by God, in whose power I am, that all that I have written, and I have left [unwritten] that they may not tax me with its being falsehood." In the following 500 years, Africa would be seen by Euroancestrals in the dichotomy of both "true" and "false" Africa and African.

After visiting the Asante Empire in 1817, the Englishman Bowditch described the great procession in Kumasi of the king's retinue thus:

> The king, his tributaries, and captains, were resplendent in the distance, surrounded by attendants of every description.... At least 100 large umbrellas, or canopies which could shelter 30 persons, were sprung up and down by the bearers with brilliant effect, being made of scarlet, yellow and the most shewy cloths and silks, and crowned on the top with crescents, pelicans, barrels and arms and swords of gold. The caboceers, as did their superior captains and attendants wore Ashanti cloths of extravagant price from the costly foreign silks which had been unravelled to weave them in all varieties of color, as well as patterns ...were of an incredible size and weight and thrown over the shoulders exactly like a Roman toga...silk fil-

---

50 this and following quotations from the book *When We ruled* by Walker, Robin, London: Every Generation Media, 2006.

let generally encircles their temples, and massy gold necklaces, intricately wrought."

Fifty-five years later another honest soul, W. W. Reade, wrote in his *The Martyrdom of Man* in 1872 that two of his colleagues told him they "...were astonished to find among the Negroes magnificent courts; regiments of cavalry; the horses caparisoned in silk for gala days and clad in coats of mail for war; long trains of camels laden with salt, corn and cloth and cowrie shells (which form the currency) and kola nuts which the Arabs call 'the coffee of the Negroes'".

Less than a century later, Africa had been turned into the Continent of Chaos, with assassinations, military coups, civil wars and political bedlam. To this day Euroancestrals seem not to be aware that the African continent is 31 million square kilometers. The DRCongo alone is as big as all of Europe, and DRCongo is not the largest nation in Africa. Whereas Europeans and the West are able to discern the German culture from that of the neighboring French, Poles or Czechs, the vast continent of Africa is miraculously a single village to them.

In 1772 a certain Samuel Estwick wrote a memorandum to the Right Honorable Lord Mansfield, with regards to a court case, "In general they are void of Genius, and seem almost incapable of making any progress in civility or science... they seem unable to combine ideas, or to pursue a chain of reasoning..." James Ramsay had this to write: "As far as I can judge there is no difference between the intellects of whites and blacks, but such as circumstances and education naturally produce."[51] Come 1787, Thomas Jefferson himself wrote, "Comparing them by their faculties of memory, reason and imagination, it appears to me, that in memory they are equal to the whites; in reason much inferior, as I think one could scarcely be found capable of tracing and comprehending the investigations of Euclid; and that in imagination they are dull, tasteless, and anomalous"[52]. Euclid, the world's greatest mathematician, was an African. In 1711, the writer Joseph Addison (who seems to have influenced Ramsay's thoughts), had this to say on the Euro-fascinating phenomenon known as Negroes with their Savage Greatness of Soul:

> "I consider an human soul without education like marble in the quarry, which [shows] none of its inherent beauties, until the skill of the polisher fetches out the colours, makes the surface shine, and discovers every ornamental cloud, spot, and vein that runs through the body of it. Education, after the same manner, when it works upon a noble mind, draws out to view every latent virtue and perfection, which without such helps are never able to make their appearance... When one hears of Negroes, who upon the Death of their Masters, or upon changing their Service, hang themselves upon the next Tree, as it frequently happens in our ... Plantations, who can forbear admiring their fidelity, though it expresses itself in so dreadful a

51 Ramsay, James, in his *An Essay on the treatment and conversion of African Slaves in the British Sugar Colonies,* London 1784, p. 199
52 Jefferson, Thomas, *Notes on the State of Vrginia,* London 11787, p. 232

manner? What might not that Savage Greatness of Soul, be raised to, were it rightly cultivated?."[53]

But Addison turns everything upside down here in favor of his own kind. The Savage Greatness of Soul in the plantations was indeed *rightly cultivated* and *raised to* a status worse than that of a dumb beast of burden who should have no emotions. The master raped his wife and daughters before him; and he couldn't do a thing to protect his family. The master sired daughters with his raped wife and daughters, and raped these incestuously as well. Meanwhile, he was to labor and look away. If he so much as looked the master's wife or daughter in the eyes, he was lynched.

In 1684, a delegation from the Gold Coast (Ghana) received a cold shoulder from Europeans for the first time. The delegation, representatives of 86 rulers of their country who for nearly 400 years had been recognized in Europe as kings, came to the Berlin Residence of the Great Elector Frederick William of Brandenburg, only to learn with what little regard Africans were now being treated. The virus that was grazing in the New World of "lower class Europeans" had by now ricocheted back to Old Europe. Africans were no longer treated as equal partners. These kings were now relegated to "chiefs," a title suggestive of primitivism. The leader of the Ghanaian delegation is registered in the official documents in Germany as "Jan Jancke," since nobody thought his African name was worth noting down. At any rate this encounter led to the first Brandenburg colony in Africa. The African had been trustful, conducted himself with decency and fought in honor. The European had acted in bad faith, cast around a covetous eye, and worked out a strategy of conquest.

Most amazing, these suggestive notions became universal, anchored in not only Western conceptions of African societies but around the world, including among Africans themselves. References to "tribes" ruled by "chiefs" and war commanders in tanks or wielding Kalashnikovs as "warlords" are familiar.

---

53 Addison, Joseph, an untitled essay in *The Spectator, Vol. 3, No. 215*, London, 1711.

CHAPTER 11. EUROPE BECOMES CHRISTENDOM, AND WHITE

At some time in the 4th century a philosopher of Christian Tyre, one
Meropius, was voyaging at the southern end of the Red Sea with the
aim of improving his mind as well as those of two young relatives,
Aedesius and Frumentius. ...the Roman ship in which they were voyag-
ing put into an Ethiopian port ...through Frumentius Christianity
eventually became a state religion of the Axumite Kingdom and after-
wards the chief religion of the peoples of Abyssinia (later Ethiopia).

— BASIL DAVIDSON[54]

No European religion has become a world religion. Most Euroancestrals harbor grand illusions, but, Jerusalem long lost or not, Christianity is Afro-Orient,
not European. Megignoarrogance tells Euroancestrals that they are the civilized
Christians of Christendom. Christianity was thriving in the Horn of Africa in the
1st century, before this religion had really taken root anywhere in Europe. The
majority of the Celts and Germanics and other European tribes were still wor-
shiping their various pantheons. On the other hand Africans compressed their
religions, with so many divinities for every sphere of their lives, into a single religious name. This then survived across the Atlantic, incorporating other elements
but with the original basic elements remaining intact. They are alive to this minute in Africa, Europe, the Caribbean and the Americas — as Candomblé. Most
Africans and Euroancestrals, with that warped view in place, are not or do not
want to be consciously aware of this.

During the Middle Ages, Christendom was a synonym for Europe. Even new
ships arriving in the New World were asked by their Euro-American cousins

---

54 Davidson, Basil, *Africa in History* (revised and expanded edition), New York:
Touchstone 1995, p. 116-117

which "part of Christendom" they came from. When I first came across this fact, I wanted to find out how and when Europeans became Christians living in "Christendom." I began playing detective, and spent most of my free time as a book spook snooping in libraries all over England, the country in which I had first been exposed to the B and W words. Through the years, I made the following observations.

In or around 1660, ladies and gentlemen of the European aristocracy developed a strange ambition. It became fashionable to make their faces, throats, breasts, hands and any other exposed parts of their bodies as white as alabaster. Soon all noblewomen and most noblemen were having rouged rosy cheeks and powdered snow-white foreheads and breasts. This was now regarded as a required component of flawless beauty, to be maintained until the grave. No treatment was too drastic. Europeans were regularly phlebotomized until they fainted. Ladies swallowed laxatives, ashes and sand and did their best to ruin their stomachs in order to look pale. Direct sunshine on the skin was avoided, white powder was applied liberally and chemical cleaning agents were cosmetic prerequisites. Masks were worn even on the hottest day to keep out the sun. Gloves smeared with ointment made of wax, almond and attar of roses were worn even while sleeping to keep the hands "white/smooth and beautiful."[55]

All this bleaching of the skin was meant to demarcate the "better classes" from the middle class, as well as the ordinary workers and peasants. They put up not only a physical but also a visible resistance against contributing to the production processes of their national economies, which still consisted to a great extent of working in the fields.

Pigmentation became one of the signs demarcating the world of the privileged from that of the ordinary folk, and this borderline was strictly kept in place. This European class-division tendency flowed smoothly into the belief that Divine Providence had ordained this separateness, this *apartheid*. It was God's will and none should meddle with it.

The trans-Atlantic slave trade was in full swing at this very period and dark-skinned people (no one asked of what class) were being traded away to be used as beasts of burden. It was since the mid 17th century that pigmentation determined who ruled and who was ruled, who was master and who servant.

The doctrine was quickly adopted in the colonies in the Americas and later in Africa and Asia, with the exception that Africans were also labeled "heathens" as opposed to Christians. Whatever their religion, Africans were

55 Martin, Peter, *Schwarze Teufel, edle Mohren*, Hamburg: Hamburger Institut für Sozialforschung 1993, Junius Verlag, p. 101

denied any real notion of the word "religion." Unlike Asians, Africans at this stage in European history didn't even warrant being labeled pagans.

The words "black" and "white" first emerged "officially" as descriptions of Africans and Europeans towards the end of the 17th century. It did not matter that the natural complexion of Africans ranges from brown to dark brown, and the natural complexion of Europeans is pink to light brown — never white, no matter how much bleached. Whether used "poetically" or "officially", it was not the Africans who came up with these terms. As recently as the 1960s, Americans referred to Afroancestrals as "Negroes" or "colored people," still labels coming from the Euroancestral turf. It was a bit of a shock when movements like the Black Panthers insisted on referring to themselves as "Blacks" to counterpoise "Whites"; it was the "deep-seated screams from the psyche and the soul," described below.

From mid to late 17th century, when the "Moor" was gradually becoming "heathen and black," many heathen practices were carried out on these "blacks" by the civilized Christian "whites." Their embryos and parts of their bodies including their heads were preserved and dissected, they were put in the circus where they were made to tear live doves with their bare teeth and eat them, kneel and pray to the head of an ox, do wild leaps and dances waving cudgels around, eat raw flesh, show their private parts — the lot. They were even made to "offer" their blood and urine to be tested in order to determine whether "black" urine and blood had the same chemical components as "white" urine and blood.

Worse things continued, even to the beginning of the 20th century. A Baltimore-born African-American who came to Berlin and went broke tells the story of how he earned his money in the circus:

> You see, boss, I'se been working here, got ten dollars a week to play wild man. I was all stripped 'cept around the middle and wore a claw necklace; had to make out as if I couldn't talk. 'Twas mighty tiresome to howl and grin all day. Then times got hard. I had to eat raw meat and drink blood. The circus man, he stood off as if he was afraid of me and chucked meat on the floor to me. I had to lean over, pick it up in my teeth and worry it like I was a dog. It was horse meat and pretty tough, boss, but it brought crowds for a while. Then it got drefful cold for a nigger with no clothes on and they put a snake around my neck. I couldn't stand that, so I'se come to the hospital."[56]

Two centuries before, European aristocracy had been in a fever about acquiring African courtiers. In the main, children between the ages of 4 to 7 were preferred. This was the hottest fashion in the Christendom as everyone from king to

---

56 Thompson, William Carter, *On the Road with a Circus*, New York: Goldman 1903, p. 70

countess was prepared to pay a fortune for a child slave. The "blacker" the better. David Dabydeen in his study of *Hogarth's Blacks* (1987) wrote:

> In van Dyck's Henrietta of Lorraine, the black is a mere aesthetic foil. The lady's tallness comes out in relation to his smallness, and his dark skin throws into relief the whiteness of her skin. In real life blacks were greatly prized for the intensity of their colour, as the "For Sale" advertisements in English newspapers indicate. The Williamson's Liverpool Advertiser of 20 April 1756 carries this advertisement: "Wanted immediately a Black Boy. He must be of a deep black complexion..."[57]

A European fairy tale speaks of a princess who so longed for "a little Moor" in vain that she finally took a little "white" boy and had him roasted until he was black enough for her. The (in her era) fashionable Isabella d'Este ordered her shipping agent in Venice to bring her a little African who was to be as black as possible. The agent finally wrote to her that he had found a little African of about four years of age, but the child was not black enough. In the end the princess did acquire an African child, but she still lamented the fact that the child was not as black as she would have preferred. A certain German lady of the courts is said to have remarked to her African female servant companion, "It was very unpleasant that you were not with me when I went for a walk, because the Baron of Schock said I would have looked even whiter than usual, had I been walking next to you." [58]

Euroancestrals till today think in this vein. They would not be "whites" if there were no "blacks." Studies of European societies fall under "Sociology," studies of African societies under "Ethnology." Armed conflicts in European societies are caused by "political self-awareness"; armed conflicts in African societies are "tribal conflicts." The modern "fast food" reportage on Africans by reporters for the Western predator papers find nothing good or even "normal" about Africa and Africans but the wildlife. While the German media reports daily of German children or infants raped and murdered, thrown into a river, buried in a forest or under potted plants, they never show the children's corpses or genital details. Yet a little Somali or Kikuyu girl screaming and twitching in pain as several women with dirty hands hold her down for an excision is close-up material. And in a manner that satisfies a voyeuristic vision of barbarism. Western media reportage will, of course, be about "Africa" and "Africans," not Somalis or Kikuyus. The image of the doped African child wielding an AK47 bigger than himself, or one starving to

---

57 Dabydeen, *Hogarth's Blacks. Images of Blacks in Eighteenth Century English Art*, Manchester, Manchester University Press 1987, p. 30
58 Rathelf, Ernst Lorenz Michael, *Die Mohrinn zu Hamburg, Tragödie*, Hamburg 1775, p. 45

death in shallow breaths as an orphan in Darfur or Ethiopia, are voyeurism trips. Up close. Closer.

Yet all through the ages, since the Europeans concocted this fall from glory of the "noble Moor" to the "heathen black," Afroancestrals in their damaged psyches seem programmed to self-destruct. Not many are protected in childhood from the affliction of "knowing" that the color of their skin is supposedly not on a par with the pink or light-brown variety. Every human being ought to ponder the effect of these B and W words on small children. What does an Afroancestral child feel the moment it learns that its complexion is not "beautiful" because it is "black", nor is its hair, mouth, nose, everything African *on* and *in* the child? Furthermore, that supposedly being "black" relegates the person and its entire people to the lowest rung of the human ladder? Added to this, the child will come to absorb abundant doses of cultural and spiritual/religious confusion, and the naked miseries hinged on the poverty that has been worked on by outsiders for at least 600 years! Anything and everything African is supposedly primitive and heathen or at best backward. Corrupted. Underdeveloped.

Many citizens of India, Sri Lanka and East Asia are darker-skinned than many Africans and Afroancestrals, but nobody refers to them as "blacks" to their face, least of all they themselves. Asiancestrals™ do not refer to themselves as skin colors. But out of whatever irreparable collective psychological damage regarding an artificial term they adopted from Euroancestrals, Africans and Afroancestrals religiously refer to themselves as "blacks." They are wonderfully doing the job of perpetuating the polarity notion that somebody else must, then, be "white."

This *was* and *is* a psychological booby-trap set up centuries ago to keep on ensnaring Afroancestrals with a constant confirmation of their "inferiority." While no one is better at setting up such psychological booby-traps than the Euroancestrals, no one is better at the servility required to adopt and haul around with them such a subtly corrosive, damaging notion than (to borrow Joseph Addison's phrase) those whose "fidelity" nobody can "forbear admiring." Afroancestrals have been religiously passing on this corrosive belief over at least the last three and a half centuries.

"I'm black and proud" and "Black is beautiful" were deep-seated screams from the psyche and the soul, trying to rid themselves of the damnation as best as they could. Malcolm did not become Malcolm X nor did Cassius Clay become Mohammed Ali out of a mere social fad. Tortured souls and damaged psyches were screaming for some kind of salvation, some rescue from a wounding trap no one quite knew how they had been caught into. And yet the booby-trap is still firmly in place.

Euroancestral or Asiancestral children also encounter this sort of programming as they grow up. But the Euroancestral child discovers that it and its people are the rulers of the world. It is part of the rulers by virtue of its *complexion and characteristics*. All the way to economic, military and technological power. The worst that can happen to it is that it grows up with superiority complexes harmful not only to others but to itself as well. These are what I call Megignoarrogance complexes — mega ignorance and arrogance combined — which are so characteristic of Euroancestrals. Especially the "I have nothing against other races" type. This is why it never even occurs to them to send emissaries to Africa and Asia who speak at least one language of the nation they are sent to. But they would never send one to a European, an Australian or North American country who does not master the languages spoken in these countries. On the other hand they would never tolerate an African or Asian emissary who does not speak the language of the Euroancestral nation of his mission.

The Asiancentral child is possibly "comforted" by the fact that it and its people are not at the bottom rung of the ladder. Not by complexion, at least, if perhaps in characteristics. Apartheid South Africa used this "strategy" very successfully, creating the "buffer zone" of the so-called coloreds — as if there is a human being who is colorless! Moreover, the Asiancestrals have religions (however conceived as against African religions) and cultures that have endured or even repelled the impact of the Euroancestral all-round hegemony.

There is great wisdom in the phrase: "Know your enemy," otherwise known as "Be prepared." And this is why the West is teeming with "Institutes of African Studies" strictly contained at their universities. Hundreds of papers on African Studies are called for in the West annually. The subjects range from Afroancestral mental health, tropical diseases peculiar to Africa, African social behavior, artistic trends both popular (read: Western) and traditional (read: African), parenting in Sub-Saharan Africa, Islam and Africa, how the African youth is expressing his emotional and political leanings in pop music and art, and so on. The West is not keeping such tight tabs on Africa out philanthropic concern. They are shaping the way Africa is viewed, even by "experts". They even give Africans (who are sometimes actually very ambitious in a positive way, but have no alternatives for higher studies at home) scholarships to study at these institutes of African studies, because the African postgraduates will leave an invaluable wealth of Western dictated dissertations behind. And they are thoroughly indoctrinated and then lured to be the next lecturers in these Western institutions, instead of going back to Africa. One such graduate with a Luo-sounding name, who studied in a Swedish institute for African studies, wrote a book about the Luos and maintained that Luos had never had central governments or kings. But (to fall back on a "universal" source), Basil Davidson, who has written about a dozen books on African history and devoted more than thirty years "to the intensive study of the African peoples," in Africa, has this to write about the Luos:

> The early Iron Age farmers of Uganda...had evidently acquired a simple form of government ... by chiefs before the thirteenth century.... These were infiltrated by migrating groups of Luo-speaking folk from the region of the Upper Nile. These Luos were looking for good land. They found it in the pleasant country of Uganda. Here their ruling clans, supported by a large number of "commoner clans" into which the local people were progressively absorbed, were able to impose themselves and to found states and dynasties of their own. One branch of the Luo, for instance, founded or at least helped to found the Bito line of kings, who are remembered as having ruled over Bunyoro for eighteen generations. Another Luo line of kings is remembered to have ruled over Buganda for twenty-two generations.... Even under colonial rule the [kings] of the Alur, another people of Luo origins, were still extending their authority over neighboring folk who had previously lived without any "central government" of their own, but who now saw a new value in the arbitration of chiefs, accepted Alur chiefly rule without resistance, or even asked for it to be extended among them.[59]

It is hard to see how a Luo who studied in a Swedish institute of African Studies could overlook all of the above. Africans live in a glass house. They can't even close their eyes in sleep without the West dissecting all the details of the process with the precision of an eye surgeon. Then they twist everything around to serve their purposes. There is a war going on out there, without even a battle to call attention to the violence being done.

Ultimately the war is against Africa and Africans, and the West simply uses a particular slant on African culture as a tactical weapon. Churchill is supposed to have said that in times of war, truth is so precious as to need a bodyguard of lies.

At the time of writing, the Sudan has allowed German archaeologists who found the ruins of ancient African pyramids in Sudan to whisk these off to Germany for "further study under optimum conditions," it is alleged. Why didn't the African Union do something to prevent this, if the Sudanese government didn't? Who is supervising what is going on in Germany? When will the pyramids be brought back to Africa — or will they be kept in Europe "under optimum conditions"? When the European archaeologists then rewrite the ancient history

---

59 Davidson, Basil, *Africa In History*, (revised and expanded edition), New York: Touchstone 1995, p. 149 ff

of Africa as suits their European purposes, will Africa have the legitimacy of complaining afterwards? Imitating the West is hardly something I recommend across the board, but if there is one thing worth aping, then it is the way they stick together. When it comes to taking a stand against the rest of the world, they stand together. Not Africans.

Take the very remarkable majority rule in democratic South Africa. The apartheid leaders did not give up their abhorrent system without making plans for the future. Secret "agreements" were drummed up from November 1987 to May 1990 between the exile ANC officials and the Afrikaner elite in Mells Park House, England. They found a way of conning Afroancestral South Africans out of true freedom by pressuring (to employ a euphemism) Nelson Mandela and his ANC bosses to keep their sooty fingers off the lily white South African economic arena. The World Bank and the IMF joined in, applying the thumbscrews as usual. The neo-apartheid principle of "group rights" was put on the pedestal *in petto*. No compromises on economic equality. Never mind that America had previously supplied computers used to run the apartheid police force, the trucks and armored vehicles used to attack townships and 40% of the oil the apartheid regime needed to run the country. America vetoed the UN Security Council resolutions against the apartheid leaders, who were even assisted in acquiring that "Big Taboo Outside the West": nuclear weapons. Britain was trotting along nicely. By the end of the 1980s British investment in South Africa had reached 50% of all foreign investments.

Nelson Mandela is said to have met the "apartheid establishment" 40 times before his release at 16:16 hours on 11th February 1990. Come 2001 (seven years after South Africa's African majority rule), at the World Economic Forum in Davos, Switzerland, one of President Mbeki's economic advisors admitted, "South Africa is in the hands of international capital." Because Africans always make reconciliation their swan song, only to earn derisive sniggers behind their backs.

The journalist and filmmaker John Pilger, who has written elaborately on this South African subject and interviewed all concerned for his book *Freedom Next Time*, published in 2006, terms it "the continuation of suffering by exclusion: apartheid by other means." When he mentioned to De Klerk in an interview that Euroancestrals of South Africa had not made any substantial changes and that many of them were better off than ever before, De Klerk's reaction was, "It is true that our lives have not fundamentally changed. We can still go to cricket at Newland and watch the rugby." To Mandela, Pilger pointed out that there had been a double apartheid in South Africa, with the economic branch of it still intact. Mandela's defense was, "You must remember that the best way to introduce transformation is to do so without dislocating any aspect of our public life. We do not want to challenge big business that can take fright and take away their money." Which is precisely why they should have been challenged. Only that would permit inter-Africa trade and production to get a fair start.

Critical decisions by the ANC elite included endorsing the apartheid regime's agreement to join GATT (General Agreement on Tariffs and Trade, the predecessor of WTO). This was tantamount to the surrender of economic independence. Other destructive decisions were: to desist from nationalization, repay the apartheid regime's debt of $25 billion, abolish exchange control (which meant that the rich Euroancestrals could take their capital overseas — something they had forbidden by law during their own apartheid regime era!) and to grant the Reserve Bank formal independence. It did not take long after South Africa's majority rule and the Ministry of Finance allowed the biggest companies in South Africa to grab their fortune and ferry it out of the country, then set up shop in London.

Meanwhile the average South African household income has risen by 15% since the majority rule, but the Afroancestral household has fallen by 19%. The pledged redistribution of 30% of farmland from 60,000 Euroancestral farmers to the rural and urban poor is so far less than 3% in the realization. In trying to explain why the ANC crumbled like a cookie, John Pilger poses the questions, "Was it simply a matter of the ANC having been in exile so long it was willing to accept power at any price? ... What exactly was the deal struck between the ANC leadership and the fascist Broederbond which stood behind the apartheid regime? What had Mandela and Mbeki and the other exiles in Zambia offered? What role had the Americans and international capital played?"[60]

Well, they did what they always do: gave an inch and took a league.

Again as an example, the president of Equatorial Guinea, after surviving the attempted coup masterminded by Westerners, did not run to Lagos or the AU headquarters in Addis Ababa for support or comfort. Africans have to engender an *esprit de corps* worthy of their unparalleled glorious ancestry. The African should at last grasp the pernicious and dangerous self-interest that oils the West's African machinery. Although not all the West is populated with Lucifers, the good and upright souls are like the proverbial needle in the haystack. One would have to look very hard and bring infinite patience along. There are, soberly observed, no trustworthy Western baby-sitters for the African infants nor Western selfless comrades-in-arms against Africa's ailments — just a lot of incurable viruses whose cures are worse than the disease, because the cures are distorted and the viruses easily mutate. As soon as

---

60 *New African No. 459* February 2007 article by Osei Boateng: *Apartheid did not die* p. 16-19

they invade African territory. If there is anything African "epidemiologists" should be terrified about, then it is these viruses.

It is time every African figuratively swore an oath to preserve, protect and defend their continent. Otherwise the legacy for future generations will be a crippling *damnosa hereditas*. Africans already know that they can depend on nearly every single one of their politicians to be a crook and very competent in state treason. It is a frightening thought, but these politicians play the power game, and disregarding the lives and livelihood of their citizens makes them feel great.

And Africans should stop being "blacks" to themselves and to the rest of the world — because they are not. Western writers are totally handicapped when it comes to describing Afroancestrals. Whether the household domestic or the Nobel Prize winner, an Afroancestral in Western writing and even ordinary speech is "incomplete" if the color of the skin is not mentioned. Africa, and especially Africans, are always treated like some special branch of fascinating pathogens — not to associate with too closely, but to be identified unambiguously.

As already mentioned, those who cannot delegate power love power far too much to handle it adequately. Power carries responsibility and this responsibility demands the highest degree of discipline. The same goes for the self-loving.

Chapter 12. Superstition In the Heart of Darkest Europe

The oldest religious rites of Indo-European peoples do no presuppose temples or idols. Nor is there a reconstructable term for "temple." But there is a "worship," conceived as a hospitable reception with a meal, consisting of slaughtered animals, and accompanying recitation of poetry, the "celestials" coming, as it were, on a visit to the "earthly ones."

— PAUL THIEME[61]

The very heartland of African spirituality.

Afroancestrals, like cobras charmed by a mongoose, are vulnerable to fatal charms including military. When Euroancestral colonizers displaced and expelled the people, those who were displaced and rendered landless would seem to have found some debilitating attraction in this. It is a long-established tradition seen also in the horrors that befell the Celtic Irish in 1565. Many Afroancestrals (at first under the power of the gun, later quite voluntarily through conditioned thinking) had gradually turned to eating lamb at Easter and turkey at Christmas, to replace the white cock at births or the brown cow at harvesting. The black and white bull at funerals gave way to the Lord's Prayer. The cross with a naked man in a loincloth was better than the ancestral carvings and figurines in bone, bronze, pottery, calabash artistry and ivory. An invisible God in a non-existent heaven was preferred over the invisible but evident Gods deep in the earth, in eclipses, thunder, in the universe, in trees, roaming the air, dwelling in the sun and the moon, and sometimes even manifesting themselves in human,

---

61 Thieme as quoted by Mallory, *In Search of the Indo-Europeans*, London: Thames and Hudson, 1999 p.128

animal or other forms. African polytheism was not treated like that of Hinduism and Buddhism. Meanwhile these so-called primitive African carvings and figurines and other symbols of ancient African art and the spiritual cosmos are sitting in European museums or private homes as increasingly precious curiosities called collections.

Nobody has ever seen God or the Holy Ghost but Christians believe in them. Is this not superstition? No, because humankind from time immemorial had "faith" in which they placed their "belief". Africans of the tropical forests are forever damned by and to their superstitious nature, it is written in the West again and again. Yet in Europe and the US, tarot cards, horoscopes and fortune-tellers have never been more popular. There is a world-class German football club with a live goat at the stadium as their mascot; Euro-Christian priests perform exorcisms to drive the devil out of the possessed. It would seem as if conducting one's superstitions via the phone or a crystal ball, cathedral or a TV screen, exempts them from being regarded as superstitions. Yet, after conversion into Christianity, Africans are still treated with contempt or with the angry tolerance one would accord a retarded but harmless child.

Armed pilgrims, to be later called "crusaders," were recruited with promises of spiritual privileges, the most important being reduced time spent in Purgatory for the atonement of sins. Ergo, guarantee for an early entry into heaven for the holy warriors, should they lose their lives fighting the good fight for the Christian faith. Where, then, is the big difference in comparison to Moslem martyrdom, except that sex has always been a dirty word in Christendom and that Moslems still believe in their paradise?

The roots remain, even if, out of convenience, one changes from eating fish on Fridays or lamb at Easter. Spilling an animal's blood on the ground or "drinking the blood" and "eating the flesh" of the Lord decidedly point to old and common roots in human spirituality. Today most of humankind "hunt" and "gather" at the supermarket, and still as a pack, not necessarily consciously. Like-minded groups hunt and gather together with a common goal: their *interest*. A word that commands powerful political meaning in the West.

So do the B and W words.

I was in a hospital once in Nuremberg, Bavaria. I was lying on my back reading a book on the bed, with my curly hair spread over the pillows. A nurse came in and whooped with admiration for my hair. Beaming, she said, "If you were blonde, you would look just like an angel!" "Who says all angels are blonde, nurse?" The nurse was completely confounded, and went crimson. Euroancestral born and bred, she had never given any thought to whether angels might be anything other than blonde.

As a result of a nasty burn I sustained years ago during a fondue dinner, there is a patch of pale pink — or should I say white? — skin on the back of my right hand. I often get the most ridiculous comments from pink people. Some kindly suggest the solarium or the sunshine. I explain that the pigmentation has been destroyed and my skin cannot produce my normally abundant melanin anymore on the burnt patch. They do not understand because in their minds Africans are "black" to the marrow. My witty husband often offers the double-edged remark, "I think the best trick is to put her in the oven for a couple of hours!"

I'm a passionate cook and enjoy having friends around for a many-course Kenyan meal. Westerners seem to believe that Africans (those nondescript residents of a single undifferentiated continent-wide village) have very simple cuisine. Why, Africans have nothing to eat in the first place! But we do have a many-course cuisine, not rarely as many as thirty or more dishes, only that all the dishes are served in one go. The diners can choose where they start the meal and where they end it according to the dictates of their own taste buds. My friends and business acquaintances love my Kenyan dishes. I do explain to them that Kenyan cuisine is a blend of the various African ethnic groups, an Arab and Mediterranean blend over thousands of years of interaction between Africans of the Indian Ocean coast with the Middle East Arabs and people of the Mediter-ranean region, the Indo-British influence, and a touch of the migrant communi-ties like the Italians, Jews and Chinese who were brought in by the colonizers as coolies or prisoners of war, or as immigrants, or to solve "the Eastern Europe Jewish Question." Still, nearly all of my friends or colleagues, including fellow Africans, keep on asking me for the recipe of that "African dish." There is no such thing as an "African dish" just as there is no "European dish," as such. But the conditioning that leads them to perceive Africa as a single country is firmly in place. Africa is the world's second largest continent, with a population of around 900 million people today, and hundreds of thousands of cultures and languages, but Euroancestrals only see their "village" Africa. And many Africans have picked it up like disciplined soldiers who hear the command: *forward march!*

In June 2005, I was invited by the television station *Bayerische Rundfunk* to discuss what chances foreigners living in Germany had in the employment or self-employment sectors. A young man from Burundi made me think about *when* an Afroancestral child realizes *who* he is to the world and *what* impact this has on his entire life. This young Burundian had studied architecture in China, spoke five languages including Chinese and — living in the country — was married to a German. An international citizen in the truest sense of the word. But asked how he felt in the German society or whether he had encountered racial problems, he replied: "I am black and I have to live with it." What did he mean? Did he feel he had been born with some incurable disease? But the television presenters obviously considered such a reply "normal."

In Europe I continue to see similar conditioned perceptions. Once, in one of my communications and intercultural training courses, the class had just done a global tour of non-verbal communication. I explained that Malawians do not look at each other directly in the eyes, as a sign of politeness — not because they are congenital liars or are forbidden to look the so-called white people in the eye. One participant then wanted to know whether my "tribe" also considers it bad manners to look another person straight in the eye. I asked him whether Franconians are a "tribe." Of course not. Friesians? Of course not. "Okay, let's take a leap over to say, the Monegasques? The people of Monaco, the smallest sovereign state (after the Vatican) with a population of 31,900 and an area of 2 square kilometers. Smaller than the smallest farm of a Kenyan rancher. Are the Monegasques a tribe?"

This time the participant asked me a question. "Monaco? But they're Europeans!" I wondered if this participant would be equally perplexed if I mentioned that many Inuits are also Danes, and therefore Europeans.

Likewise, policemen in Germany may arrest a *"Schwarz Afrikaner und ein Marokkaner."* A black African and a Moroccan. A ZDF television newscaster stated (when the Italian authorities refused Sudanese refugees permission to get out of the *Cap Anamur*), *"Sogar die Afrikaner kann man das nicht antun."* "Even Africans shouldn't have this done to them." It is so "normal" to the newsreader that he does not realize what he is actually saying. A slip like that would never be heard in Germany had it been about the Sons of Moses. It would also never be publicly uttered by a British, French, Belgian or Dutch newscaster without causing a public uproar. For the German public it is quite normal.

My Euroancestral colleagues ask me what dialect my so-called "tribe" speaks. I say they speak a language known as Dholuo, not a dialect. Is that *"afrikanisch?"* they ask. I tell them it certainly is not *"europäisch."* Many of my seminarees can't un-knot the fact that a woman from Africa is lecturing them about communication and culture in their own good old Europe — particularly the so-called resettlers of German stock coming from the former Soviet Union polyglot. To such people I'm the living proof of why German culture is deteriorating. To them I'm rummaging about in the family silver cupboard where I have no business poking my brown (excuse the Nazi pun) nose. When I am stuck in traffic jams, driving my own car, loud remarks have been hurled at me about what kind of relationship I have with the owner of the car. My skin shade and the nice car just don't tally.

In Germany, anybody who does not look "German" is automatically assumed a foreigner. I've calculated strategies to deal with this, so that I now send my staff to negotiate business deals on my behalf until the final signing of the contract. I finally put my signature on the contract with the remark, "You have been negotiating with magnificent generals — I'm their commander-in-chief." And my "generals" and I have good laughs over this.

A German television station still tells viewers (in a program that is supposed to be educational) that coffee originated from Arabia, and its name, from Turkey. So do dictionaries. Is it because nobody would want to drink a beverage that originated in Ethiopia (Ethiopia's Kaffa region, which also gave coffee its name) or is it simply part and parcel of the marginalization strategy?

As already mentioned, the EU sent troops to the DRCongo in 2006 apparently to ensure peaceful democratic elections. They sent these troops not for the Congolese people but for their own governments and multinationals, with stakes in the wealth of the Congolese people's abundant natural resources needed for the Western economy. But the clever global propaganda is that selfless and philanthropic Euroancestrals, once again risking life and money for the wretched of the earth! The Congolese people end up with some malleable Western stooge at the helm and it is business as usual. Otherwise the reward is another resounding "tribal conflict," another Patrice Lumumba, another debilitating Kwame Nkrumah, another Robert Ouko, another spider-webbed Felix Moumié case, another Thomas Sankara or Thomas Joseph Mboya, another Sir Mark Thatcher & Western Mercenaries. The endless list of business as usual.

In the discussions that follow readings of my first German-translated novel — *Khiras Traum* — I am always questioned about female genital mutilation. When I answer that I know nothing about how it is done nor why, that I've failed to find any person or literature that could explain this practice to me, the audience can't grasp it. I come from (all one village) Africa, don't I? All of us African ladies are presumably walking around with mutilated genitals.

I wrote another book, the true and moving story of a Kenyan grandmother who lost her son and daughter-in-law in the terrorist bombings in Nairobi in August 1998. The two deceased were the breadwinners of the family which included the couple's five small children. My editor rejected the typescript, boldly stating that an "inner Africa" story with no Euroancestral as the protagonist is a surefire flop. No readers would be interested. But had this story been written by a Euroancestral, or had it been an "inner African" story about African female genital mutilation, the editor would have grabbed it.

Thus even literature must serve the public relations goals that posit Africa and Europe as counter poles, with the imperative structure emphasizing "we" are civilized and "they" are savages. Euroancestrals as protagonists in such savages stories are of course the selfless ones risking their lives to live among these savages in the jungle and teach them how to read and write. With pens and paper donated from some Western "humanitarian" group living in an old people's home. It is of no consequence that the barter-trading savages do not have, and will never see, a post office.

Binyavanga Wainaina writes, in part, in his article: "How to write about Africa":

> After celebrity activists and aid workers, conservationists are Africa's most important people. Do not offend them. You need them to invite you to their 30,000-acre game ranch or "conservation area," and this is the only way you will get to interview the celebrity activist. Often a book cover with a heroic-looking conservationist on it works magic for sales. Anybody white, tanned and wearing khaki who once had a pet antelope or a farm is a conservationist, one who is preserving Africa's rich heritage. When interviewing him or her, do not ask how much funding they have; do not ask how much money they make off their game. Never ask how much they pay their employees. Readers will be put off if you don't mention the light in Africa. And sunsets, the African sunset is a must. It is always big and red. There is always a big sky. Wide empty spaces and game are critical — Africa is the Land of Wide Empty Spaces. When writing about the plight of flora and fauna, make sure you mention that Africa is overpopulated. When your main character is in a desert or jungle living with indigenous peoples (anybody short), it is okay to mention that Africa has been severely depopulated by Aids and War (use caps).[62]

When the hunt was on for a new Pope early in 2005, ZDF television ran a program on the possible candidates. Each candidate was described with their names, ages, the entire curriculum vitae which included of course their nationalities. Then the presenter — now finally come to the bottom of the ladder — announced: "It could also be a black." Full stop. An *it*. A nameless pigmentation, possibly from Pluto. Or an inexplicable apparition. A pathogen that should be approached in a space suit.

It must be quite something to live in the world of such journalists. I wrote to the TV station and received an explanation that as long as the *basic points* were correctly presented, nothing was wrong. I didn't know that six little words constitute *basic points*. I have archived these letters from the various television stations. So much Megignoarrogance deserves to be immortalized!

---

62 Wainaina article: http://www.granta.com/extracts/2615. Accessed 14.04.06

Chapter 13. The Wages of Science – "Race" and other Misnomers

> *That all the claims of superiority of the whites over the blacks, on account of their color, are founded in ignorance and inhumanity.*
>
> — BENJAMIN RUSH *(1745-1813), a signatory of the American Declaration of Independence*
>
> *This Aryan family of speech was of Asiatic origin.*
>
> — A H SAYCE, 1880
>
> *This Aryan family of speech was of European origin.*
>
> — A H SAYCE, 1890
>
> So far as my examination of the facts has gone it has led me to the conviction that it was in Asia Minor that the Indo-European languages developed.
>
> — A H SAYCE, 1927[63]

Racism as a poisonous belief is a reality that is both abhorrent and powerful. But "race" in terms of "different humankinds" does not exist. Humankind's imagined differences are indeed skin deep — no more. There is no scientific basis for the notion race, much less *pure* race. Yet the notions of race and racism have developed into a "real and abiding influence on our collective psyche and continue to wreak havoc globally," writes Dr. Charles Quist-Adade, PhD, a university professor in Canada.

---

63 Mallory, *In Search of the Indo-Europeans*, London: Thames and Hudson 1989, p.143

Ever since Europe's *Age of Enlightenment*, which paradoxically was an 18th century philosophical movement stressing the importance of reason, Europeans have come up with as many as eleven different human "races." The pioneer "race scientist" Francois Bernier even excluded the Lapps from, but included the Native Americans in, the white/European/Caucasian "race" category. "Facts" were churned out which led to "convictions" as to who is who in humankind's zoo. Before the arrival of the Euroancestrals, the Native Americans did not even imagine that they were *red Indians*.

But if you can go back far enough there was only one humankind, living on one landmass — Gondwanaland. Things simply got mystified by interested parties digging up a site here, collecting Vedic writings there, unearthing some ancient bones on the other place and grinding them to powder for lab tests. There was much debating on the probability of "Indo-Aryans" of Western Asia migrating eastwards to wander into India. Or whether they divided at some earlier stage down in the south, somewhere, with one branch going east to populate "India" while the other strode smartly to western Asia. Different versions of the story flatter different egos, suggest different patterns of "natural" alliances, have different implications for who "owns" what.

Quite an effort has been made to reduce Afroancestrals to savage beasts. And not by ordinary merchants or peasants but by the learned, the nobility, and the clerics. Edward Tyson (1650-1708) of the Royal Society, whose works later influenced Linné (a.k.a. Linnaeus), actually took great pains analyzing the anatomy of a pigmy as the missing link between humankind and the anthropoid apes. In 1699 he wrote his "great work," *Orang-Outang, sive Homo Sylvestris: or, The Anatomy of A Pygmie compared with that of a Monkey, an Ape, and a Man*. It turned out later that the "pygmie" had actually been a chimpanzee. But his fellow scientists still regard this "great work" of Tyson's as one of the best anatomical comparisons of those days, the argument being that Tyson only wrote about what he had actually observed.

When it comes to influencing the psyche, the scientist Johann Friedrich Blumenbach of Göttingen University (1752-1840) holds the candle. In his work, *De generis humani varietate nativa* (*About the Natural Differences Between Human Beings*), Blumenbach scaled the number of "races" down to five: the Caucasian or "white" category which embraced the greater part of Europe and Western Asia; the Mongolian or "yellow" variety occupying Tartary to China and Japan and so on; the *Aethiopissae/Guinea* or "black," inhabiting Africa (excluding North Africa), Australia, Papua New Guinea and other Pacific Islands; the American or "red" people of North and South America and the Caribbic; and the Malayan or "brown" category occupying the Indian Archipelago. Blumenbach, concentrating on the "aesthetic hierarchy-classification," put the Caucasians at the top of the ladder of human "races" by contending that Europeans were the most beautiful race of men. He apparently was unaware of the fact that his definition of "most beautiful" could not be universal. The other four categories were believed to be degenerates of the Caucasian stock. Ridiculous theories and technologies such as *phrenology* which determined that the size and shape of the brow bone was indicative of character and criminality, and *craniometry* — the measurement of the bones of the skull — led to determining one's intelligence. Like in a chamber of horrors tale, these so-called scientists pulled unborn "Negro" foeti out of live pregnant women and put "Negro" sperm under the microscope after chopping the testicles off their live owners. Whatever had to be done to support "racial" differences and unhinge any common affinities as a single species of humankind was done, regardless of the consequences. Only the envisaged future "advantages" of exploitation counted.

According to Dr. Quist-Adade, the founder of ideological "racism" was Arthur Gobineau, who identified three "races": European/Caucasian, Mongolian/Asiatic and Ethiopian/African. The race on "races" was on. Linnaeus, a.k.a Linné, (1758) who placed Africans *below* the domestic dog, grouped four categories plus three imaginary ones. Even in the 20th century, Hooton (1926) came up with three and Garn (1965) had nine plus two lower levels.

But "race" has no genetic foundation. The modern scientists of the Human Genome Project have buried all notion of "scientific racism." All human beings have one and the same gene pool. This is why they can interbreed right across the color bar. For better or worse. A Dinka of southern Sudan and an Icelander of Northern Europe can interbreed and produce a Dinka-Icelander child; whereas a crocodile and a tortoise cannot interbreed. Race in human beings is an arbitrary and artificial concept invented by human beings.

The Dinka has acquired dark skin through a gradual evolution involving thousands of years. His ancestors acquired the high level of melanin (the skin-darkening agent) that was needed to keep out the sun's ultraviolet heat. The Icelander's light complexion on the other hand allows the highly abundant production of the chemical known as Vitamin D, which helps him to thrive despite the little sunshine available in the far north. This chemical helps him to absorb calcium which is the essential constituent of bones and teeth. The farther people are from the equator, generally speaking, the lighter their complexions. Thus complexions according to Dr. Quist-Adade are a continuum from dark to pale, with no clinical way to pinpoint where "black" ends and "white" begins. Moreover, gradually, over thousands of years, people of different climatic zones learnt to dress a certain way, move a certain way, breath a certain way, talk a certain way and eat certain nourishment a certain way. The African athletes have a nimble gait and run differently from their Euroancestral counterparts. The Maasai's graceful bearing while standing on one leg for hours would never have been cultivated if he had to stand on snow or frozen ground. Nobody wears mini skirts in the hot Sahara, but they also don't wear floor-length furs, either. Long loose robes with little underneath are perfect ventilators in a hot climate.

But once Western scholars came up with the concept of "race," it was only human nature that Euroancestrals used this notion to give them the right to use their "might" to establish themselves at the top of a hierarchy. To this day humankind (even scholars and authors who ought to know better) keeps on confusing ethnic groups, languages and nations with this fictitious "race." History was segmented into successive ladders of "races," with each "race" in a sort of relay race, each wielding power for a period of time before passing on the crown to a more "superior" variant. And now this Western variant is overwhelmed with terror at the thought of ever having to pass on this power to a new "superior" variant. So they eat more, arm themselves to above the teeth, acquire more material wealth, and install time-saving gadgets in their homes to avoid losing a minute in cooking, dishwashing, doing the laundry. They watch TV while driving to the supermarket and simultaneously keep tabs on their adolescents by cell phone, with automated timers and reminders for everything. All that and more; but they *have no time!* Not even for each other.

If this scene of the highest Euroancestral lifestyle seems over the top, consider scenarios painted by writers like Scholl-Latour about "cannibalistic Africans." Such writers attribute organizational talent, orderliness, beauty and intelligence to physical features such as the breadth and gradient of one's nose, the width of the mouth, the thickness of the lips and the (lighter) shade of the skin. What would Kim Basinger and the UN special emissaries, the Ohovens, say about their bee-stung lips! I wish Africans all the wealth they long for, but I would not want them to lose their humane and open nature, their love of companionship and togetherness, their acceptance of sharing as an obvious human trait, their innate elegance and proud humility. The current "Modernity" thoroughly confuses many African traits and renders most Africans "lost" in some Limboland.

In this classification of the 18th to the 20th centuries (which seems to continue clandestinely these days), was concocted by an assortment of scientist cabals that included archaeologists, paleontologists, Indologists, historians, linguists and philologists. They were broad minded enough to include the fabrications of medieval monks who had done their holy best to interpret the Book of Genesis literally. I quote Dr. J P Mallory: "When the Greek word for oak is the same as the

Germanic word for beech and the Russian word for elder, on what grounds does one ascribe an original Proto-Indo-European meaning to the word?"[64]

Back in Eurasia of some 6,000 years ago, an ancestor was found who spoke the languages of the Proto-Indo-Europeans. But especially in Europe, there was a near-universal desperate longing for an illustrious ancestry all their own, according to Dr. Mallory. To begin with, Troy gave the Romans their illustrious past. Come the Middle Ages and the Spanish aristocracy, and *only* the Spanish aristocracy, had their ancestral blood dripping directly into their veins from the veins of the superior Visigoths. Caught between hell and a big furnace that gave them chronic schizophrenia, the French didn't know whether they should head off towards the pedigree of Vercingetorix and his Gauls/Celts or make a run for Charlemagne and his Franks (Germans). The Germans were careening all over the European landscape anyway. I quote again from Dr. Mallory:

> The Germans, on the other hand, saw their own history begin with those expansions that provided the Visigoths, Franks and Saxons — the illustrious ancestors — of their neighbours. When Tacitus maintained that the Germans were pure of blood, unmixed with other races and autochthonous, there was little reason to deny that their origins lay in Northern Europe. If the Church required a Biblical link, then Ashkenaz, a grandson of the prolific Japheth, could be found to trek his way to Northern Europe and establish the German people. [65]

The English were the regular (so to speak) Europe's Mestizos, octaroons and quadroons and whatever other "-roons" they themselves were so meticulously fussy about in the New World. The English were a dandy mixture of Anglo-Saxons, Britons, Normans, and Whoever. Mutts. In a land of devoted dog breeders, this was so unacceptable that, to overcome it, the English turned to the Holy Land and brought, from across the seas, some lost tribe of Israel just to make their ancestry even more ancient. Notice the oscillation between pseudo-sciences and the Bible.

The Caucasians were furiously concocting theories and positing them as facts. They had indeed recovered from their historic inferiority complexes against the sophisticated and richly endowed "Mussulmans and Ethiopians." By the 19th century, physical anthropologists measured "racial" superiority or inferiority by using the cephalic index: Dolichocephalic (long-headed) Nordics and their brachycephalic (broad-headed) southern neighbors. The blond blue-eyed fellow who had previously been relegated to the caricature of the dreamy romantic was

---

64 Ibid., p.112
65 Ibid., p. 266

flipped over. Around 1870, he became the stereotype of the virile Nordic Garth types.

Again to quote from Dr. Mallory:

> A superior Nordic physical type had been discovered by science; it remained for the philologists to provide him with an ancient and illustrious ethnic identity. The discovery of the Indo-European language family did more than simply elucidate the historical relationship between many Europeans and Asian languages. It severed once and for all the fantasy of deriving all languages from Hebrew, and by extension, Adam. The indivisibility of the human race was being destroyed not only by those who profited from exploiting different peoples, but by science itself. Following the West's discovery of the wealth of Indic and Iranian literature, European scholars looked beyond Eden to seek their own more illustrious forebears in Central Asia, Iran and India. Although Indo-European and Indo-Germanic had both been coined early in the nineteenth century, Max Müller, and other linguists, encouraged the use of Aryan to describe the ancient Indo-European. Naturally, if these early Aryans were the ancestors of the Europeans, then they too must have been part of the superior white race.[66]

Superiority of physical type, culture and language aside, other elements were missing for full-blooded Aryanism. The word-based language of the Chinese had been found "simple" and dropped to the bottom of the ladder, but Asia was not quite appropriate anyway. Asia was too far from Europe and frankly not pink enough. The intellectual environment of 19th and early 20th century Aryan "fitted with mental endowments" and "promoters of true progress" (V. Gordon Childe) was pulled away from the Hindu Kush or Himalayas and slotted in by Canon I. Taylor as "an improved race of Finns." Theodor Poesche was of the view that if one could locate the spot in Europe with the highest cases of albinism, that would be the center of the Aryan "race." A European homeland was found in the Pripet marshes of Eastern Europe; but in 1883 one Karl Penka ruled out any possibility of the "powerful, energetic blond race" ever developing from the unhealthy environment of a swamp. After rummaging through archaeology, mythology, etymology, linguistics and anthropology, the good fellow had it: Aryans originated in southern Scandinavia and could not be derived from anywhere else. Soon all of European society agreed: Aryans had from the very first cell been "blond Dolichocephalics."

The Indologist Max Müller vehemently rejected this construct being placed atop the foundation he had built, "But it was too late. The Indo-Europeans and racism had become inseparable in the minds of many scholars... the superiority of the ancient Aryan Nordic race had entered popular political culture," concludes Dr. Mallory in his book about the search for the "Master Race."

---

66 Ibid., p. 267

CHAPTER 14. PHYSICIAN, HEAL THY HYPOCRISY FIRST

> *Archaeology can offer nothing new to the study of Proto-Indo-European civilization. For any candidate culture advanced by archaeologists as the Proto-Indo-European culture, only two types of evidence can be offered: evidence that conforms to the evidence offered by linguists, which will be tautological (although helpful as support and external validation), or evidence that differs from the linguistic evidence, which will then call into question whether the candidate ought not to be rejected in favor of another that better fits the linguistic evidence.*
>
> — BRUCE LINCOLN[67]

There are always two sides to the coin, and there are innumerable coins around. When Europeans first set foot in inland Africa there were about ten thousand independent African kingdoms, great and small — none of them as small as European nations like Lichtenstein or Monaco. But it was this compartmentalized and overcrowded, warring, disease-ridden and starving Europe that loosed Europeans on the four corners of the earth. By the second half of the 19th century they had reduced these African kingdoms into forty colonies, and the bloody conflicts in Africa today were pre-programmed. In other even more unfortunate continents, the Europeans totally pushed the indigenous people out of the way and made these continents Euroancestral.

With their innate conceit and self-centeredness, England in 1890 promised its German Reich relatives possession of Rwanda (without even bothering to let the Rwandan king know of this fact). Then, seeing that the Nilotic Tutsis were

---

67 Ibid., p. 189

politically and socially advanced and organized, the Germans promptly claimed that the Tutsis couldn't possibly be Africans. They had to be some entity called *Europäide Afrikaner*, according to the racist grading methods of the Hamburg Colonial Institute. With this kind of Megignoarrogance, the British once blundered by declaring the East African island of Zanzibar independent and belonging to the Persian Gulf Sultanate as part of the Arab world. Euroancestrals seem to suffer from Africa-phobia. But they fear what they themselves have made of Africa and Africans, not what Africa and the Africans actually are. How did Jean-Paul Sartre put it? "It is sufficient to show what we have made of them in order to recognize what we have made of ourselves."

The US declares itself the "global policeman" and endeavors to "bring democracy" to others. Democracy? From a country that stops at nothing to control the private lives of its own citizens clandestinely and otherwise, decides for the citizens what books not to read and what films not to see, and makes a mockery of the election process.

The war in the DRCongo threatened to be an Africa-wide war, yet the so-called world community simply looked on because they had their oil, diamonds, gold, coltran and whatever other concessions, safeguarded. DRCongo is still poised to erupt. Supposed criticism and indignation about corruption and capital flight are false. Corruption and capital flight are among Westerners' best means for funding the bank loans that enable them to build big new houses; or their military budgets. But their public relations grip is unshakeable because they control all channels of information. The poster of the German soldiers in Kinshasa showed Euroancestral faces and hands towering over the Afroancestral heads and faces in some perverted patronizing gesture of "protection." Apart from the ridiculous election monitoring in the DRCongo where they sent their soldiers, the West's usual path is to pay the UN for soldiers from Bangladesh, Ghana, Pakistan or any other developing (read: poor) country to risk their lives in "conflicts" around the globe. But the oil, diamonds and a dozen other natural resources, especially those used to produce airplanes, computer chips, mobile phones, play stations and video recorders, are too precious to be left in the "protection" of the developing countries and are not destined for them, except as expensive finished products.

It is a game you have to have a certain type of heart and mental makeup to play.

Afroancestrals commit political violence their way, Euroancestrals do it their way. The latter may not drop handcuffed youths into the ocean, but they bomb whole towns and villages. To think in the vein of: "they are not like us" is a universally worrying prospect for any culture. Up north in Hamburg, I first heard this joke: "Do you know the difference between an Austrian and a Bavarian? A Bavarian is in the transitional stage between Austrians and humankind." In this sense, Euroancestral "tribalism" is not limited to people from other continents.

What seems to be Euro-specific, however, are the conflicts. In the last decade there were only four wars, as far as the West was concerned: the Gulf War in 1991, Kosovo in 1999, and the ongoing wars in Afghanistan and Iraq. It is easy for the Westerner to mistake the media accounts for the real "wars." The media is the scale with which they measure the importance of a news item — one minute, two? And the media manipulate and polarize the people by creating "us" (the good) and "they" (the evil). It is an aggressive public relations campaign.

But the truth is that in the 1990s there were much more than 100 wars around the globe that killed millions of people either through weapons or through displacement and torture. The horrendous wars in Africa and South America simply did not count because they did not touch the lives of the rich Northerners or diminish their economies. Except when DRCongo or Sierra Leonean diamonds were bypassing Western established dealers as "blood" or "conflict" diamonds. These wars supported Western economies through arms trade, then reconstruction, lending facilities, and so on. Wars have become investments for the rich and their citizens through even cheaper imports of raw material and unprocessed edibles, and markets for subsidized products that ruin the local producers. Such facts, of course, are never in the mainstream media.

For the West, issues get attention only when they negatively involve them in one way or another. This is the stage at which they start coining phrases like "rogue states," "war of values," "collateral damage," "democratic rule," "good governance" and so on. Their media then become "embedded" for the government propaganda and public relations department. Furthermore, it is not the issues that are treated as important but *who* (ethnic group), *where* and *what* is going on in the "conflicts." The Middle East is a good example. The region definitely receives more detailed coverage than African "conflicts" do, yet the glaring partiality of the West shows in which direction the wind blows.

The Palestinians voted democratically in January 2006 to elect whomever they wanted as their political leaders. Hamas was their democratic choice, not because Palestinians did not want to live in peace with Israelis but because they wanted to rid themselves of the corrupt and rivalry-ridden Fatah. But instead of accepting this electoral result, the West, who had pushed for the elections in the first place, was out ranting and raving with all their might from the media, and turning off the financial faucet for Hamas while turning it on for Fatah. Refusing to recognize Hamas was the best way to get Palestinians butchering each other and Israelis "legitimately" engaging in battle. The Israelis, who more than anybody else in the world should know what it is like to be a pariah in your own land, believe in tit-for-tat at the ratio of at least 100 to 1. It seems beyond their grasp that continually adding fuel to the fire is not the best way to calm the Palestinians and give them confidence in less radical approaches. "So long as they were smart enough not to openly exercise terror, no one touched them," said the senior Israeli military officer, referring to Hamas. "But now they've gone back to it, so we have the right to deal differently with this terrorist government and try to remove them." That is, remove a democratically elected government by the power of weapons and tall tales.

Today, Israel is not just an ally, it is part of the West. On June 29, 2006, Israeli aircraft fired missiles near the town of Khan Younis in the southern Gaza Strip. The seizures were partly intended to warn Hamas leaders that they could lose not only their power and liberty but also their lives, unless they allowed Israelis to reign supreme. Israel had not only bombed the Palestinian Interior Ministry, it had left Palestinians with no electricity and no water on the sizzling hot days in the Gaza Strip. They had abducted dozens of Palestinian cabinet ministers and members of parliament as if these were common criminals. I do not condone the despicable act by the Palestinians in abducting an Israeli soldier who was only nineteen years old. But the ratio of offences on both sides only serves to stir up feelings of humiliation in the Palestinians and those who sympathize with them. Yet violence seems to be the only language of communication between these two biblically warring tribes. There are more than 8,000 Palestinian prisoners — of which the Palestinians were demanding the release of only 100. The Palestinians are well aware that one kidnapped Israeli soldier causes a major storm, while thousands of Palestinians in Israeli prisons, or even the Israeli occupation itself, hardly ruffles a blade of grass. Israelis were alleging violent acts that deserve being "treated differently." But they would not say what would happen to the Palestinian prisoners whose freedom was demanded if the young soldier were to be released. Was their arrogance more precious to them than the life of the young Israeli soldier in captivity?

When it comes to coverage of news events in Africa, it is sometimes harder to see which way the wind is blowing, and what the actual game is. Saving lives is certainly not a goal. Back in June 1998, Mekki Kuku, a Nuba teacher living in northern Sudan, was arrested for converting from Islam to Christianity and he faced the death penalty. No country in the West or in Africa offered him a home among fellow Christians. Was it because he couldn't be (mis)used as a political/religious pawn or was it because he was a bit too sun-drenched? After all, the Afghani Abdur Rahman, the new Christian who had not even been threatened with death for abandoning Islam, was immediately offered a home among fellow

Christians in half a dozen Western countries. The non-Muslim Sudanese, mostly those in southern Sudan, refuse to embrace Islam and have been fighting back for nearly half a century since Sudan gained independence from the British. Omar al Bashir's government maintains that they may be enslaved and all their property be seized as booty. As independent witnesses to the massacres in northern Bhar El Ghazal, Lady Caroline Cox of the British House of Lords and the US Congressman Tony Hall made a trip to the crime scenes in May 1998. Congressman Hall said: "I felt numb as I walked over the bodies and skeletons [of the people murdered by Arab raiders]. If the United States is truly sorry for doing too little to stop Rwanda's atrocities, we should act now to stop Sudan's."[68] The US and the West has done less than too little — they have made the situation worse since the scramble for southern Sudan's oil began, with the Chinese jostling as energetically as the rest. Bashir's government is still represented in both the United Nations and the African Union.

The physician needs to first heal himself of his pathological hypocrisy before curing others.

There are dark strings of deeds that do not lead to win-win results for all of humanity. The French President Jacques Chirac opened a museum in June 2006, the Quai Branly Museum, showcasing stolen works of art from Africa, Asia, the Americas and Oceania. The good man refers to the thefts and the chronic Euroancestral violence accompanying them as follows:

> "France wished to pay a rightful homage to peoples to whom, throughout the ages, history has all too often done violence. Peoples injured and exterminated by the greed and brutality of conquerors. Peoples humiliated and scorned, denied their own history. Peoples still now often marginalized, weakened, endangered by the inexorable advance of modernity. Peoples who nevertheless want their dignity restored and acknowledged. This is in fact the spirit behind the declaration on the rights of indigenous peoples that we are drafting in Geneva, a declaration to which I know the Secretary General of the United Nations, Mr. Kofi Annan, is especially committed."

To the victims, this may sound hypocritically humble. Further in his opening speech, Chirac said:

> "Central to our idea is the rejection of ethnocentrism and of the indefensible and unacceptable pretension of the West that it alone bears the destiny of humanity, and the rejection of false evolutionism, which purports that some peoples remain immutably at an earlier stage of human evolution, and that their cultures, termed 'primitive', only have value as objects of study for anthropologists or, at best, as sources of inspiration for Western artists. Those are absurd and shocking prejudices, which must

---

68 University of Pennsylvania African Studies Center, http://www.africa. upenn.edu/ Hornet/irin427.html. 12.06.07

be combated. There is no hierarchy of the arts and cultures any more than there is hierarchy of peoples. First and foremost, the Quai Branly Museum is founded on the belief in the equal dignity of the world's cultures."[69]

This parchment from Ethiopia is a 1st century piece showing the "Four Gospels". In the 1st centruy, no single Briton was a Christian, but this stolen parchment is now in the British Library.

No lesser person than HM the Queen owns this bronze head from Benin, given to her in 1973 by Yakubu Gowon, a former Biafra War military leader. It was not his personal possession to give away, it is the property of Nigerian citizens. The bronze head is 1,600 years old.

In the British Museum alone, there are about 140 objects of art stolen by British soldiers or administrators, from Kenya, Uganda, Mozambique, Ethiopia, Tanzania, Somalia and Burundi. These were loaned out to Kenya's 2006 art exhibition *Hazina* (Kiswahili for "treasures"). The pieces were withdrawn during the bicentenary commemorations of slavery abolition, March 2007. As always when the West perpetrates a crime against other peoples, they have a perversely fantastic way of asserting that they are absolutely *bona fide*, legal, entitled. These stolen African artifacts are some of the "written" history and genealogy the West

69 Opening speech by President Jacques Chirac of the Quai Branly Museum on 20 June 2006

would like to rob Africans of. These are the very rich evidence of the tapestry of Africa and Africans' wealthy history which is deliberately denied. The West is quick to re-write history or to provide panaceas like "slavery was legal at the time." In Durban, South Africa, during the UN Conference on racism in 2001, the British government said exactly this and concluded that the trans-Atlantic slavery industry was not a crime against humanity. The abducted Africans had merely been Christendom's merchandise. Now the British Museum also maintains that looting African art was "legal at the time." The UNESCO outlawed stolen arts after the UN agreement only in 1970. The British Museum's spokesperson announced that they have campaigned vigorously against the continued looting of archaeological sites across the globe — while stressing that this pre-1970 material was legally acquired under international law at the time it was collected. Collected or stolen? Where was the international law enacted, and was the African continent part of the "international" entity referred to?

The British Museum was created largely to serve as a repository for artifacts looted from Africa between the 17th and 19th centuries. Such plunder included large amounts of famous artifacts from Egypt which, it is now ascertained, are the undeniable proof that the inhabitants of ancient Egypt were dark-skinned Afroancestrals. Apart from the famous Greek Elgin Marbles, equally valuable objects for the Museum included the Ashanti artifacts including the King's Golden Stool, many Ethiopian religious icons stolen in the 1860s and the complete plundering of the Magdala Fortress by British troops following the defeat of the Ethiopian Emperor Tewodros. A cap and slippers decorated with gold have been identified as having been stolen by British forces from an Ashanti king in 1897. They were sold in December 2003 at Christie's in London, such history now becoming a "commodity" sold into private collections.

One of the countries that most interested the West was the DRCongo, whose people the invaders regarded as backward in comparison with Egyptians and East Africans. The British Museum and other Western institutions practically hired bandits and organized hordes like the Compagnie du Kasai to criss-cross the Congo basin, pillaging and murdering. The Bakongo people had expertise in metallurgical arts in ancient Kongo. They were aware of the toxicity of lead vapors, and devised both preventive and curative methods by pharmacological use of pawpaw and palm oil. They also mastered mechanical methods by which they exerted pressure to free the digestive tract to combat lead poisoning. People living in the eastern Kongo and the neighboring areas made delicate crafts, manufacturing damasks, satins, taffeta, sarcenets, and clothes of tissue and velvet which the Europeans of the 16th and 17th centuries wrote about.

The European psyche at the time totally denied that of the Africans, so that even private collectors like Herbert Lang and Frederick Starr had no qualms about absconding with objects considered by the Africans as sacred, such as those venerating the departed. During an invasion of Benin in 1897, British army officers applied the same Megignoarrogance that the US applied in plundering humankind's legacy in Baghdad more recently. The British soldiers exercised excessive violence and ransacked the many Benin Bronzes now in Glasgow Museum, after deposing the leader of the great ancient kingdom. The British helped themselves to over 3,000 ancient artworks from the king's palace before torching the palace. Then Ergo — Africans had never built palaces!

When I visited the Museum of Musical Instruments (Africa and Asia) in Munich in early 2007, a trusting curator allowed me to leaf through thick files where the "history" of each musical instrument was recorded. I came upon a memo written as recently as 28 October 1985 listing the acquisition of the *apala* ensemble of the Yorubas of Nigeria, complete with the *ndundu* drums, *agidigbo*, lamellophone and *senkere* (rattles). In the same files I read how the German Embassy in Kampala, Uganda, received instructions in the same year to locate a blind musician called Waiswa Lubogo of the Busoga ethnic group. After being located, the embassy received further instructions to make arrangements for Waiswa Lubogo with two other musicians to be flown to Germany with ALL their instruments and ANY OTHER INSTRUMENTS of the Busoga people that could be found. The memo reads in part, "...eine grosse Anzahl von Musikinstrumenten aus ihren Heimatgebieten, wenn möglich alle bei den Basoga üblichen Typen mitnehmen, auch ein grosses *emabire* Xylophone...und die dazugehörigen Trommeltypen ["... to bring with them as great a number of musical instruments from their home area, and if possible all the usual types of Busoga instruments including the huge *emabire* xylophone...and the complementary types of drums belonging to it"). Moreover, a certain Evaristo Muyinda was found and he assisted in acquiring the *ennanga* (bow-harp), *entongli* (lyre) and other Ugandan instruments.

Demands by African members of parliaments, ministers or heads of states for the return of valuable artifacts are brushed aside as not amounting to official claims. When the plunderers have the decency to return various items, it is often done on the "Q-T". In 2006, for example, London quietly returned to Kenya some ceremonial garb belonging to the East African Nandi ruler Koitale arap Samoei, whom the British beheaded in 1907. The African public should be notified as to what has been returned, so they can protect it. It is an open secret, for example, that Nigerian curators have conspired with thieves to steal returned valuables. Governments of Africa and the Caribbean need to prepare in advance for the safe

return of artifacts, and the African community must first put itself in the position to be the real custodians of artifacts wherever they are *right now*.

Some of the ancient African musical instruments in Munich Museum of Musical Instruments

A British member of the Museums and Libraries Archives Council, Arthur
Torrington OBE, has said that art institutions do not "want to accept the objects
were stolen because if they do it for one, they'll have to do it for all." Further, "A
lot of this art would be extremely popular in Africa, yet they are here and a lot of

us don't even know they're there." He added that, "Unfortunately, many African governments' thinking about heritage is not that advanced."

What story does this musical instrument tell? The musician's, the craftsman's or the ruler of the realm's? The Munich Museum of course reveals less than little to the public.

Torrington's remark is true especially of the elite. This brings us back to the Africans' collective psychic damage. They have been so successfully indoctrinated with the "worthlessness" and "primitiveness" of their own heritage that they let it slip away without a second thought. It is such damage that blocks the formation of a communal front in the fight for reparations, as well as fights elsewhere. As in chess, each African move can be seen in advance. Champions think as far as six moves ahead. It is not coincidental that a different standard is applied to Nazi loot, where claims raised in civil court by individual robbed Jews find international acceptance. The Jews can put their heads together and decide on a common course of action and abide by it to the death, if need be. The Africans can put their heads together and decide on a common course, but without two valuable characteristics: trust in each other and determination to resist the Masters of the Game. These Masters know what incentives to offer, and they can crumble any African unity.

An 11th century Queen Mother head from Benin, now in Liverpool

Kongo Art that was stolen by hired invading Europeans. Sudan, now in London

If those are the only two options, it is probably preferable to have the African arts remain safe in the likes of Quai Branly than to have them slipped back into Africa with no guarantee they will not end up disappearing into the "private market." That way, at least, Africans can eventually visit Europe to see their heritage.

Kadaru pot from the Nuba Hills

The post of World Bank President is in the hands of the US administration, while the IMF Managing Director is traditionally a European. On the surface all humankind are represented since the two continents are superficially the home of almost every ethnic group on earth. But the stitch-up has been widely criticized by governments, academics and the staff of the institutions themselves. Long-time Bank watchers were, at the time of Wolfowitz's appointment, asking whether this move signaled the Bush administration's intentions to convert the Bank into a grant-making institution, running down its resources and prestige. Dnavid Waskow, Director of Friends of the Earth International, observed that, "Wolfowitz has shown nothing but disdain for collaboration with other countries. How's he going to run the World Bank, and to what end? (quoted by Paul Blustein and Peter Baker in "Wolfowitz Picked For World Bank," The Washington Post)"[70] We now know how and can say "Good riddance, Wolfowitz" with a sigh of relief. Wolfowitz has been replaced by Robert Zoellick, former vice chairman of Goldman Sachs, former US Trade Representative and former US Deputy Secretary of State. There's not much question whose interests he will be pursuing. Meanwhile, nearly 2 billion human beings live on less than $1 a day. For ordinary Africans, it's still the devil and the deep blue sea.

There is an inquisition team squatting down in the White House. It consists of high ranking US government officials and diplomats, and one of their priorities is the vetoing of UN decisions, if such decisions are contrary to US American interests. They keep the leaders of the UN and all its bodies under thorough observation. Whoever, in such presumed world organizations, goes against the grain is stopped on his tracks or pulled out altogether. Jean Ziegler, in his book *L'Empire de la honte*, tells the interesting story of how this inquisition team forced the then UN Secretary General Kofi Annan to do

---

70 *Washington Post*, Paul Blustein and Peter Baker in their article *Wolfowitz Picked For World Bank*, 17 March 2005 (http://www.washingtonpost.com/ac2/wp-dyn/A39858-2005Mar16)

their bidding by threatening to drop all US contributive responsibilities in Pristina, Kosovo — at the time an inferno.

Why? Because the European Union Council of Ministers, responsible for the task, had chosen a new head of mission in Kosovo and the Secretary General, as a mere formality, had ratified the appointment. The new appointee was the top-notch Swedish former minister for cooperation and immigration, who had also been Sweden's ambassador at the UN: Pierre Schori. The US didn't want Schori to have this post in Kosovo, apparently because in his youth Schori the Socialist had publicly demonstrated against America's attack on Vietnam. Since then he is marked down in the inquisition team's black list as *an enemy of America!* The Secretary General was pressured to annul Schori's appointment, with no fewer than four consecutive visits by US Secretary of State Colin Powell. The UN was once again blackmailed by the White House and had to annul Schori's appointment. The famous world community looked the other way. The European Union didn't even dare to clear its throat.

The son of Germanicus, Gaius Caesar, also known as Caligula, had spoken.

Chapter 15. ESF = Extra Slums Facility

> *It is what is also called aid parturition.... How does a community that
> has received substantial food aid and Medicare learn to sustain itself
> once the agencies withdraw? That is the issue here. What precautions
> must be taken by the donors to make sure that adequate logisti-
> cal provisions remain in place and no undue deprivation results?*

— JOHN LE CARRÉ[71]

The Royal African Society put it succinctly in their *Message To World Leaders*:
"It's not just about thinking up good things we should do to Africa — it's about
the bad things we should stop doing." ESF is or are one of the bad things in many
ways.

In a lecture delivered on 10 April 2006 at the Kiel Institute, northern Germany, the Fund's Economic Counselor and Director of Research Raghuram Rajan
talked at length about reviving the quality of multilateral dialogue and economic
patriotism (protectionism). Rajan went through the entire litany of ebbing internationalism, lack of sustainability, myopic policies of politicians, fund surveillance and floating exchange rates, mentioning the Unites States as one of the
"offenders...running a current account deficit of 6.5% of GDP [meaning it spends
far more than it saves], in the process absorbing 70% of world external savings."
But the rest of the world has to "accept that the United States is special..."

And for those of the poor world who are not "special" and who are therefore
used to getting shocks, a compensation mechanism has been created by the IMF
to assist them in dealing with such shocks. It has the exotic name of Exogenous
Shocks Facility, or ESF.

---

71 le Carré, John,*The Constant Gardener*, New York : Pocket Books 2001 p. 304

"In November 2005," reports the Bretton Woods news article of January 23, 2006, "the IMF's board approved the establishment of the Exogenous Shocks Facility (ESF) to provide quick-disbursing funds to countries experiencing exogenous shocks. The Fund defines an exogenous shock as 'an event that has a significant negative impact on the economy and that is beyond the control of the government. That could include commodity price changes (including oil), natural disasters, and conflicts and crises in neighboring countries that disrupt trade'. The board agreed that shocks due to shortfalls in aid flows 'would not normally qualify for the ESF'."

The German NGO Erlassjahr is concerned that the definition of what constitutes a shock, the amount of funds that a country requires to tide it over, and the structural adjustment needed to address the underlying cause of the shock are all left "up to the discretionary assessment of the Fund." The appropriateness of the timeframe for assistance, eligibility criteria which would exclude many disaster-prone countries, and the sufficiency of the resources available are questionable. All 43 contributors to the PRGF (Poverty Reduction and Growth Facility) trust subsidy account have consented to the activation of the account. Donor contributions totaling $700 million are needed to subsidize planned total lending of $2.8 billion over the first five years. So far, the UK has pledged $85 million, Japan $29 million, and France and Saudi Arabia have pledged to follow suit. UK chancellor Gordon Brown has encouraged oil producers to pay into the fund.

In fact Erlassjahr, in an article headed "Shockingly Weak Shock-Facility for the Weak," by Jonas Bunte,[72] lists the positive and negative points of ESF. The negative outnumber the positive. Analysts are said to welcome the idea in principle but to be concerned about the details of implementation. But if one adds the fairly inevitable debt services, the sums are enormous. The old IMF merry-go-round. Unlike development banks, the IMF purports not to "lend for specific projects..... Country authorities describe the objectives and policy programs for which they seek financial support from the Fund in a Letter Of Intent..." So where does this leave the ordinary African? Outside the door of corruption where these so-called country authorities and the money-lenders are rubbing their hands. The IMF, despite its "surveillance functions," has basically no means of hindering bribes or keeping money from being hidden in bank accounts abroad. At the end of the day Africans and pro-Africans who wish to oppose corruption are like new recruits battling the very army who trained them in warfare. The "teacher" knows exactly what strategies

---

72 Bunte article, Schockingly Weak Shock Facilities for the Weak, ff (http://www.erlassjahr. de/content/publikationen/dokumente/20051205_esf_analysis.pdf), Accessed: 21.12.05

and tactics he has taught his "pupils," but — even better — he knows what he *did not* teach them.

Positive Points As Listed By Erlassjahr

A facility to provide assistance in the case of exogenous shocks is need-ed, as developing countries are especially vulnerable.
It is furthermore encouraging that the assistance will now be given on concessional terms.
Providing assistance in the basis of "first give, then look"- is appropriate as the slow disbursement of funds was a problem with previous compensation mechanisms.

Negative Points As Listed By Erlassjahr

However, this attempt of a quick disbursement is contradictory to vari-ous conditions that need to be met in order to trigger the disbursement.
Whether these conditions are met is subject to discretionary judgments by the Fund as there are no definitions given, e.g. of what constitutes an exogenous shock.
The timeframe of the assistance is inconsistent with World Bank and IMF findings on the persistence of exogenous shocks.
No justification is given why only LICs [Low Income Countries] should be eligible for assistance under the ESF.
The amounts available to the eligible countries might be insufficient.
It is not clear how the loans given under this facility relate to the G8-plan to wipe out all debt owed to the IMF by Post-CP HIPCs [Highly Indebted Poor Countries]. Similarly, it is unclear how it relates to the DSF.

As Jonas Bunte of Erlassjahr (the German NGO) puts it, it looks as though the ESF will go like this. Initially, "the characteristics of the ESF will be pre-sented. Then a critical assessment of the proposal is undertaken starting with addressing the speed of disbursement. Questioning the timeframe of assistance follows this. Section 4 [of the IMF ESF] reviews the eligibility criteria and Sec-tion 5 whether the resources provided are sufficient." He suggests that assis-tance based on the characteristics of the ESF does not even possess the funds it is supposed to put at the disposal of the patients who have through this convo-luted process been recognized as the shocked-needy. Countries are limited to receiving no more in ESF resources than 50% of the country's quota in the IMF; yet such limits on the one hand can be exceeded in "exceptional circumstances" according to the Fund. On the other hand the disbursement "shall also take into account the size and likely persistence of the shock" and this will of course be determined by the IMF. The form of assistance as shown in the table above shall be of a concessional credit with a 0.5% interest rate and initial repayments beginning in five and a half years after the first disbursement, in ten semi-annual rates. No rescheduling of repayments is allowed. "Loans shall be disbursed up to one year after the original request with the option to extend the assistance up to two years. The decision on the extension is made by the Fund given a detailed program by the country on how to use the resources in the second year."

All PRGF eligible countries (thus with a per capita income of less than $895) are qualified to obtain assistance under the ESF. However, these countries may only receive disbursements if there are no other outstanding repayments to the IMF. Furthermore, "a country may not obtain assistance from the Trust under the PRGF and the ESF at the same time." Similarly, a country may not have more than one ESF arrangement for the same shock.

In the Africa continent, this is a shock in itself. Which of Africa's problems is not exogenous? The current PRGF-Fund, in true IMF fashion, is to be renamed a PRGF-ESF-Fund for the accounting, which can be accessed by both the PRGF and the ESF. Additionally, a PRGF-Fund and an ESF-Fund shall be created, which can be accessed only by the respective programs.

Bunte explains how the mechanism is supposed to work. First the country asks for a specific amount of assistance due to balance of payments or reserves difficulties as a result of an exogenous shock. The amount is to be granted without being challenged by the IMF, if the following criteria are met:

- [The IMF] needs to be satisfied that there is a balance of payment(s) problem whose primary source is a sudden and exogenous shock.

- [The IMF] needs to assess that there is no structural adjustment needed, which normally would be implemented by a PRGF-agreement.

- The country must have submitted an I-PRSP (an Interim Poverty Reduction Strategy Paper) preparation status report, a PRSP, or APR plus an analysis in the form of a Joint Staff Advisory Note concerning these documents within the previous 18 months. (It is possible to make exceptions to this step, but this procedure needs then to be completed before the first review).

And then this nice shot from the Fund: in case a disbursement takes place in the absence of need, the country is expected to repay the amount plus interest within 30 days.

If the country fails to repay within that period, "the Managing Director [of the IMF] shall promptly submit a report to the Executive Board together with a proposal on how to deal with the matter."

The IMF's attempt to create a concessional facility that would disburse resources quickly after a shock is laudable, as the document reads: "The Trustee shall not challenge [this] representation of need prior to providing the member with the requested disbursement." However, there is a significant contradiction implied: Funds are supposed to be disbursed without challenge — but only if certain criteria are met beforehand?!

The ESF sounds like a job-creation measure for the Fund's stuff. The result, once again, is that the voiceless, uneducated African citizens have just acquired another debt they will have to pay back but don't even know about. Because they have all that oil, gold, diamonds, bauxite, uranium and so on which they know equally little about.

Bunte argues that, according to the document, assistance will be given when the IMF determines:

1. That there is a balance of payment(s) problem, and that it is "caused by an exogenous shock."
2. That the situation would not be better remedied by "structural adjustments" that would normally be prescribed under a PRFG-Program. Only if this is not the case, assistance can be given.
3. How the requested amount should be disbursed in order to deal with the shock.

After the assistance has been given the Fund determines whether there was really a need for disbursement. If, in the view of the Fund, the assistance was provided in absence of a need, the money must be returned within 30 days.

No definition is given for what would constitute an "exogenous shock." No comment is made on shocks that are a combination of endogenous and exogenous factors? These determinations are largely up to the discretionary assessment of the Fund. Similarly, no guidelines are available for determining when a "structural adjustment normally prescribed under a PRGF-Program" is needed and on what criteria. As these points are not clear it is not possible to determine if the amount of money requested by the country can be released very quickly. This depends on how thoroughly the Fund wants to examine whether the criteria described above are met — and on questions such as: When does a decline in commodity prices present a shock, as opposed to normal market conditions?

The third argument is what has been described as adequate time-frame for assistance. ESF loans, the IMF maintains, are supposed to be given only for a year or a maximum of two years with repayment starting five years after the first disbursement. However, "shocks tend to be more persistent," says Bunte. A World Bank staff paper "reveals that the maximum effect of a commodity price shock is typically achieved only after about four years." Furthermore, the most common type of shock to LICs (Low Income Countries), a drop of commodity prices, tends to be persistent with average half-lives that typically exceed five years. The questions go on.

In the light of other emergency assistance programs primarily concerned with natural disasters, it is understandable that the ESF shall not cover the total loss by an exogenous shock. But the increasing magnitude and frequency of exogenous shocks to developing countries over the last decades should be remembered. It should equally be remembered that countries face not only natural disasters, but even more frequently commodity price shocks, Terms-of-Trade shocks or exchange-rate shocks, with similar costs. Each of them will require not a full, but a partial compensation. In this regard a comparison does give some indication of whether the assistance will be able to actually help.

Since the ESF is supposed to be funded by donations from industrialized countries, the matter remains theoretical, in any case. Currently, only $2.8 billion is committed by 2009 (25% of the total amount supposed to be made available to all countries), with annual contributions of $700 million by donors not further specified. Gordon Brown already clarified that he expects the oil-producing countries to share some of their windfall earnings due to the high oil price. By now "eight industrialized countries" have endorsed the ESF — of which only three are known. The resources available through the ESF would not be sufficient to cover the various kinds of external shocks experienced by developing countries, nor is the funding actually secured.

Most citizens of the poor countries, especially in Sub-Saharan Africa, will not benefit much from such funds, anyway. Several months after the ESF funding was announced, Kenya's President Kibaki was on the world media posing with the usual trademarks — starving people with their ribs bent on being more prominent than the president is — in the semi-arid North-Eastern province of Kenya. Apparently drought had hit the region and ushered in starvation. A recurring problem, but nobody has ever thought of a sustainable counter-action. Except begging, of course. African leaders have made a profession out of begging and they are pretty good at it. Most ordinary Africans I talked to prefer "assistance for self-help," which they are prepared to pay back. In the case of Kenya, the problem was not so much the drought in North-Eastern Province and even much less, lack of food. There was enough grain produced in Western Kenya to feed everybody. The problem was Kenya's lack of infrastructure and the horrendous cost of transportation. Instead of whisking himself off to beg the world for help, the president would have done better to whisk a few hundred sacks of maize to the area.

During the 9th Commonwealth Heavily Indebted Poor Countries (HIPC) Ministerial Forum in Livingstone, Zambia, representatives of the civil society from Ghana, Kenya, Malawi, Sierra Leone, Uganda, Zambia and a regional network headquartered in Zimbabwe, the African Forum and Network on Debt and Development (AFRODAD), all met in Lusaka on April 6-9, 2006 and in Livingstone on April 10-12, 2006, to prepare for participation in the 9th HIPC Ministerial Forum.

On the question of ESF, they came up with a good number of statements. They considered the facility as having a wider reach than similar predecessors and could assist in maintaining future debt sustainability, but only through concessionality. It negates its purpose when it becomes what AFRODAD regards as a catalyst for other forms of assistance. The avenue African countries should at last avoid like the plague is the old one of the euphemistic "assistance programs." But the AFRODAD sounded as if ESF was some sort of green light for more borrowing, although debt is one of the major factors crippling the continent. If more debts are accumulated, then this is the *damnosa hereditas* that future generations of Africans will receive as their legacy. And then — remember the words of John Perkins, the Economic Hit Man — the owed will simply walk into the continent, claim it as the debt repayment, and turn it into a timber farm.

The ESF are of the least use for countries off track in their PRGF programs and facing unanticipated shocks on top of all that. Perhaps Africans are not yet digging their own graves, but if they continue to gnaw at this perpetually dangled debt carrot, they are definitely digging the graves of their progeny.

AFRODAD raised important questions. Why the lack of consultation with the potential beneficiaries and stakeholders before establishing the facility? Why does the discretion lie solely with the IMF? Why are the many shocks experienced by LICs that have no or limited balance of payments implications not covered? Why the short duration for alleviation, when many shocks may be protracted? If the ESF is a loan, why is it being paraded as a concession? Why is the access limited to a maximum of 50% of the IMF quota? Why is the influence of the upper credit tranche (the portion or installments for a loan or credit) utilization conditionality of ESF constraining? Because, while it is called a concession, the ESF still remains a loan, not a grant or gift. And lastly, why this non-inclusion of some middle-income Small Island Developing States (SIDS) that face massive shocks? Africans should put their heads together and look for the answers, keeping in mind that the IMF is an opponent and a master of the chess board. It has probably thought out a dozen moves ahead.

Nor should any African be encouraged by the Gleneagles, St. Petersburg or Heiligendamm Summits and their cheese on the rat trap pet named MDRI (Multilateral Debt Relief Initiative). Africa must avoid being the rat. Even more urgently, Africa should put little faith in the Gleneagles Agreement by the G8 leaders. Remember that Africa, according to Tony Blair then, was a scar on the conscience of the world.

African governments should by all means follow the AFRODAD bid to create or strengthen contingency mechanisms that will take care of the immediate effects of shocks, but not as an interim while holding their hands out for ESF support. "Make Poverty History" is a lovely lullaby. So is "Millennium Development Goals." Unless Africa spits on her hands and grabs the hoe herself, that row is never going to be dug.

Chapter 16. The Machinery of Corruption

> *The poor people in those [developing] countries would be stuck ulti-*
> *mately with this amazing debt that they couldn't possibly repay. A*
> *country [...] owes over fifty percent of its national budget just to pay*
> *down its debt. And it really can't do it. So, we literally have them*
> *over a barrel. So, when we want more oil, we go to [the country] and*
> *say, "Look, you're not able to repay your debts, therefore give our oil*
> *companies your Amazon rain forest, which are filled with oil." And*
> *today we're going in and destroying Amazonian rain forests, forcing*
> *[the country] to give them to us because they've accumulated all this*
> *debt. So we make this big loan, most of it comes back to the United*
> *States, the country is left with the debt plus lots of interest, and they*
> *basically become our servants, our slaves. It's an empire. There's no*
> *two ways about it. It's a huge empire. It's been extremely successful.*
>
> — JOHN PERKINS, [73] *Confessions of an Economic Hit Man, 2004*

Raymond Baker in an oral testimony to the AAPPG (All Africa Party Parliamentary Group) as far back as January 2001 said, "We have been putting some
$25 billion a year of foreign aid into Africa in the most recent years. Compare
that with my estimate of the amount of money that goes illegally out of Africa
and ultimately into Western coffers, $100-200 billion. In other words, for every
$1 of foreign aid that we are generously handing out across the top of the table,
we are taking back some $4-$8 in dirty money under the table."[74]

Just before the Gleneagles G8 meeting in June 2005, the London-based
Royal African Society conducted several seminars, the contents of which

---

73 Perkins interview in *Democracy Now!* by the commentator and activist Amy
Goodman, on 11 November 2004.
74 "The Other Side Of The Coin" http://www.africaappg.org.uk/download/
other%20side%20of%20the%20coin%20PDF.pdf Accessed: 9.12.05

were summarized in a pamphlet entitled, "A Message to World Leaders: What about the Damage We Do to Africa?"

"It's not just about thinking up good things we should do to Africa — it's about the bad things we should stop doing." In these seminars, the RAS discussed with experts the damages the West is doing to Africa in the 21st century and analyzed five damage factors that the West inflicts on the continent, actively creating Africa's poverty. The "Damage Factors" are the fostering of corruption and money laundering, the poaching of Africa's professionals, provision of arms and mercenaries in Africa's conflicts, exploitation of natural resources, and lastly the New Global Politics and the War on Terror.

Although Tony Blair and Gordon Brown urged the G8 members to double the amount the rich world gives to Africa in aid, the two must know by virtue of their offices that one could triple or quadruple the amount to no avail because of the Damage Factors. Africa does not suffer from lack of aid; it suffers from showing very little for the billions that it receives. Africa and Africans show the characteristics of victims and recipients of charity unable to look after themselves. This image offends most Africans who, according to the Royal African Society pamphlet, are asking: "Instead of salving your consciences by giving charity to Africa, why not stop the damaging analyses that hold Africa back and stop us earning our own living in the world?"

Some aid experts apparently claim they *now* know how to utilize aid effectively so that it really brings education and health, and reduces poverty. The chaos in the "Chaos Continent" is always being freshly manufactured by these external experts, and Tony Blair's Megignoarrogant utterance should be quite the other way round: the world, especially the rich world, is a festering wound on Africa's collective conscience.

Africa confronts many barriers to growth and development. These barriers range from a) the ravages of the slave trade which has left Afroancestrals with a collective inferiority complex, b) the artificial division of the continent which separated homogeneous peoples and jammed together people of various ethnic groups with different cultures and languages, c) colonial rule and the seizure of not just the land but also the resources, d) Euroancestral support of tyrants, and e) the continued support of corrupt leaders of countries with abundant natural resources.

Exogenous shocks have been plentiful all through history, not just since the 2005 tsunami. All these factors sum up to "a history of exploitation by outsiders," opines the RAS pamphlet. It is well known that Africa's debts, "incurred with the complicity, even encouragement of Western leaders and officials, have been a burden for African countries for decades. Some have debts so unsustainable that servicing them — just paying the interest — takes up more resources than governments spend on the health and education of its citizens."

Rich countries' trade barriers shut African exports out from their markets; high tariffs on processed goods and agricultural subsidies bring down world prices of food and cotton, making African crops — many of which are of better quality than Western ones — uneconomical. Subsidized food from rich countries continues to be dumped on African markets, further undermining the economies. Holland, as an example, exports 90% of her onions to West African countries, thus preventing African farmers from growing and selling their own product. Tilapia, a Nile River and Lake Victoria fish, is routinely sold in Europe and the US as a product of Thailand. Multinational fishing cartels poach in African fishing waters and then ship their booty to the rest of the world as their own products. Britain, Belgium and Holland do it with diamonds from long-suffering Sierra Leone, DRCongo or "white economy" South Africa. So why not the Thais and Chinese?

And the snowball gathers ever greater momentum for "the lesser breed of men." (Lesser in what?) Europe and America practice the free-market principles they preach only when it is in their interests to do so. The West seems to think the word *interest* is their prerogative. Health officials in Ivory Coast say 16,000 people became ill and, at the time of writing, six died, after inhaling poisonous fumes from toxic sludge dumped in the port of Abidjan by a Dutch firm, using a Panamanian-registered freighter that discharged more than half a million liters of chemicals at open-air sites around the end of August 2006. The ship apparently was sent careening around from one European port to another with the toxic load, trying to get rid of it, before ferrying it off to Africa. No European nation publicly condemned this crime nor apologized for it, as far as I know. The African Union too, kept a low profile.

In 1999 in Cologne, the G8 termed "justifiable" their cancellation of debt to the poorest countries in Africa by heaping on these poor countries the ridiculous figure of 150% of their export income as annual repayment. And when the poor try to knock on the doors of the rich who prescribed their poverty, they are shot, as happens along the US-Mexican borders, in Spanish Ceuta, or Mellita, or they drown in the ocean or die of thirst in the desert, trying to make it across.

The World Bank estimates that $1 trillion is paid throughout the world in bribes. Untold sums are shifted through the embezzlement of public funds or theft of public assets by corrupt officials. Yet another additional $1.5 trillion the Bank lists under "tainted procurement" and an unquantified volume of fraud within the public sector. African countries are prominent among those judged to be corrupt in Transparency International's Corruption Index. This malady is further compounded by the fact that such ill-gotten funds are ferried out of the continent. Mobutu Sese Seko of former Zaire and Abacha of Nigeria embezzled around $5 billion *each*. There is also petty corruption whose extent varies enormously and is even harder to quantify. But corruption presupposes the giver before the taker.

Ordinary Africans themselves seem to accept petty as well as grand corruption as "normal." I remember the day in Kenya in September 1997, when I was concentrated in driving during a Nairobi rush hour traffic jam with my shopping and handbag in the backseat of the car. People were suddenly banging on the car and shouting that I was being robbed. Being robbed? How could I be robbed while driving? It took a bit of time for me before the coin dropped. I looked at the back seat where the banging mob was pointing. The car doors were all closed. But the seat was empty. All my shopping plus my handbag were gone. When I stopped and got out of the car, the mob surrounded me, screaming a purple streak. "It's people like you who create thieves and all sorts of criminals! How can any grownup person drive around so foolishly!" The crowd kept on and on in a jumble of accusations about my foolishness, the veins worming in their necks and their enraged spittle spraying in my face. It transpired that my complicity in theft and the creation of thieves manifested itself in the fact that I had had the audacity to drive in the city of Nairobi, this city in the sun, without bolting all the car doors and winding all the windows up — in the tropical heat! I had spent practically all my life in Europe, so that my mentality had acquired deficits that completely negated the current Kenyan local coinage. To my great confusion I was not the victim of daylight robbery but the perpetrator and creator of thieves and robbers.

And then I had a lesson on petty official corruption. Since both my husband's and my passport, credit cards, and driving licenses were gone, I had to report the robbery to the police. To begin with, the police officer taking down my statement kept on telling me that the one relevant form (which he had in his hands) for filling in the necessary details of the robbery, was the only one available. So he needed to make a photocopy of it for my case. It took me about a quarter of an hour to realize what he was saying. I asked how much the "photocopy" would cost, and I paid. When the form (the very one he had in his hands) was filled in, it transpired that the inkpad for the stamp was as dry as firewood. But another police station about five kilometers away had a pad with ink and we could drive there for the rubber stamp. Except the problem of the police car having no petrol... I went through quite high adventures because of the robbery that I had personally orchestrated. And played my criminal part in corruption.

Corruption is the single greatest obstacle to development and the biggest impediment to investment, according to the World Bank. The developmental cost goes beyond the actual money lost and extends to investment losses, private sector development and investment growth. The Bank estimates that between 300% to 400% "governance dividend" can in the long run follow good governance and corruption control, which translates into a three- to fourfold increase in income per capita and major reduction in other manifestations such as child mortality. An annual growth of 2% to 4% can be shaved off by corruption, according to the researchers. The African Union estimates that the continent loses about $148 billion a year to corruption. The money ends up in the international banking system, often in Western banks. In 2002 the Africa expert groups recommended that corruption proceeds in Africa should be classified as "crime against humanity" because the impact of the practice is on ordinary citizens. These corruptly acquired billions are laundered and "made respectable" by some of the most renowned banks in London, Washington or the discreet personal bankers of Geneva and Zurich. The Swiss have lately been cleaning up their banking system, leaving, in Europe, London as the favorite laundry for dirty money. One third of Sani Abacha's $5 billion loot which was found in Swiss banks by the Swiss authority had been first "made respectable" in the British banking system before being transferred as clean money to the Swiss bankers.

Corruption can reduce tax revenue by as much as 50% and thereby reducing government's public spending which directly affects poor people, because public services are undermined and the cost of provision is inflated. A study revealed that water utility provision in Africa had such high graft in the sector that nearly *two thirds* of the operating costs were due to corruption. Such extra costs are dumped on the consumer, and other services are simply not provided, all due to corruption. The poor are the ones who most rely on public services and who are worst affected by lack of same, by over-pricing and underperformance. When corruption causes the inflation costs of consumer goods, sometimes to as much as 20%, these costs greatly deplete the incomes of poor families. In petty corruption, bribes are demanded from the poor and such payments gobble up a higher proportion of their incomes. They have to bribe schoolteachers to secure places for their children in school, or hospital staff in order to get treatment. According to Transparency International, Kenya, where the average GDP per capita has not been more than $500 in the last ten years, the expenditure on bribery (termed the "bribery tax") amounted to a monthly average of $52 in 2002. This figure decreased in 2003 to $16 whereas the average cases of bribery solicited increased.

Corruption on business pushes up the costs of capital investment. Recurrent payments on corruption increases business risks because agreements sanctity obtained corruptly is questionable and legitimate agreements are threatened if a corrupt official receives better offers from elsewhere, especially in cases of oil, mines and gas concessions. Increase on the cost of goods can then be as high as 20%.

Another study proclaims that corruption can have an impact on foreign direct investment amounting to an extra 20% in tax, and this discourages investment and reduces profit margins. According to the Fund, corruption reduces investment by about 5%. An increase of 1 point in the corruption index can mean a reduction of foreign investment by as much as 8% and has negative effects for a country's ability to compete in international trade. Internally, smaller companies tend to suffer more because bribes take up a larger proportion of their revenue and leave them unable to compete with larger companies able to pay large bribes to secure a contract. This means that in African countries, where the domestic companies tend to be smaller than foreign competitors, the domestic companies are biased against. This produces the two-pronged factor of retarded domestic business growth and at the same time the discouragement of foreign business investment. The London-based All Africa Party Parliamentary Group (AAPPG) reports that, "The possible impacts of corruption on democracy are impossible to quantify. But corruption can undermine democratic systems by infiltrating the higher levels of governments and the most basic levels of public services. The links between corruption, money laundering, organized crime and security including terrorism, are also yet to be fully explored."[75] The RAS is of the opinion that "corruption may actually kill more people and wreck more lives than both drugs and terrorism."[76]

The nine-eleven shocked Western leaders to the point that they finally made bribery of overseas public officials illegal in a section of the Anti Terrorism Crime and Security Act (2001). But the law is made a mockery of because of non-enforcement. The Western leaders have cracked down on terrorist financing, and rising drug crimes spurred them to allocate resources into tracking the huge funds of this trade. Computerization has made the task much easier. Yet these leaders display an obvious lack of political will to combat corruption in Africa. Such investment of staff and resources has not been organized for the fight against corruption, as for the fight against

---

75 AAPPG Report, *The Other Side and ff*, London 2005: http://www.africaappg.org. uk/download/other%20side%20of%20the%20coin%20PDF.pdf 9.12.05
76 Royal African Society report, *The Damage We do June* 2005 ff: http://www.royalafricansociety.org/documents/ras_damagewedo.doc Accessed 9.12.05

terrorism, although corruption is indeed a global problem and no country can delude itself and its citizens that it is free of corruption. But Africa has a particularly virulent brand of it. The whole continent suffers from this bad reputation, causing it a reduction in business confidence and investment. Of the 20 countries rated in the Transparency International Index as most corrupt globally, 10 of them are found in Africa, even if one could argue that Africa is the second largest continent in the world. The tiny continent of Europe boasts 68 countries against Africa's 54, although Europe's borders are hard to pin down — Europe has scattered itself on islands on the Atlantic as well as the Indian and Pacific Oceans.

Between 1960 and 1999, Financial Crimes Commission estimates that Nigerian past leaders alone stole or misused £220 billion sterling and much of this was held overseas. This figure, according to the AAPPG report, is similar to the amount international aid has given to the entire African continent in *four decades!* And it explains why a resource-rich country like Nigeria, with around $300 billion earned in oil since the mid-1970s, had an average per capita income in 2002 amounting to one quarter of the mid-1970s peak and, furthermore, *below* the level it was at independence in 1960. But even smaller amounts cause enormous damage. For example, a study indicates that Tanzania's annual loss through corruption could be nearly as high as its total annual revenue collection. Weak African countries' governance and lack of institutional structures have contributed to and may perpetuate corruption. Several countries in Africa such as Eritrea, Ethiopia, DRCongo and Somali, to name but these four, are recovering from conflicts and therefore need to concentrate on security insurance. Yet corruption undermines such endeavors. In the DRCongo, one of Africa's potentially richest country, only 3% of government procurement contracts go through proper tendering processes, so that opportunities for corruption without such safeguards are enormous.

Capital flight may contribute to Africa's number one financial problem. The $148 billion estimated by the AU as leaving the continent through corruption represents one quarter of the continent's GDP. AAPPG reports: "Other estimates of the amount of total illicit proceeds coming out of Africa (including corrupt, commercial and criminal proceeds) are in the order of $100-200 billion. This dwarfs the aid and debt relief Africa is receiving. Furthermore, in Africa's case, the outflow of illicit money tends to be permanent — estimates suggest that 80% of the illicit outflows are not returned to the continent. It is also estimated that African political elites hold somewhere in the range of $700-800 billion in accounts outside the continent. The RAS puts it even more poignantly: "When a country's health budget is stolen clinics are left without drugs, hospitals without equipment, doctors are left unpaid and babies are not immunized. Corruption is a threat to the economic stability and security of countries whose resources have been stolen or diverted." Unlike the African expert groups defining it as a "crime against humanity," Transparency International defines corruption as "the abuse of entrusted power for private gain." This may apply to actors like Mobutu who once told his party conference that it was acceptable to steal as long as the fact remained in informal limits. Mobutu saw no distinction between his private and state bank accounts. In such kleptocracies, the citizenry quickly follow suit. The policemen who fleeced me in Nairobi probably had not received their salaries for several months, let alone supplies of equipment and stationery, so that inkpads had to be shared across the city. Policemen in Cameroon took to charging taxi drivers for imaginary crimes such as "having double windscreens" for drivers wearing prescription spectacles or sun glasses — to augment the police's meager wages. When the taxi drivers finally went on strike in 2004, it was to protest against "greedy" policemen who were not adhering to the sums that had been agreed upon for the "offences." My beloved Africa!

There are certain situations, certain human mental conditions that can be found only in Africa. In 2002, I shipped twelve used computers to Kenya, intending them as a present to a school I had previously visited where I watched schoolchildren learning on cut-out and "painted" keyboards on cardboard cartons. No screen, of course. When I flew to Mombasa for the used computers, which I had solicited from various German companies, the customs officials demanded customs duty from me that would have bought more than twenty brand-new computers. In what I have termed the damaged African collective psyche, they did not believe that I, an African, could simply give twelve computers as a gift to schoolchildren not even related to me — I surely meant to sell them! I finally shipped the computers back to Germany and gave them to a Balkan country's computer school. The school administrators not only came and collected the computers, and me; they promptly made me an honorary citizen. In Kenya, I can't even send friends or relatives a birthday present larger than the card, and that too often gets tampered with, just in case there could be a Western currency banknote hidden in it. Even a used blouse would cost the receiver a fantastic sum as "customs duty."

Before they were sent off to monitor the elections, I discussed the DRCongo EU troops with a friend from Guinea Conakry, and he said, "Let the Europeans go there even if they will only be in Kinshasa. When an African knows that a European is somewhere in the neighborhood, he behaves himself." I couldn't help but agree. The old collective psychological damage. The victor and the defeated.

In the entire Sub-Saharan Africa, the most popular jobs for the citizen outside the mainstream political field are those in public services where petty corruption is "easy" and just about part of the job description: the police, the army, the private and public lawyers, the judiciary, customs and immigration, the civil service, health and education (not necessarily in that order). A Congolese judge is quoted as having said, "There are three sorts of judges here in Kinshasa. One gives judgment on the merits of the case and does not ask for anything. These are very rare. Then there are those who talk to the litigants and give the judgment to the highest bidder. There are many like that. The third category are those who try to make a fair judgment but then go to the winner afterwards and ask them for some payment. This is what I do. If I did not I could not feed my family."

In Africa corruption, petty and grand, affects all sectors. Yes, corruption is avoidable and no, the African culture of reciprocity does not include grand-scale robbery, embezzlement and theft. In some cultures in Africa even petty thieves lose their thieving hands, liars their lying tongues. Petty corruption is not the result of cultural but rather of economic factors.

But the ones particularly prone to the grand corruption which involves high level officials or politicians and their foreign front men are the construction, security, military and the extractive industries. Transparency International has identified 13 features of the construction sector that make it particularly prone to grand corruption. The size and complexity of construction projects which include various phases and layers of different contractors and subcontractors endows this sector with more opportunities for corruption at each stage, both by the foreigners and the governments, that is hard to detect. Some projects are unique so that there are no comparable pricing scales. Shady terminology like "anticipatory awards" or "mobilization fees" often amounting to *half* of the total cost of the full contract have been disclosed in audit inspections in Nigeria, because corruption does not end with the awarding of the contract but continues for the duration of the construction and operation phases, including maintenance and spare parts. It is not rare to have "anticipatory awards" or "mobilization fees" paid to projects that are then scrapped.

The AAPPG reports a construction expert describing the situation:

> You need certificates every month of what has been done and someone is certifying that. To get your certificate you may have to pay every

month. Once you have your certificate you need to get the payment, but to get your payment you may have to pay. In order to get your equipment through Customs & Immigration you will probably have to pay and to get your visas. This is perpetuated all the way down the contractual hierarchy, through the sub-contractors. You also have fraud occurring in that claims put forward may be enhanced or inflated for false reasons and false costs. You get this whole contractual structure of hundreds of companies... That is why costs can overrun by 50 or 100 per cent sometimes.

And that translates into higher costs.

Without goodwill or principled actors, it is hard to pinpoint what proceeds are banked or spent overseas instead of domestically, but the tendency is that the proceeds are banked overseas. Non-existent companies receive funds or present fake or mispriced invoices for payment. With such non-existent companies, Kenya was, in the Goldenberg scandal involving leading politicians and officials in the Moi government, fleeced of an estimated $600 million to $1 billion in just three years. The practice is continuing in the Kibaki error as the published Githongo Report on the Anglo Leasing Affair recently proved.

Former Zaire should have had boosted profits in the 1990s when the copper price rose, but instead lost hundreds of millions of dollars annually to Mobutu. The dizzying volume of money in oil has been the propellant of grand corruption in countries like Nigeria, Equatorial Guinea, Angola and the DRCongo. In fact at the time of writing, the oil earnings in Equatorial Guinea remain a "state secret." When an oil company agreed to reveal how much they pay Angola, the Angolan government reprimanded it. But as long as such conglomerates cringe at corrupt governments' reprimands, corruption prevails. In primary resource exploitation, corrupt leaders undersell their national wealth for a lump sum. Other sectors, such as public health, can become so criminal as to offer citizens fake drugs. This is now a big problem in Nigeria.

Then there is the corruption connected with the aid industry. Aid agencies often have to pay bribes to customs officials for their shipments to be released or in order to get permits. The aid to Africa through the World Bank in the last 40 years comes to some $54 billion, while during this same period Africa's economic situation has only worsened. Misuse of aid — the Bank and donor countries call these "leakages," or "uncompensated sales" when it comes to a country's natural resources — plays a contributory factor to the ineffectiveness of financial inputs. During the Cold War years the donor nations turned a blind eye to corruption, human rights abuses, bad governance and kleptomania as long as the man at the helm was "their son of a bitch." Funds were deliberately (mis)used to keep the son of a bitch in power. Today it is not rare for African political leaders to use aid funds to finance the extensive of the patronage system which inflates political and civil service staff to ridiculous proportions, to the detriment of true democracy. The number of "nominated members" of parliament is often double the number of the "elected" members. When direct budgetary support for a project is involved, the risks and opportunities for corruption are even greater, starting from the selection of *which* project *where*, and then design, procurement, formulation, execution, evaluation, implementation and financial management by *who*. Aid is indeed part of the problem and not part of the solution.

Chapter 17. Elements Inhuman II

> *The ancestors of the Aryans cultivated wheat when those of*
> *the brachycephalics were probably still living like monkeys.*
>
> — GEORGES VACHER DE LAPOUGE, 1899[77]

Since the days of de Lapouge and the atrocities of Nazi Germany, one would expect that the Aryan myth is long since dead. But an Internet search corrects that impression.

Latent racism boiled over in a small incident in 2004, when my husband's political rivals found a way of slinging mud at him through their media adherents. He was head of a charity organization that arranged language courses and other integration and cultural training, mainly for the so-called immigrant community. That in itself was no sin. The sin was that my company let office space to the charity organization. The media used this, and me, to stoke up public emotions. My name was all over the affair with the usual racist and Megignoarrogant phrases like "banana republic" and "foreigners" and "African wife" (I couldn't simply be a "wife"). And out here, Africa is one village that only looks huge on the television screen and on maps. None of the media bothered to solicit my opinion even by a phone call. I decided to take a supreme stance and simply rose above the situation.

During the 2006 Football World Cup in Germany, some of the country's politicians came up with the phrase "no-go-areas," meaning places that dark-skinned visitors to the World Cup should avoid. There would have been danger of being

---

77 Mallory, J.P. *In Search of the Indo-Europeans*, London: Thames & Hudson, p. 266

attacked by racism-driven Germans. Most Germans, especially the politicians, prefer using the euphemism *Ausländerfeindlichkeit* — hostility to foreigners, instead of the word racism. Apart from the right extremists, there would seem to be a lot of *Ausländerfeindlichkeit* where one would not expect it — in the German bureaucratic system and the police force. In the last couple of years many African asylum-seekers have been mistreated or killed in police cells or in the streets, and so far the courts have left the culprits to walk out Scot free. Asylum-seekers' quarters have been repeatedly set on fire, the latest one in Saxony-Anhalt. Since the German reunion, 135 people have died through right extremist violence.

The Bavarian state government is out to ban Muslim women teachers who wear headscarves to the classroom. They claim this does not tally with occidental Christian ethics, and the argument that nuns wear their head gear into classrooms is rejected with the counter-argument that nuns cannot be compared to ordinary Muslim women. Until just a few decades ago, mature European women routinely covered their hair and nobody suggested they stop doing so. They stopped it of their own free will. At times, the bullying goes too far.

When their media offer them opportunities to assuage their vague sense of guilt through donations for the "less fortunate" by showing them mass killings and famine in countries like Ethiopia, Westerners organize "charity" gala dinners and balls where they adorn themselves in "blood diamonds," and hairdos the cost of each of which, alone, would feed several African families for months. When their governments inform them of some new assault on the roots of poverty in Africa, they actually believe that they are the planet's leading philanthropists. But they are angels who seem to have been schooled by the devil himself. They muscle the rest of the world out of the way, then blame the same people for their poverty.

The West conveniently forgets that all humankind come from the ancestral home in the Rift Valley. The mendacity and malevolence of Euroancestrals when it comes to separating the chaff from the wheat and firmly underscoring the "us" against the "them," the putative "good" against the "evil," is observable in the never-ending Middle East war. The freak arm of this latent racism shows in Germany's attitude towards different crises. The Germans are forever at pains to atone for the past. But when it comes to Africa, the German minister for development assistance, Heidemarie Wieczorek-Zeul, told the Hereros that Germany will not pay a single cent in reparation for the atrocities of von Trotha and his German colonialists. Nobody in the West is prepared to pay reparations to Africans because, as with stolen artifacts from the continent, one such gesture would touch off a landslide of demands for reparations, for the most part entirely legitimate and impossible to shrug off. The Germans committed their first genocide against the Hereros, then used the lessons learnt against the Jews. There is even evidence confirming the genocide, issued at Ozombu Zovindimba on October 2, 1904. The extermination order read:

> I, the Great General of the German troops, send this letter to the Herero people. Hereros are no longer German subjects. All Hereros must leave the land. If the people do not want this, then I will force them to do so with the Big Gun. Any Herero found within the German borders, with or without a gun, with or without cattle [the cattle belonging to the Africans had been stolen from them at gunpoint and then they were forbidden to own any cattle], will be shot. I shall no longer receive any women and children. I will drive them back to their people, or I will shoot them. This is my decision for the Herero people. Signed by the Great General of the Mighty Kaiser Wilhelm II, 2 October 1904. [78]

A rare case in history where the perpetrators actually put down in writing their intention to commit genocide. And as if this was not enough, the German soldiers at the time poisoned all the waterholes in the Kalahari Desert to kill the fleeing men, women and children of Namibian ethnic groups.

This same minister, Heidemarie Wieczorek-Zeul, gave a television interview from the donor conference in Stockholm about the Lebanon-Hezbollah-Israeli war. The bad guys, to her and her government, were the Hezbollah. But in all fairness, the only innocent party to this mess is Lebanon's citizens. Israel has no right to simply attack a sovereign state, destroying the entire infrastructure and 15,000 innocent people's homes, just because armed criminals live in Lebanon. There is not a single country on earth without armed criminals living in it, organized as well as unorganized. Apart from the homes, 78 bridges and 630 kilometers of roads were damaged. In the agricultural sector there were damages of up to $185 million of crops, $1 million in poultry and an unvalued 25,000 lost sheep and goats. Lebanon's forecasted 6% per annum economic growth will plunge and unemployment rise.

If the Israelis have suffered centuries of discrimination, it is understandable that they are determined to have a land they can call their own. But blackmailing the West, taking more and more territory from others, and indiscriminately bombing innocent human beings in their own four walls does not pave the road for a peaceful existence in that land.

There are many parallels between the Middle East and Sub-Saharan Africa, whenever Euroancestrals are involved. The same pseudo-arguments once used to dehumanize non-Euroancestrals in general and Africans in particular are still the benchmarks for inclusion and exclusion.

---

78 *New African*, October 2006 No. 455, "Focus on Namibia", p. 70

In the Middle East, as in Africa, there are elements inhuman on the part of the West as well as elements of corruption. Contracts for rebuilding the infrastructure are allocated to Western companies. The OECD Convention on Combating Bribery of Foreign Public Officials in International Business Transactions (1997), Phase Two Review (2005), is rendered ineffective because "for a bribe to be illegal the bribe giver must believe that the official would act 'primarily' because of the bribe." But who can prove this in a court of law, and how? Bribes are often paid through intermediaries or for the benefit of a third party.

As long as the West is unable to bring its bribe-givers before the court, as long as extremely high levels of proof are required to open an investigation into suspicious transactions, it has no right to pin corruption on anybody else. The AAPPG report mentioned in the last chapter states:

> The French and US authorities have opened investigations into allegations of bribery by a major consortium, TSKJ, in securing contracts for a liquefied natural gas plant in Nigeria at Bonny Island. The UK authorities have not opened their own investigation even though one of the consortium member companies, MW Kellogg, is UK based and the agent alleged to have facilitated the bribes is British, resides in the UK and uses a company registered in Gibraltar. Furthermore the UK's ECGD gave 127 million [British pounds] worth of support to MW Kellogg, the UK subsidiary of US Halliburton, for the project... Because the French investigating authorities have made public much of the information it is known that the agent is a UK based lawyer named Jeffrey Tesler, whose fee, subject to securing a contract for TSKJ, appears to have been $51 million. It is alleged that the agent was the channel through which bribes were paid to Nigerian officials in order to secure the contract. Halliburton has admitted to the US Securities and Exchange Commission that such payments were made...[79]

A lawyer earns $51 million simply by securing a contract. And Africa is the *7K Kontinent* — a politically incorrect popular German-language description of Africa (Kriege, Krisen, Katastrophen, Korruption, Kriminalität, Kapitalflucht, Krankheiten — the continent of wars, crises, catastrophes, corruption, crime, capital flight and disease), and poor.

Sir Patrick Darling wrote in his evidence to the AAPPG (to be read under the same website above): "With one hand, the West has pointed its finger at corrupt African leaders, whilst, with its other hand, its bankers, lawyers, accountants, art dealers, health authorities, universities, estate agents and embassies have been actively or passively encouraging wealth out of Africa into the West's economies."

The West should put its own house in order and design an effective policy coherence when it comes to non-Western regions. The report of the Commission

---

79 AAPPG report, *The Other Side Of The Coin* http://www.africaappg.org.
uk/download/other%20side%20of%20th.) Accessed: 20.11.06

for Africa (March 2005) lists down recommendations for the West to fight the supply side of corruption and money laundering which a decent and civilized West could effectively adopt and fulfill. But instead, even the OECD Convention on Combating Bribery does not mention which or what categories of individual public officials it identifies. It would seem as if they are patting their backs with some perverse satisfaction in the arena of their special social Darwinism. The suffering of innocent Africans or Arabs is but a confirmation of their "superiority" and "ability" as against the "inferiority" and "disability" of the others.

A small but proud country in southern Africa, Lesotho, shamed the world when it exposed a bribery scandal, invested time and money in the prosecution and took legal action against large scale corruption in its Highlands Water Project. Lesotho prosecuted several senior officials in the government. International companies were implicated as bribe-givers in the construction project, including German and British firms Balfour Beatty, Sir Alexander Gibb & Company, Stirling International Civil Engineering and Kier International. Lesotho has already prosecuted a Canadian as well as a German company, and it is still gathering evidence against others. The West should assist Lesotho in its noble endeavors not only in investigation but also in prevention and enforcement. Dr. Susan Hawley, in her oral evidence to the AAPPG in December 2005, described the current situation thus:

> Because it is so hard to get evidence on overseas corruption, we have a situation where you do not get evidence unless you open an investigation, but you cannot open an investigation unless you have evidence, and that is a vicious cycle. I think that is what the intelligence gap is, that there is a need for someone to be building up the evidence from when an allegation first comes in. The question is: Who should do it and do they have the resources to do it?[80]

The OECD has criticized some countries, especially the United Kingdom, for placing too much importance on the impacts of effective investigation on the countries' "economy and relations with other states." Such considerations only impede effective investigations because "crime should not be investigated so selectively." This is one of the typical double standard that the West pulls out when Africa and other regions are on the scene. When it suits their purposes, they invest whatever it takes for the crime to be investigated thoroughly and culprits are made to resign their jobs and punished by a court of law. The AAPPG recommends setting up "an EU-wide database to exclude companies convicted of corruption from public procurement across the EU." This is a hard nut to crack. The Siemens company has been caught (2006-2007) in an overseas

---

80 Dr Susan Hawley's written evidence p. 6, 7, & 13 of the AAPPG Report, December 2005

bribery scandal they have admitted, but it cannot be imagined that the German government would keep Siemens out of public procurement nor allow any of their EU fellow members to do the same to this multinational firm. It is one of the big movers and shakers!

There are more elements inhuman in the West's dealing with other regions. Sitting in the Indian Ocean is an archipelago named Chagos. With an ordinance as straight as a corkscrew for its legal underpinning, the British sold the archipelago to the US in 1965 to be used as a military base. And that is what it is, to this minute. Americans wanted the islands but not the Chagossian people. These "lesser breed of men" were driven out of their islands and shoved down the throats of Seychelles and Mauritius, who did not want the unlawfully deported Chagossians either. Everybody was told that this was merely a temporary arrangement. Forty years later, no alternative has been found. In November 2000 a high court in Britain granted the Chagossians the right to go back to their islands and begin a new settled existence. The US said no, Britain got hold of a group of lawyers of its own, and the case is rolling anew — against the Chagossians. Whenever the Americans are asked to give the islanders back the land of their ancestors, the Americans say: Any time, but the British are the landlords, not us. Over to Her Majesty's Government, and the British say: Any time, but it is American territory. The Americans in fact occupy only one of the islands, Diego Garcia, where they lead a paradisiacal life. But they don't want anybody looking over the shoulder of Pax Americana.

As always, when the West makes other people's lives a catastrophe, they turn around and accuse the world of causing the disasters by creating a dynamic that requires a "new world order"! Even a fool stops erring at some stage. But not the so-called superpower and their mastiff who refuse to see this human crisis (or any other crises for that matter) in its magnitude and shape. Rather, they see it in shades of human pigmentation. Moreover, Mauritius and Seychelles are also not happy with their lot as hosts to the kidnapped. Who would be? This time not in Israel and Palestine, but right in the middle of the Indian Ocean. Britain and America are now back to doing everything in their power to twist things around against the Chagossians. To quote Tacitus, "They make a desert and call it peace." As Stalin put it, one death is a tragedy but a million deaths is a statistic. And Thomas Jefferson said, "There is not a truth existing which I fear or would wish unknown to the whole world." But this is the truth. Britain and the United States are staunch believers in propagating lies and ridiculous cover-ups for the rest of the world. Even when they know that they cannot fool all the people all the time. Yet as long as one has very big guns to uphold the cheatings and fabrications, then one is *Capi di tutti Capi.*

Let us take a quick look at another two-faced Western stance in Africa. One of the current Darling-of-the-West African country is Ghana, the "star pupil". Now, compare one or two things that bind Ghana and the Demon-of-the-West African country, Zimbabwe. *New African* in its June 2007 issue, does it splendidly and asserts, "Ghana and Zimbabwe have similar variables in many aspects...the two countries have a vitriolic private press vying for honours with the state-owned media. They also have an opposition not shy to speak its mind. But the strange thing is that while Ghana is talked about in glowing terms in Western capitals, Zimbabwe is said to be a 'dictatorship' ruled by a 'tyrant'...In April 1983, Ghana devalued the cedi [Ghanaian currency unit] under intense pressure from the IMF and World bank. At the time, the cedi was exchanged for 5 cedis to 1 pound and 2.75 cedis to US$1. Today, the cedi is exchanging for 18,400 to 1 pound, and 9,240 to US$1... the princely sum of 184,000% has been the depreciation of the cedi in 24 years! [Yet] Today, [the Bank and the Fund] and other Western opinion formers point to the 1,750% inflation rate, recently revised to 2,200%, in Zimbabwe, [as] the worst since Hitler committed suicide in his bunker in Berlin...!"

Hunger, thirst, diseases and armed conflicts are apocalyptic riders of underdevelopment in Africa which annually destroy human resources. Globalization is forcing this new millennium under its yolk and it is controlled by transcontinental capitalistic oligarchs. Humankind is for the first time (possibly the last) undergoing a transitional period of their lives as intelligent, dignified and proud travelers on this planet. The planet is groaning under the weight of abundance in food, housing, commodities and health services, yet more than 100,000 people die daily of hunger or malnutrition. Nearly each ticking second, a child under the age of ten dies of hunger. More than 858 million people are undernourished with about 35 million of them living in the rich North, 517 million in Asia, representing 24% of the continent's population. In Sub-Saharan Africa, 34% of the population are chronically undernourished and this interprets into 306 million people of the present population of Africa. The FAO terms the African case "extreme hunger" since their daily nourishment has 800 calories less than a human being needs to *survive*. A child who lacks sufficient nourishment in the first five years of its life will have poor health and damaged brain cells for the rest of its life and possibly not live to be 40 years old. But the cycle does not stop here. Mothers who as children were undernourished and brain damaged give birth to hundreds of millions of damaged infants. A study has confirmed that enough agricultural products are harvested on our planet to feed 12 billion people adequately.

In the West surplus food like grains, meat or dairy products are incinerated, simply go up in smoke instead of being donated to the starving. Why? The euphemism is "price support," in other words, to avoid hurting profits. Prices have to be kept stable, not human communities.

A German poultry farm kills 3 million seven-day-old chicks daily. Why? Because they will grow into cocks. Cocks cost too much to keep alive since they don't lay eggs, and only a few hundred thousand of them are needed to accompany their millions of lady hens. And yet in the Southern Hemisphere there are at least 2 billion people who would be prepared to personally dig up worms to feed these killed chicks if the people could get their hands on even a single one, in the hope of one day owning a cock. Jean Ziegler writes that the perpetual hunger and undernourishment are caused by human beings. All the deserts, the floods, and the droughts would leave nobody starving if human beings practiced solidarity and shared the abundant nourishment produced on the planet.

According to UNDP, over 2 billion humans live in "absolute poverty." They have no schools, no access to medicine, no constant income, no drinking water, no regular employment, no adequate shelter or nourishment. Responsible for their fate are the lords of globalization and their political and financial lackeys. Their ultimate goal is to privatize the entire Planet Earth since they practically each already own fifty villas, ten castles, twenty yachts, half a dozen islands, ten private jets and any number of limousines, around the globe. No king, queen or emperor, no empire has ever been as powerful as they are. Nor as ruthlessly brutal and immoral. But they believe they should be worshipped for it all. Bill Gates' fortune is as huge as that of 106 million poor US Americans put together. And his fortune is growing by the minute while the poor are getting poorer. The end of communism has presented the world with a capitalism gone dizzy. A capitalism that regards complementariness, reciprocity and solidarity among human beings as gross sins. A capitalism bent on the accumulation of wealth and power and the height of despotism. Their weapons are mergers, fusions, privatization, hostile takeovers, dumping prices, WTO, IMF, World Bank, and corrupting of the political elite worldwide. And best of all as a tool, the US military empire which watches the whole planet for them via satellites, patrolling the world's oceans in carrier battle groups and fights their wars in countries who refuse to bend to their wills. For their financial expansion, they have their mercenaries at the WTO, IMF and the World Bank as well as in the stock market exchanges from Tokyo to New York, London, Paris and Frankfurt. They even have their muscle men in the cellar of the White House specifically for the United Nations and its Secretary General, whom they loose on the UN every time the world organization does or proposes something that goes against their capitalistic grains.

The Nobel Peace Prize laureate for 2006, Professor Mohammed Yunus, remarked optimistically that the UNO Millennium Development Goals of halving the number of the world's poor by 2025 is one of his aims. He predicted that one day poverty will disappear and poverty museums will be built to show children what poverty looked like. A wonderful dream. He is right when he maintains that poverty is not created by the poor, that it is the failure at the top rather than lack of capability at the bottom. What he does not say out loud is that the top does not wish to have a capable bottom. A capable bottom is the top's nightmare. Professor Yunus himself must be the worst horror to neo-liberalists because the good professor is actually allowing poor borrowers to own the bank they are borrowing from! It is possibly worse to the oligarchs than being asked to pay taxes from profits someone else sweated for, for them to accumulate.

There is no sphere of life where the West is not actively strangling Africa and other developing regions. The Chairman of the AAPPG, Hugh Bayley, opined in the above report that, "Corruption is bleeding Africa to death and the cost is borne by the poor. The African Union calculate that $ 148 billion a year is corruptly spirited out of the continent. *This is six times what Africa receives in aid* [emphasis mine]. Much of the money is banked in Britain or our overseas territories and dependencies and sometimes British citizens or companies are involved in corrupt deals."[81] Large-scale corruption has the corrupt West in the background. With it comes capital flight leading to the true trickle down effect — the unpaid army and police force harass the innocent citizens for petty bribes, the hungry orphan will steal or pick-pocket to feed itself, the undernourished HIV-positive parent or child will die of malaria, TB or even the common cold because governments cannot afford the expensive Western medicines and are forbidden by the West's patent system to produce cheaper medicaments.

It is not uncommon that these medicines were poached out of Africa in the first place, such as the diabetes medicine Acarbose, better known in the US as Precose or in Europe as Glucobay. The bacteria called *actinoplanes sp.* or SE50, which enables the biosynthesis of Acarbose to activate fermentation, comes from Lake Ruiru in Kenya. Once the German transnational pharmaceutical company Bayer got hold of the bacteria, they patented it in 1995. Bayer's profits from Arcabose in the year 2004 was a staggering 278 million Euros. In the Republic of Congo (Brazzaville), the Canadian firm Option Biotech in Montreal took the seed of the *aframomum stipulatum* and patented it to produce their potency pill known as Biovigora, which is not a chemical

---

81 AAPPG Report, *The Other Side and ff*, London 2005: *http://www.africaappg.org. uk/download/other%20side%20of%20the%20coin%20PDF.pdf. Accessed 20.11.06*

medicament. These seeds had been used by the Congolese and other African groups of people without any side effects since time immemorial. A bottle of Biovigora containing 24 pills costs $30. The Congolese were never even compensated following the patenting of the seed of their *aframomum stipulatum*.

In 2004 the French luxury goods producer Dior Group, plus American and German cosmetics and drug producers, patented the resin of the *okoumé* tree which they use in the production of creams, gel, balsam, mascara, nails products and so on. The *okoumé* tree is used in Gabon and other western and central African countries to make ceremonial torches, as a substitute for incense, and for making skin creams such as Shea Butter. The African Shea Butter is the best and purest, not having been garnished with scent and other chemicals as preservatives and so on. Dior knew this but still the resin was patented by the Western companies.

One famous African phenomenon is the baobab tree, whose leaves have a mucus extract with a sedative effect. The German multinational concern Cognis, who also have a patent on the Moroccan tree *argan*, have patented the baobab extract. The baobab has a great symbolic importance for many Africans who also use the extract in their traditional medicine and as cosmetic for the hair and skin. Cognis uses the extract in cosmetic products for hair, skin, eyelids and nails. The Cognis argument that they were the first to "discover" the cosmetic use of the mucus in the baobab leaves is therefore a load of nonsense. The San people of South Africa, Angola and Namibia used the *hoodia* cactus to quench their thirst while out hunting in the Kalahari Desert. The South African research center CSIR used the traditional San knowledge to find out about five different parts of the cactus and patented them. They then sold the usufruct to the British company Phytopharm and production license to the American company Pfizer. The San got zilch. When the matter became public, the media put pressure on Phytopharm, who came up with the Megignoarrogant argument that the 100,000 Sans were long since extinct. In 2003 the CSIR pledged to give the San part of the income from Phytopharm, which amounts to 0.003% of what Phytopharm makes in retail sales from the five different parts of the *hoodia* cactus. Pfizer sold their licenses back to Phytopharm, who sold them to Unilever, the producer of Slim Fast with the properties of the *hoodia* cactus, and other diet foods, for an initial $12.5 million and a further $27.5 million to come, plus the income from the Unilever products in the retail markets.

The writer/"conservationist" Kuki Gallman describes in one of her autobiographies how she went poaching for African medicinal knowledge with a group of Westerners in tow. She brought them to the simple hut of the old

Kikuyu medicine-woman and finally coaxed the woman into revealing what herbs, resins, saps, leaves, barks, roots and everything else she used to cure what ailments and diseases. Free of charge. And this old lady often treated "my Africans" for Kuki Gallman, the Kenyan of Italian/British descent who owns private-property Africans and their wildlife. If this old woman had been advised to get hold of a lawyer before revealing her secrets, she would have become a Kenyan multi-millionaire overnight.

The wars fought in Africa are Western wars fought by proxy, either for geo-strategic territories or for control and share in Africa's abundant natural resources. Somebody outside Africa is manufacturing and selling the weapons. Somebody outside of Africa is accepting whole forests, oil reserves and mines as the currency of payment for the weapons. The trickle down effect here is the series of inevitable crises spewing millions of "displaced persons" across borders. Other catastrophes include the environmental pollution engineered in or by the West, such as in the Niger Delta.

The West in general, the globalizers, and the neo-liberals, have one parameter: their negotiations and no-holds-barred approach have undermined Africa's fragile democracies and incapacitated the African people's determined endeavors to achieve sustainable development. They are the clear winners in these destructive undertakings. The exploitation of Africa, even in the 21st century, is of course blamed on Africa and the Africans. Exactly the mental framework employed over the last 600 years. "[The] ravages of the slave trade, the European carve-up of the continent, followed by colonial rule and the seizure of African land and resources, the support of tyrants during the Cold War, all add up to a history of exploitation by outsiders."[82] (Royal African Society Report in 2005).

By some tacit agreement the West veils itself in defiance or contrariness.

The West, particularly Europe and the United States of America, owe Africans apologies. The reparations would possibly be colossal but not more than the West can afford, and above all they are justified. Those who dismiss this on the grounds that Africans and Arabs were engaged in slave trading anyway forget three things: one is that the scale was incomparable with the trans-Atlantic trade, two is that European merchant ships making stops in the Indian Ocean islands gave a heretofore unknown impetus to the Arab slave trade for the European — not the Arab and Eastern — market, and three is that Africans and Arabs bought, sold and owned slaves but never forgot that the slaves were God's creatures and were human beings just like

---

82 Royal African Society report, *The Damage We do* June 2005 ff: http://www.royalafricansociety.org/documents/ras_damagewedo.doc Accessed 14.4.06

them. African slave girls gave birth to sons who became caliphs and generals in the Islamic Empire, whether in palaces in Persia, Constantinople or elaborate villas in Al-Andalus. African slave men married whomever they wanted to marry and had the opportunity to break out of bondage on their own social and intellectual merits, which was often in less than two years even if they had been captured in boyhood. Slaves in African households were treated like kin. They had the right to speak their minds, which often led to being appointed as advisors.

This is a world apart from dehumanizing a fellow human being.

Reparations should not be given to governments. They can be in the form of a trust fund for small loans to those in the microeconomy, in meeting the payments of school and college fees over an agreeable period of time, in building schools and health centers, and can be monitored by the civil society or appropriate local NGOs. The Africans should not squabble over the details of who is entitled and who is not; they should negotiate with a single voice. The damage done, especially psychologically, affects the whole continent as well as the Diaspora.

Britain, obviously acting on behalf of its US masters, blocked the EU from issuing formal apologies for the trans-Atlantic slave trade since 2001, suggesting "a more modest expression of regret," whatever that means in a matter as grave as this. Both Britain and the US have militantly rejected demands to call slavery a crime against humanity, in order to avoid legal processes that would lead to reparations. The Church of England had the first sugar cane plantation in the Caribbean, on the island of Barbados. Named Codrington, it comprised 700 acres and made annual profits of more than £200, estimated at $325,000 in current money. All of it was realized from slave labor, most of whom were women whose short lives were recorded by the Codrington clerks on the same list as those for horses, cattle and hogs. One record from 1743 says that "three negro ... were suffocated to death by the steam of a receiving cistern in the distill house." Adam Hochschild in his book, *Bury the Chains — The British Struggle to Abolish Slavery*, writes that "The Caribbean was a slaughter house."[83] Early deaths and low birth rate made the Caribbean slave masters import a flow of new slaves, more than the American South plantation owners.

These deaths were the result of what the "repenter" John Newton (who wrote the hymn "Amazing Grace" and 279 other hymns) and his fellow slavers described as "little relaxation, hard fare, and hard usage, to wear them

83 Hochschild, Adam, *Bury the Chains — The British Struggle to Abolish Slavery*, London: Pan Books 2006

out before they become useless, and unable to do services; and then, to buy new ones, to fill up their places..."

The Church of England finally publicly apologized for their role in the slave trade early in 2006. In a bid to bring reconciliation between Afroances- trals and Euroancestrals, a European delegation of Christian leaders from countries including Britain, France, Holland, Portugal, Spain, the US and Germany traveled to Harare in Zimbabwe to apologize for the atrocities committed against Africans during the slave trade and colonial rule. They did so before an audience of hundreds of delegates including representatives from 24 African states, President Joachim Chissano of Mozambique, the President of Zimbabwe's Council of Chiefs and Dr. Olivia Muchena, Zim- babwe's Minister for Science and Technology Development. Chris Seaton of Britain and the chair of the European African Reconciliation Process deliv- ered the apology:

> We repent for robbing Africans of their history and identity. Today we ask for forgiveness in Jesus' name before you and God. We repent for taking rather than giving. We repent for taking the riches and the lands of Africa. We repent for dehumanizing Africans, treating them as goods, calling them black ivory.[84]

The European delegation, some of whom shed tears, knelt before President Chissano asking for forgiveness of their sins against Africa and her people. Yet it was a religious delegation who apologized, not a governmental one. On the other hand, Africa has learnt her lesson and learnt it the hardest and most painful way. When dealing with the West, she is tensed and her ears are pointed and alert. The Executive Secretary of the Heads of Christian Denomination, Father Fred- erick Chiromba, commented on the European delegation's apology as being "a good beginning for the creation of a better understanding among people of differ- ent races and nations." But, and this is a very big but, Reverend Simon Modhiba of the Methodist Church of Zimbabwe put in, "If the move is meant to build bridges, I see no problems with it. It is important to understand the motives and goals of the initiative as well as the target group. This is important before Africans acknowledge and accept apologies."[85] How apt. This time, Africans are not going to kneel down, fold their hands, close their eyes and pray while their land is being occupied and stolen.

---

84 Seaton as quoted in *New African* No. 455, October 2006
85 Ibid.

Chapter 18. Economic Progress and Beyond

> *Past economic growth is crucial to the material aspects of our exis-*
> *tence: the best predictor of the living standard that a newborn baby*
> *can expect to enjoy is the accident of where he or she is born. There is*
> *very little in common between the quality of life that can be expected*
> *by an average person born in, say, rural Cameroon or urban Java, and*
> *one born in Greenwich, Connecticut or Oslo, Norway. The difference*
> *is captured by a somewhat artificial statistic concocted by economists*
> *known as national income or gross national product per capita.*
>
> — JOEL MOKYR[86]

Our Common Interest is, as already mentioned, Tony Blair's Commission for Africa report in 2005, which proposed cash transfers and various measures that Western governments were to launch in combating Africa's poverty — like can-celling debts (a euphemism the West should abandon — the bank doorman can hardly repay the bank's stolen reserves overnight!) — tackling corruption and increasing aid. The continent's media visibility went up, but only in the usual cavalcade of famine, wars, and mass killing in the familiar lands like Uganda, DRCongo, Ivory Coast, and Sudan who uses the Janjaweed ethnic group militia in the counter-insurgency as proxy fighters. For ordinary Africans, it was the same old story of living on the edge. The Sudanese government, in January 2005, concluded a peace agreement in Nairobi with the Sudan's People's Liberation Movement to end the twenty-year civil war between the mainly Christian south and the mainly Moslem north. They were aware of the fact that the West would

---

86 Mokyr, *The Lever of Riches*, Oxford University Press Inc., New York, 1990 p. 3

not want to jeopardize this agreement by putting international pressure on their government about Darfur.

Warning against generalizing, the report goes on to generalize that Africa "has suffered from governments that have looted the resources of the state; that could not or would not deliver services to their people; that in many cases were predatory, corruptly extracting their countries' resources; that maintained control through violence and bribery, and that squandered or stole aid."[87]

Then why increase aid? Philanthropic PR? And why *has suffered*? It is still suffering. Corruption and violence has not stopped. And where did the loot go? Is *Our Common Interest* meant to serve Africa's or as usual the West's interest? Blair's Great Britain and their offshore territories and dependencies are some of the world's most notorious in the giver side of corruption; London is said to be the biggest money-laundering city in Europe. The "corruptly extracting" the resources companies are Western ones. The report seems to conveniently avoid specifying the countries, the loot and the plunder. Its list of Commissioners includes the former president of Tanzania Benjamin Mpaka and Ethiopia's Prime Minister Meles Zenawi. It treats the diverse polities of Africa as a single entity. The philosopher Kwame Anthony Appiah says that treating the continent as a single country is a fantasy born of European colonialism, a notion adopted by romantic imperialism and epic dreamers such as the pan-Africanists and Rastafarians. Now Blair and Gordon Brown would seem to increase their number.

John Ryle in his article "The Many Voices of Africa," writes:

> Africa is far less homogenous — geographically, culturally, religiously and politically — than Europe or the Americas. South Africa and Burkina Faso have as much in common as Spain and Uzbekistan. In a number of African countries things do seem to be getting better. Across the continent civil wars are fewer and gross national product is on the up. The mistake is to generalize. The very word Africa — that sonorous trisyllable — seems to invite grandiloquence. Because the continent has a clear geographical unity it is tempting to hold forth about it. Cecil Rhodes wanted to colour everything imperial red from the Cape to Cairo; since then the tendency has been for Westerners — and often Africans too — to seek to impose a single reality, a general explanation, on the whole place."[88]

Yet despite this "clear geographical unity," the West is more determined than ever to artificially maintain Northern Africa as part of the Middle East. To say that Africa has "never been more dangerous" when wars are being fought in

87 *Our Common Interest*, Report by The Commission for Africa.
  Full report: http://news.bbc.co.uk/2/shared/bsp/hi/
  pdfs/11_03_05africa.pdf. Accessed: September 2006
88 Granta Magazine: "Introduction: The Many Voices of Africa" by John Ryle,
  http://www.granta.com/extracts/2614. Accessed: September 2006

Darfur or DRCongo is like saying that Eurasia "has never been more dangerous" because of the war in Chechnya. Ryle argues that the generalizing is what is dangerous. Those responsible for the looting and embezzlement should be named and the exceptions be applauded. Culture, according to *Our Common Interest*, is a driving force in the fate of nations, meaning political culture. All too often other very important African cultural areas like art, languages, culinary and music are merely scratched on the surface or pushed aside altogether.

There is no Sub-Saharan African who does not speak at least three languages, including one of the four European languages in Africa — English, French, Spanish and Portuguese. Here, Africa has an edge over Europe and America, but the West with their Megignoarrogance are not appreciative, they book this asset on their "superiority/conquest" column. In international conferences whether at the UN Security Council or WTO negotiations, African representatives speak European languages while most non-African countries' representatives speak their native tongues. According to some estimates[89] there are more than 2,000 African languages, not dialects, which amounts to one third of the total number of languages on the entire planet. The Commission for Africa refers to African proverbs as "tangible cultural heritage" but nobody has ever troubled themselves to count them, least of all the Africans themselves. The single ethnic group, the Akan people of Ghana, have a published collection of 7,015 sayings. Ryle writes that "if every African language boasted as many proverbs as the Akan do there would be 14 million altogether, enough to tie several government commissions in knots." Westerners living in the kind of luxury in Africa that they would never have back in their countries of origin, and earning a fortune there as employees of companies, embassies, organizations and the media, as a rule do not bother to learn any African language.

Everything valuable in Africa is grabbed by the West, even music. John Ryle in his article quotes Stephen Brown, a musicologist, describes it thus:

> One of the most important events of the twentieth century was the marriage of African and European musical languages. It wasn't just one marriage, but a series of marriages — in the American South, in Cuba, in Jamaica, in Brazil, and, of course, Africa. There is something about each of the two music cultures that seem to need the other ... European music provided harmonic progressions organized round a tonal centre — an idea which, once you've heard it, is irresistible. African music offered its polyrhythms, rhythms that occur in layers — a kind of beat which, once heard, is hard to live without."[90]

---

89 2,580, according to www.ethnologue.com
90. Granta Magazine: "Introduction: The Many Voices of Africa" by John Ryle, http://www.granta.com/extracts/2614. Accessed: September 2006

And the continent of Africa itself, too, is hard for the West to live without. It is time that the people of Africa were included instead of being left out in the cold. Or the heat.

The invented notion of "race" is still a popular subject in studies and writings, whether *The Bell Curve*[91] by Charles Murray and Richard Herrnstein or Professor J. Philippe Rushton's *Race, Evolution, and Behavior*[92]. Important to note is how such Westerners always look for differences rather than similarities of humankind. Divisions instead of unities. Professor Rushton[93] writes extensively about something termed the r-K strategies. His view is similar to that of Richard Lynn of the University of Coleraine in Northern Ireland, who dwells on "racial" differences and gender differences in intelligence. The professor suggests that "racial" differences came from evolution in different climates and he leans towards the single-origin theory that we all evolved from relatively recent African ancestors, and that the African/non-African split occurred about 110,000 years ago, the European/Asian split perhaps 41,000 thousand years ago. The cold northern environments were much harsher than that of Africa so that the northern dwellers had to make clothes, build fires and shelters, and store food for the winter. It was much more important to hunt in the north, he claims, because cold-climate fruits and nuts were highly seasonal. Hunting was also made much more difficult since there was less cover for the hunters. To this day hunter-gatherers of the north are supposed to use more sophisticated tools than those in the south. Because the hunters had to share the meat, much more cooperation was required than would be in fruit gathering by individuals, which in the tropics can be done all year round.

Professor Rushton concludes that Asians developed particularly high intelligence and have especially good visuo-spatial abilities because the northern Siberian environment where they lived and hunted was even harsher. The Native Americans who are supposed to be related to the Asians apparently lost the high intelligence and visuo-spatial abilities because, after crossing the Baring Strait into the Americas, they steadily moved southwards where they were not subjected to the rigors that sharpened the Asian mind. Additionally they found large mammals that had never been hunted and could therefore be killed easily. By this theory the Native American is now pre-

91information and review: http://www.mediatransparency.org/personprofile.php?personID=3
92 Ibid. Accessed: November 2005
93 review: http://www.hartford-hwp.com/archives/45/019.html Accessed: February 2007

sented as the culprit who decimated the giant sloths and mammoths that once inhabited the Americas.

But if the cold climate is crucial for the development of high intelligence and visuo-spatial abilities, then the Eskimos should be the most advanced people on the planet. Yet Professor Rushton's stumbling explanation is that human life in the Arctic is relatively recent (how recent and from where?) and therefore the harsh climate has not selected Eskimos as keenly for intelligence and cooperation as it has done Asians and Europeans. Ergo, ethnic differences in intelligence are hereditary genetics rather than environmental. This is contradictory. In the r-K theory, he argues the pattern on "Asians-whites-blacks," where at one extreme is the r-strategy by which an organism produces a very large number of offspring but provides them with little or no care, so that only a few survive. Furthermore, in the current era of social mobility in which hereditary social privileges have disappeared, the failure or success of individuals depends a lot on their native abilities. Children of the rich are clever and talented because they inherit the qualities that assisted their parents in getting rich. When the unintelligent children of the rich go down the social scale, they take on the habits and values of their new class rather than keep those of the class they had been born into, maintains the professor. Another about-face argument. K-oriented parents can therefore have an r child, the symbol r being the maximum rate of increase in a population. The offspring of the r organisms, he argues, must mature quickly because they get no help from their parents, and when conditions are favorable the r-strategists can increase their number at a terrific rate.

The other extreme is the K-strategy, where the number of offspring is much smaller but enormous effort is expended to give each one a good chance to survive. Professor Rushton maintains that the r- and K-strategists are therefore very different in both biology and life histories. K-strategists, unlike the simpler r-strategists, live longer, have larger brains and take longer to reach sexual maturity. They tend to have social organization abilities. Adults fight predators together, may share food and cooperate in the hunt. The K-symbol represents the carrying capacity of the breeding area and the production of few offspring who are carefully nurtured for a particular environment. All humankind generally belong to the K-strategy, but Asians apparently show more K behavior than "whites" who in turn show more than "blacks" consistently with virtually no departure from this pattern. The "racial differences" in the reproduction physiology run along an r-K pattern from Afroancestrals to Euroancestrals to Asians, so that human fraternal twin births come under the r-strategy, producing more and smaller offspring likely to be miscarried, born underweight, die in infancy and receive less parental care. And of course according to the professor, fraternal twin births is twice as common among "blacks" as among "whites," triplets more common among "whites" than among Asians and seventeen times more common among Africans, where multiple births account for 60 out of every 1,000, than among "whites."

The offspring of the different "races" gestate and mature following the r-K strategies, where Afroancestrals are born earlier and smaller than Euroancestrals, but are stronger and better coordinated (?) — they sit and roll over sooner than Euroancestrals who in their turn manage these sooner than Asians. Allegedly Afroancestrals walk at 11 months, Euroancestrals at 12 months and Asians at 13 months. Rushton has Euroancestrals placed firmly in the middle — they are never *the bad* nor are they *the best*, but the other two groups are also permanently *the bad* (Afroancestrals) and *the best* (Asians) — right down to permanent tooth eruption whose lateness present a "near-perfect" correlation to longevity, brain size, years to maturity and complexity of social organization. Afroancestrals attain sexual maturity sooner than Euroancestrals who in their turn are there faster than Asians. The average US American woman produces 14 children, grandchildren and great-grandchildren while the figure rises to 258 in Africa, which prodigious African reproductive effort occurs in a shorter life-span, and so on and so forth. The Asians have the least children, grandchildren and great-grandchildren and live longest. Rushton even delves in the age-old subject of male genital size, confirmed to him by no lesser phenomenon than the AIDS pandemic and international organizations discovering that one size condoms do not fit all of the planet's males. The reader can easily guess who has the largest and longest, and who the smallest and shortest of this organ. Ditto the length of the vagina, frequency of sexual intercourse, number of sexual partners and the quantity of sperm production. These traits are apparently not cultural or environmental but rather "at least partly genetic." Rushton is said to have "exhaustively surveyed recent studies of heredity, which suggest a powerful genetic influence on virtually all aspects of human behavior." There are no differences in the frequencies of identical twin births in the three ethnics groups, and when these twins are brought up apart they resemble each other in virtually every way more than fraternal twins brought up in the same household. Personality traits that are influenced by environment reflect personal surroundings that differ primarily because people shape their surroundings to match their genetic predilections. Here's one for Charles Darwin, Jared Diamond and the environmentalists to scratch their heads over!

When it comes to IQ studies, the professor kindly remembers other ethnic groups and arrives at the following averages:

"Whites"	100
Asians	105
American "blacks" who are 25% "white" (?)	85
African "blacks"	70 - 75
"Amerindians" including Central and Latin America	x
Americans with little or no European blood	89
Polynesians, Micronesians, Melanesians and Maoris	80 - 95

Rushton contends that although IQ tests tend to give disparate results by ethnic groups, there are biological indicators of intelligence that cannot be accused of cultural bias, and such an indicator, which he allegedly studied in depth, is brain size. Larger heads contain larger brains and are positively correlated with intelligence. Asians have a higher intelligence than Euroancestrals but the difference is mainly in visuo-spatial performance which makes Asians good engineers and mathematicians rather than shining in verbal ability. A 1980 survey of professions in the US found that Chinese-Americans were over-represented in the sciences at a rate of six times their proportion in the population, but there were only a quarter as many Chinese-American lawyers as their numbers would suggest. Afroancestrals of course were minimally represented in both fields. As groups, Euroancestrals and Asians have larger brains than Afroancestrals. Apparently Afroancestral children in the US, at age seven, are 16 percentile points taller than Euroancestral children but their head circumference is 8 percentile points smaller. Here Rushton confuses again by maintaining that a small person with the same size of brain as a big person can be thought of as having a "larger" brain because smaller bodies require less brain to maintain basal functions! The Asians are likely to have larger brains than Euroancestrals, but some indicators of the larger size appear only after correcting upward for the fact that Asians are smaller than Euroancestrals.

Reading Rushton's book makes one feel that Euroancestrals always want to have a monopoly, even when it comes to intelligence. All the same he tells us that on average Euroancestrals "probably" have about 100 million fewer cerebral neurons than Asians, Afroancestrals 480 million fewer than Euroancestrals. The Afroancestral/Asian difference is claimed to be "especially significant" because of differences in body size. The Afroancestrals, having small brains in large bodies, "are at a serious intellectual disadvantage compared to Asians because a larger proportion of their already-smaller brains is probably occupied with basal functions and not available for conscious thought."[94] (Imagine a female *African* at five-foot-eleven!)

It keeps on getting better. Another directly physiological assessment of intelligence is the type of reaction-time test pioneered by Professor Arthur Jensen of Berkeley.[95] These tests require people to make simple choices when a light goes on. Intelligence is correlated with both speed and consistency of reaction time, and Asians perform better than Euroancestrals, who perform better than Afroancestrals. In the variables below, I've left in Rushton's concept of middling "whites" and rearguard "blacks."

He applies the concept of "regression towards the mean." People with extreme ratings in a normal distribution of any trait are likely to have children who are not as extreme as themselves. As an example, very tall people are likely to have taller-than-average children, but perhaps not as tall as the parents — the children's heights tend to move towards the average for the population. Another study has proved that African Americans regress towards a mean of 85 while Euroancestrals regress towards a mean of 100. Another indicator that ethnic intelligence differences are susceptible to genetic influence is the "inbreeding depression scores," where such children have unusually low scores on certain intelligence tests. These proved that the *greatest intelligence differences* are found in the Afroancestral-Euroancestral turfs. It must be a wonder that all the members of the European aristocracy are not complete imbeciles to the last person. Nobody has been more consistent in marrying their own blood-related family members throughout the centuries than the European monarchs. And, although I have no idea how African Americans pair off in marriage, I do know that in Luoland, as in many African societies, one never marries one's cousin no matter how distant. It is taboo to marry a son-in-law, daughter-in-law, step-father, step-brother, step-sister, step-mother and so on.

As if all of the above were not enough to demonstrate the Euroancestral high intelligence hallmark of *K*-strategy, Professor Rushton explains that the "races" with more *K* traits have more complex and cooperative social organizations, are more restrained and law abiding, and show more altruism.

In terms of *r-K* strategy, altruism and social cooperation permit individuals to bring up their offspring under more dependable and peaceful circumstances, a precondition for groups that have staked their survival on producing small numbers of large-brained but slow-maturing offspring, so the mes-

---

94 review: http://www.hartford-hwp.com/archives/45/019.html. Accessed: February 2007
95 review: http://www.isteve.com/jensen.htm. Accessed February: 2007

sage. It continues that for traits like altruism and aggression to be properly included in an *r-K* pattern, they must be shown to be, like intelligence, at least partly controlled by heredity and to differ from ethnic group to ethnic group. Suggestions in research are that these traits are greatly influenced by heredity, and that they appear early in life. But if this is so, then we are back to environment, not genetic heredity! In one study, children who were rated as "aggressive" by their peers at age eight were rated the same way by a different set of peers ten years later. By the time they were 19 years old, those in the "aggressive" group were three times more likely to have a police record than those who were not considered "aggressive."

The classification madness of the 18th and 19th centuries seem to be back in full swing in the 21st century, especially in countries like the United States.

"RACE" AND r-K VARIABLES

Variable	Asians	Whites	Blacks
Brain size	Large	Intermediate	Small
IQ	105	100	85
Decision Times	Fast	Intermediate	Slow
Cultural Achievements	High	High	Low
Gestation Times	?	Intermediate	Short
Development	Late	Intermediate	Early
Age of first intercourse	Late	Intermediate	Early
Life Span	Long	Intermediate	Short
Twinning per 100,000	4	8	16
Hormone Levels	Low	Intermediate	High
Genitalia	Small	Intermediate	Large
Intercourse Frequency	Low	Intermediate	High
AIDS/Syphilis	Low	Intermediate	High
Aggressiveness	Low	Intermediate	High
Cautiousness	High	Intermediate	Low
Dominance	Low	Intermediate	High
Self-Concept	Low	Intermediate	High
Marital Stability	High	Intermediate	Low
Criminality	Low	Intermediate	High
Administrative Ability	High	High	Low

Conclusion

> *Integral human development, sustainable development, depends more on harmonious human relationships than on the organization and operation of an unfettered free market. A fundamental fault with globalization as experienced in Africa is that it is not rooted in community but structured from above according to abstract economic laws.*

— PETER HENRIOT, S.J., Jesuit Centre for Theological Reflection, Lusaka[96]

As already mentioned, the damage to the African collective psyche needs to be "healed" because it is responsible for an incredible degree of elements inhuman, especially in the continental African. There are, among Africans, many who are good, honest and devoted to Africa's cause and wellbeing. Downright admirable are the ordinary African people who are able to hold onto hope in the face of one catastrophe after another, and their extended familial solidarity amid all the unbearable suffering. But such Africans are getting even fewer as the younger generations are born into ever deepening doldrums in Africa's economic progress and cultural advancement, and a desperate lack of positive role models.

I don't believe that Euroancestrals commit twice as many suicides as Afroancestrals and Asians twice as many as Euroancestrals because the latter two somehow inherited genes that make them more self-conscious and introspective. But in the African's acquired "boss culture," whether remnants of slavery and colonialism or not, there would seem to be an overdose of self-opinionatedness,

---

96 Henriot in his article and speech, *Globalization: Implications for Africa* of 12 January 1998, in Lusaka, Zambia

ruthlessness, aggression and the kind of narcissism I describe in Chapter 5, and a lack of responsibility and consciousness as well as conscience.

Personality and ethnic differences should be explained under environmental and psychological influences and definitely not under genetic heredities. Experiments in altruism for example confirm that people are more willing to help like people. Ethnic solidarity can be likened to a sort of extended nepotism, a genetic similarity and the desire to preserve a common ancestry. But Africans are increasingly more likely to assist a non-African than a fellow African. Unlike the Asians and Euroancestrals, modern Africans are less restrained, less cooperative and terribly aggressive — to their own kind. But with the other ethnic groups, they try to make themselves invisible or over-cooperate.

Just shortly before the 2006 football World Cup Championships, the president of a West African country turned up out of nowhere to force his "protégé" on the coach of the national football team as a new World Cup team footballer. What goes on in the head of a president who behaves thus? The coach, a Euroancestral, summarily resigned. His "Excellency" possibly interpreted that act of resigning as the confirmation of his power. Had the trainer been an African, he wouldn't have resigned, he would have accepted the new "team member" — either out of fear for his employment future or out of a lack of moral responsibility.

In Tom Clancy's novel *Executive Orders*, he writes:

> What people call "the initiative" is never anything more or less than a psychological advantage. It combines one side's feeling that they are winning with the other side's feeling that something has gone wrong — that they must now prepare for and respond to the actions of their enemy instead of preparing their own offensive action. Couched in terms of "momentum" or "ascendancy," it really always comes down to who is doing what to whom, and a sudden change in that equation will have a stronger effect than that of a gradual buildup to the same set of circumstances. The expected, when replaced by the unexpected, lingers for a time, lingers in the mind, since it is easier, for a while, to deny rather than to adapt, and that just makes things harder for those who are being done to. For the doers, there are other tasks.[97]

There are examples of tasks in Africa that should have been regulated and implemented but are ignored. When I visited my old "temporary" school in Kenya several years ago, I found something unexpected. The Latin motto on the main entrance of the now run-down colonial classrooms building had faded but was still legible. The windows of the cubicles no longer had curtains and were broken. The swimming pool was still there, supporting a small hill; it was now the rubbish dump. Nobody had taken the initiative to invest in renovating the school since the 1970s. Where is Africa's foresight? Or economic investment? In-

---

97 Clancy, *Executive Orders*, New York: Berkley Books 1997

stead of allotting funds to schools, health services, roads and other infrastructure, monuments of rulers crop up, erected by themselves with public money. Such as the misplaced replica of St. Peters Cathedral in the middle of the African landscape and at odds with it, built by the late Felix Houphoüet-Boigny of Ivory Coast. These Africans are out of touch not only with a country's governance methodology but also with the rest of the world. How do they get away with decades of cruelty, oppression and plunder while Ahmadinejad is pressured and Saddam Hussein is killed?

In 1948, Cameroon and South Korea were comparable on the macro-economic scale in terms of per capita income, population, rate of urbanization, education, health, infrastructure (few in both cases), natural resources, the trauma of colonialism and so on. By 1998, Cameroon was still in the league of the poorest nations of the world while South Korea was an emerging economic powerhouse not only to reckon with but also to doff your hat for. How did South Korea get out of the mire and into the donor-nation side in the OECD and why does Cameroon remain wallowing in the mire? The reasons lie in the cultural environment that weakens and divides one nation and strengthens and unites the other. The one nation has a population that is individually prepared to make sacrifices for the good of the entire community whatever the cost (Confucian–Buddhism), the other nation has individuals who have relegated themselves to thinking "with the stomach." Africa's proud progenitors traditionally had the noble cultural characteristic of solidarity and held highest this commitment to the welfare of the entire community. They didn't need cheerleaders to inspire them in their duties or to underscore their achievements. Such Africans now seem extinct. Today enthusiastic participants in national celebrations and ethnic dancers are sweating in the African midday sun in order to, at least for this one single day, have a bite and a drink. And hope. But hope for what? A miracle? Hope in whom? The FAO and Medicare?

A culture is relatively stable when the norms mirror the values of the group. But when this fails, then the road to becoming unstable is paved. Many successful modern Africans complain about their domestic helps, whom they fashionably refer to as "houseboy" or "housegirl," terms that confirm the fact that Africans have neatly stepped into the colonial masters' shoes. The complaints dwell on such matters as theft of sugar, flour, salt, soap, baby food and so on. Research has shown that Euroancestrals, whether foreign or local citizens, solve similar problems by supplying these commodities to their domestics, say, once a week, and counting that as part of the domestics' salaries. Or simply by talking to their domestics about this problem and offering them the alternative of borrowing whatever commodity they were short of and giving the equivalent back later, when they were in a position to do so. Somehow it works. At least no one is in the position of accusing someone of theft, and no one is in the position of being accused of being a thief. As a result, over the decades, Africans prefer to work for/with Euroancestrals, even if the pay is less than that offered by an Afroancestral.

Africa has the Boss Culture. Everybody is more equal than everybody else, everybody a divinity to the subordinates or those presumed under them: men to women, parents to children, brothers to sisters, the car owner to the petrol station attendant, the bicycle owner to the pedestrian, "their excellencies" to the entire nation including the wildlife. These "excellencies" — the role models — expect the police force to function even when salaries are six months in arrears, and the army to remain loyal and disciplined on endless supplies of cheap alcohol and guns. Their entire judiciary generally auctions crimes and charges alike. They decide whether a crime has been committed or not, depending on the highest bidder, while pocketing bids from all involved. And the ordinary citizen seeking legal assistance enters a lawyer's office as if entering God's throne room, amazed to have been granted audience. Only to be conned and ripped off, with no guarantees. And, miraculously, it all "functions" accordingly in the Boss Culture. Nobody seems to complain much, if at all, and everybody is so very busy hoping, always hoping.

Hope is a good thing and should never be lost. But hope also incorporates belief. There is freedom of choice here, for Africans. Yet in whom or in what do Africans *really* believe, after the psychological and spiritual conflict that has been poured down their throats? When they close their eyes and pray, what imagery do they have of God? Their Ancestors and their Gods, the Arab Ancestor and Allah or the pseudo-Icelander Ancestor and the imaginary white-bearded God in some imaginary heaven? The foregoing are all mediators between humankind and their symbolic Invisible Creator(s) with whom humanity cannot communicate directly. Africans have the right to choose their spiritual world, their cosmic union and their religion of choice where they feel protected and experience a sense of belonging. Why not have The Son of Man as a Maasai Mountain God, instead of a pseudo-Icelander? We have the freedom of denomination in Africa, including in the primarily Muslim north. Africans have the wide spectrum of every religion in the world being practiced in the continent from Candomblé to Hinduism, Buddhism to Christianity, Jewish followers to followers of the Aga Khan. The religious images should be ones that Africans can identify with without grading themselves lower or higher in their spiritual make-up and spiritual family. These images must impart to them the longing and pride to be a projection and projectile of all the images from time immemorial. The words with which they communicate with God must be theirs and reflect their cultural values, not those words dictated to them. God in whichever religion, presumably understands all languages. Selected outsiders' cultural traits should be carefully incorporated into Africa's multitudinous cultures. African cultural traits that have become obsolete or even downright harmful in the modern world should be reformed. Africans have embraced alien Euroancestral traits piecemeal. This has brought them to the stage where they are like the painted Easter eggs — hollowed out and extremely fragile. They break at the slightest pressure, whether from within or from without.

One who has neither knowledge nor faith in his own culture is an empty vessel that anybody can fill up with anything. South Korea has made it to the arena of the emerging economies because it held onto its cultural and spiritual attire. Cameroon, and Sub-Saharan Africa adorned and continue to adorn themselves with borrowed plumes. Africans too have to separate their chaff from the grain themselves, for only they know which is which. Religious reforms have occurred very often ever since Luther King turned away from Roman Catholicism in 1517.

Africa is neither poor nor powerless. All that the continent needs are the right kind of sons and daughters who are prepared to channel this wealth and power diligently for the welfare of the people and use the political clout of Africa's enormous natural resources over the rest of the world. Wealth is might. One of the worst enemies of Africa is nepotism: some of us — friends, relatives, peers — are supposed to be artificially more equal to us than others despite rules, law and order. This is the primary step towards disintegration of the regulated system. Here is where exceptions to the rule are made arbitrarily and with impunity.

When we talk of culture, we, as geographic groups of humanity, bury ourselves in the delusion that we mean one and the same thing. We don't. The word "culture" says it all — some norm each group has CULTIVATED for themselves. One can domesticate and sow millet and yam. But one cannot then expect to harvest maize and asparagus, or reject one's millet and yam harvests for being "different."

This is what Africans have also done piecemeal — they increasingly reject what they have cultivated and force themselves into cultural attires that do not fit their physique nor conform to the makeup of their psyches. They should find the right ingredients to mix a suitable recipe of old traditions and modern trends. The Asiatics have done this very successfully.

The fatalism so general in Africa has become a chronic disease. It manifests itself in a thousand ways from profound resignation to the kind of patrimony that strangles all Africans. Instead of taking their fate in their hands and deciding on a course of action, they fold their hands on their laps and expect "those up there" to "do something" for them. It is time to come to terms with the fact that "those up there" are not going to do anything unless the African populations corner them. Humility may be good for the soul, but death is definitely bad for the body. The Darling-of-the-West dictatorships in Africa would not be so arbitrary if Africans got up and acted. African sons and daughters have many causes and, united, they can bring these to the fore. If the West installs inept marionettes to govern them or assassins to kill their good leaders, then it is up to the Africans to organize themselves and form a forum with cohesive arguments, collect evidence, and lay these out for all to judge. Those who suffer in silence cannot expect to be heard. Many people in the world would be on Africa's side and would join in the fight if Africans showed some backbone by taking the initiative.

A couple of years ago there was a television documentary about the Sudanese slavery racket. A woman slave "bought" free by some Christian religious organization and brought back south to her people was interviewed. She had been cursed and beaten. Among her other duties, she was regularly sent off to go and buy food for the household. Money, she said, was pressed into one hand, a shopping basket in the other, and her child was strapped to her back. But why didn't she then escape, the journalist asked. She said it was because she didn't know anybody up there in the north to show her the way back south. Typical! Someone else has to help. She had cultured a dependency which seemed to her the easier way out in her life, a dependency she valued more than her freedom.

In late August/the beginning of September 1997, some unknown entity dumped tons of toxic maize somewhere in the area of Embakasi Airport in Nairobi. When the starving masses discovered this, they scrambled for the maize on hands and knees to the last member of the family. And to the last grain. All the media issued warnings that the maize was not fit for human consumption. The warning fell on the deaf ears of the starving. In interviews, the people insisted that they would hang onto their sacks of poisoned maize, declaring either that they did not believe the maize was toxic or that they would wait and see if somebody else consumed and died from it. Unbelievable that the once oh-so-proud Kenyans had been reduced to such desperation. They were willing to risk death for the entire family. How high must the degree of destitution in one be, for one to welcome such elements inhuman in oneself? The Kenyans should have demanded that the culprit be found and brought before the law. They have the right and the power to do so. Again, the ordinary Africans normally resort to the wrong reaction or place their hands on their laps.

The greatest resource that Africa has, even paramount to the continent's abundant natural resources, is also being abused and misused: the children. Mothers are too busy trying to find a means of survival and fathers are normally not around.

The Kenyan Affiliation Act, repealed in 1969, provided that a woman must prove that the man is the father of her child in order to claim child support from him. Or the father has to voluntarily acknowledge paternity. Most Kenyan mothers do not have the means to utilize a DNA test even if she managed to nick some hair from the father's comb or grab his freshly-used toothbrush. If the government is serious about this, then it should set up such facilities as public services to carry out the tests. Since the repeal act (a repeal act that was presided over, not surprisingly, by men only), the position has remained precarious for women. The applicant often needs to produce "evidence of a marriage," not of a divorce, not of a liaison, to obtain maintenance. And here comes the most ridiculous part, verbatim: "The Subordinate Courts (Separation and Maintenance) Act permits a woman to claim maintenance from the father of her children *if he is her husband*" (emphasis mine). If he is *not* her husband, the child is not even considered.

No doubt there are parents as well as politicians who, however rich or poor, give their children all the love and care they can afford to give. But there can never be enough of them. Paradoxically, parental love and care, and the continent's political protection and catering for Africa's children, have degenerated since the end of the colonial era, like every aspect of life in post-colonial Africa. As the judiciary, the buildings, the bridges, the entire infrastructure, the educational and health care systems, deteriorate, so do the emotional, cultural, moral, socio-economic and spiritual life of the continent's children through no fault of their own. One who has not known love can neither love nor appreciate love. One who has never learnt the values of trust cannot trust nor be trusted. One who has never known responsibility cannot act in a responsible manner nor take responsibility for anything. One who has only reaped the fruits of contempt and been fed bellyfuls of fear knows no respect nor the dignity required in dealings with fellow human beings. Orphans of AIDS roaming the streets or the countryside are easy pickings for the "field marshal" plagues who give a child a gun and teach the child how to kill for a bit of food.

It is also time to knock on the portals of the African Union and take stock — or a cudgel, if need be. They are not enthroned in Addis Ababa for extravagant and grandiose posturing, for orchestrated conferences and grandiloquent speeches which say nothing to the populations of Africa. Africans cannot expect someone else to battle for them. It is time they rose up for their human rights — the basics of which are food and shelter. When a group is driven out of their ancestral land to make way for prospectors panning for natural resources, they should be offered assistance by the whole community, including legal assistance, to see that they are adequately compensated and have a new home. Africans too should aspire to die of natural causes instead of cloaking themselves in fatalistic resignation. The rest of the world's population is living ever longer and healthier. Why shouldn't Africans?

Finally, time is a limited commodity and one never knows how much of it remains. The credo is to spend what you have as mindfully as possible, as long as you have it. Africans had better spend theirs in a concerted effort to turn things around, urgently, before Africa as a whole is turned into an Euroancestral or Asian plantation. Many multinationals already have their own enclaves complete with private professional armies and infrastructure. African citizens cannot get in without a permit showing that they are laborers or other kind of employees. The enclaves are treated like sovereign nations within sovereign nations. Who said that apartheid has been wiped out?

Africa is vast, and rich in natural resources, wildlife and best of all in different groups of people with different cultures and languages. Yet most Africans remain among the poorest people on earth. Apart from the many physical diseases that plague Africans, their worst contagion is a collective psychological trauma of spiritual and sociological oppression. The lack of self-esteem and self-worth engenders self-negation, self-hatred, fatalism and resignation. What a person hates he cannot respect and will seek to mistreat or destroy.

Many African politicians in their narcissistic delusions believe they possess their nations, its citizens, wildlife and natural resources. They have little conscience, if any at all. Most Africans, but especially the politicians and the elite, are practically incapable of welcoming commitment, true friendships, dedication, love, perseverance, emotions, attachment, intimacy, planning or any such human investments as a common people with common goals. The generations born after independence know no other Africa but "the Continent of Chaos." Schools and hospitals are not built or repaired. The elite send their children to school in the West and fly to private clinics in Switzerland when they need medical attention. The last pupils in East Africa to have their exams put together and then corrected in London were in the early 1970s. They were the last batch who underwent the Cambridge School Certificate set and corrected fairly. Today, with exams being set and corrected locally, a family's wealth and political clout influence which pupils pass examinations and which pupils fail. This further lowers the quality of university graduates. The later "after-independence" generations of young people inherit an even more intense inferiority complex that is particularly paradoxical because the true wealth of their cultural and material heritage is unparalleled.

Asians have become tigers, so the West is lining up to be their *partners*. Not converters, advisors in looting and pillaging, or big brothers through charitable causes. The West is being "forced" to speak Asiatic languages, to recognize and embrace Asiatic cultures, and not only in the business world, because certain things are so interwoven that one cannot effectively separate them. The now-popular multi-million-dollar cross-cultural training courses sidestep Africa — except for one or two exceptions like South Africa and Nigeria. But even in these two countries, nobody has to worry about what African language to speak or how to dress. Very few people from other cultures want to know about African mores and traditions. In fact there is a school that does not perceive South Africa as "an African country," a school to whom the country's economy is "not third world" economy, Africans included. Africa is fair game for the rest of the world. It is understandable that the West chooses to economically orientate itself to the Asiatics and sidesteps Africa in intercultural spheres. Why invest when you can simply collect? Sub-Saharan Africa is a *quantité négligeable*. Whatever they want from there, they can have, by merely dangling a villa, a few hundred AK47s or a paltry little bundle of banknotes. One former Ugandan minister permitted a project that was environmentally a catastrophe — for the bribe of just $10,000.

In 1985, multinational export producers in Africa employed 45,000 Sub-Saharan Africans compared to 950,000 Asians and 760,000 Latin Americans. The African figure diminishes yearly while the other two are on the increase. This trend is not arbitrary. Germany, the most economically powerful European nation, wants to "import" computer experts from India. This time the West is not commanding Indians to come over as coolies to build their roads and railways. India has seen the golden path and taken it, priming the best resources any country can have — the country's citizens. All other arguments for and against India's remarkable economical achievements aside, one has to agree that this is foresight. The West is so intrigued with this that their media and economy experts have established a kind of observation "watch tower" for India — and China.

The only way to assist Africa in a sustainable sense is to strengthen the backbone of the Africans because only they can get themselves out of their misery. In world history, societies have managed to get out of poverty without outside assistance. China and India are currently doing just that. No African ruler is willing to leave the throne upon which immeasurable wealth is heaped and can be taken literally without lifting a finger. Unless the person's name is Nelson Mandela. And this stolen wealth is sitting in Western banks, not in Africa. The most urgent and concerted efforts should be made especially in the following spheres:

Democracy and the Electorate

The mistake being made again and again over the last couple of decades is the sending off of ineffective "election observers" to African countries, who stick close to their luxurious international hotel suites in the capital cities. On average around 80% of the electorate are in rural areas. The majority of these are illiterate. The electorate is not in the least enlightened as to what elections, political parties or democracy are all about — not to mention even the basics of human rights, including the right to pursue personal happiness. Another 35%-50% of the urban population, depending on the country, have no or very little knowledge of what democracy is. "Democracy means voting Candidate AB whether you like him or not. Forget Candidate XY — that's all!" the electorate are told, by the politicians and their campaign troops who may be wielding batons and AK47s, who may be in the uniforms of the police or armed forces. The electorate's lack of knowledge and their illiteracy are abused to misinform and mislead them, much as the Western electorate's consumer desires are deliberately used to manipulate the voting.

Cognitive skills are those skills that make it possible for people to *know*. Cognitive skills must be *taught*. By the same token Africans have to be taught about their rights and about the true characteristics of the current amorphous word democracy, about the electorate and the functioning of the judiciary. In nearly every Sub-Saharan African nation, the police are not your friend and helper; they are your worst enemy and are "terrorists" right next to the armed forces. Africans have to learn to shake off their often slavish subservience to those in authority, to ethnic groups who are not Afroancestrals, and to their so-called "big men." They need to be enlightened, in courses and workshops, right down to the remotest village. This is another area where reparation funds could be channeled to the benefit of all. Afroancestrals should pick up their ancient cloak of dignity and put it on permanently, like their ancestors before them.

Sustainable Self-Assurance

A second program which should also be implemented for the long term would aim at repairing the psychic damage that has been done to all those of African descent. Adults, the youth and especially schoolchildren should be invited to participate in programs geared at awakening and sustaining their self-esteem, neighborly love, self-worth, pride *in* and the value *of* their African heritage in arts, music, writing, philosophy, and history, all that the African culture and people have contributed to the rest of the world. Blatant lies like, "the Africans had no writing," should no longer be heard. (In Benin and Meroe old forms of writing have been found, not to mention the "writing" in their artifacts as well as elsewhere, in the form of signs engraved in pottery, architecture, sculptures or other works of art.) Africans should be made aware of how many objects of African art, some over two millennia old, are in Western museums or private collections.

The next generations are the ones who will either welcome and perpetuate fatalism and resignation, and believe that it is acceptable to steal and cheat in order to survive, or they will die on barbed wire or drown at sea trying to get into Europe.

The repeated hurt that may lead to the development of a narcissistic personality must be stopped. Instead, Africans must be helped to stand up for democratic rights and social justice — despite the resistance from Western and African elites who risk to lose their golden geese. It is almost impossible to subjugate a people who are knowledgeable and strengthened with self-assurance.

The founder of AfriAvenir, Cameroonian Kum'a Ndumbe III, put it succinctly when he maintained that "only a balanced, self-confident and sincere citizen of Africa would be in a position to propel forward the development of his country." The current Western hand-picked "leaders" are only out to propel their own interests forward, in a complete reversal of African tradition.

The authentic African system has always been a democracy of representation and discussion — even under the baobab tree. The colonialists left Africa chained to imported forms of governance. Now the West is accusing African governments of autocracy, when all the African leaders are doing is perpetuating the game of their mentors. Indeed the lived and experienced colonial legacy was not a model on which democracy and equality could thrive.

Information technology which should fuel Africa to soar higher is not made readily available. This only cements fatalism and resignation in Africa. So far the tiny nation of Rwanda is the only one making IT a compulsory part of the school curriculum. All African countries should do so, and immediately.

Sanitation and Energy

There are simple, ecologically friendly installation systems for generating diesel oil from plastic and organic wastes which can further be turned into energy production. These systems can be installed in any remote village in Africa and maintained at very low costs, in conjunction with waste collection and sanitation systems. Waste and rubbish especially threaten to smother the slums ringing the larger African cities. These are the "raw materials". Apart from the energy this could produce, it would contribute much to the health of the villagers as well as the city and slum dwellers. Development aid that is truly intended to help ought to focus on this as a priority.

Somebody must take the initiative. Not an individual "somebody" but a consortium of individuals, and of nations. Africa has to pull together and become the doers, not the done to.

Bibliography

Anderson, Roy and Robert May, *Infectious Diseases of Humans*, Oxford University Press, 1992

Armah, Ayi Kwei, *The Eloquence of the Scribes*, Per Ankh Publishers, Popenquine (Senegal), 2006

Baker, Raymond, Oral testimony to the AAPPG (All Africa Party Parliamentary Group) in January 2001

Brunner, Linus, *Die Gemeinsame Wurzeln des Semitischen und Indogermanischen Wortschatzes* Bern, Munich, Francke, 1969

Bunte, Jonas, "Shockingly Weak Shock-Facility for the Weak," article on December 5, 2005 in the German NGO *Erlassjahr*.

Carré, John le, *The Constant Gardener*, Pocket Books, New York, 2001

Clancy, Tom, *Executive Orders*, Berkley Books, New York, 1996

Curtis, Mark, *Web of Deceit — Britain's Real Role in the World* Vintage, London 2003,

Darling, Sir Patrick, *Written Evidence* to the AAPPG, London, January 2001

Darwin, Charles, *Descent of Man*, 1871, Chapter VI — On the Affinities and Genealogy of Man

Davidson, Basil, *Africa in History*, Touchstone, New York, 1966

Diamond, Jared, *Guns, Germs and Steel — A Short History of Everybody for the Last 13,000 Years*, Vintage, London, 1997

Donovan, Alan, *My Journey Through African Heritage*, Kenway Publications, Nairobi, 2005

Fantina, Robert, *Desertion and the American Soldier*, New York, Algora Publishing, 2006, pp. 172-173. Fantina is himself quoting from Jeff Syrop, 1991. The New Order. http://www.zenhell.com/GetEnlightened/stories/neworder/neworder.htm. Accessed October 11, 2005

Fasold, Ralph, *Sociolinguistics of Society*, Basil Blackwell Publishers, Oxford, 1984

Henriot, Peter J., speech at conference in Lusaka on "*Land and Globalization in Africa*" of January 12 1998, in Lusaka, Zambia

Herodotus, *Historien*, Munich, Goldman Taschenbücher (1961)

Herrnstein, Richard, Charles Murray, *The Bell Curve*, Washington, Free Press , 1994

Hilsum, Lindsey, *Capitalism Magazine*, http://www.capmag.com/search.china, Accessed: June 2005

Johanson, Donald, *Australopithecus afarensis*, so named in 1978. http://www.msu.edu/~heslipst/contents/ANP440/afarensis.htm Accessed April 2006

Leakey, Richard, *The Origin of Humankind*, London, Phoenix, 1994

Pilger, John, *Freedom Next Time*, London, Bantam, 2006

Linné (a.k.a Linnaes), Carl von, *Systema Naturae*, 1735

Littauer, M. A and Crouwel, J. H., *Wheeled Vehicles and Ridden Animals in the Ancient Near East*, Cologne, Leiden, 1979

Mallory, J. P., *In Search of the Indo-European* London, Thames & Hudson, 1989

Martin, Peter, *Schwarze Teufel, edle Mohren*, Hamburg, Junius Verlag, 1993

McNeill, William, *Plagues and Peoples*, New York, Doubleday, 1976

Mokyr, Joel *The Lever of Riches*, Oxford University Press, Inc., New York, 1990 p. 3

Rogers, Everett M., *Diffusion of Innovations*, New York, The Free Press, 1962

Rushton, Philippe J., *Race, Evolution, and Behavior*. 2nd Special Abridged Edition, Published by the Charles Darwin Research Institute Port Huron, 2000

Ryle, John, "*The Many Voices of Africa*", *Granta* http://www.granta.com/extracts/2614. Accessed November 2006

Scholl-Latour, Peter, *Afrikanische Totenklage - Der Ausverkauf des Schwarzen Kontinents*, Munich, C. Bertelsmann Verlag, 2001

Shaw, Thursta, Paul Sinclair, Bassey Andah and Alex Okpoko (editors) *The Archaeology of Africa: Food, Metals and Towns, Journal of Field Archaeology*, Vol. 23, No. 2, Summer, 1996

Sterne, Laurence, *Letters of Laurence Sterne*, Oxford, Clarendon Press, 1965

Smith, Andrew, *Pastoralism in Africa*, London, Hurst, 1992

Taieb, Maurice, Australopithecus afarensis http://www.geocities.com/palaeoanthropology/Aafarensis.html Accessed: April 2006

Trompenaars, Fons, *Handbuch Globales Managen*, Munich, Econ Verlag, 1993

Tshibangu, *UNESCO General History of Africa Series* Vol. 8, ed. A. A. Mazrui

Tupy, Martin, *"Trade Liberalization and Poverty Reduction in Sub-Saharan Africa"*, CATO Instittute paper No. 557, December 6, 2005

Wainaina, Binyavanga, "How to write about Africa", Granta http://www.granta.com/extracts/2615 Accessed November 2006

Yakobson, Sergius, *Russia and Africa*, New Haven, Yale University Press, 1962

Ziegler, Jean, *Le nouveaux Maîtres du Monde et ceux qui leur résistent*, Paris, Fayard, 2002

——, *L'Empire de la honte*, Paris, Fayard, 2005

INDEX